D1606315

LITERACY ACROSS LANGUAGES AND CULTURES

SUNY Series, Literacy, Culture, and Learning:
Theory and Practice
Alan C. Purves, Editor

LITERACY ACROSS LANGUAGES AND CULTURES

edited by

BERNARDO M. FERDMAN
ROSE-MARIE WEBER
ARNULFO G. RAMÍREZ

State University
of New York
Press

Published by
State University of New York Press, Albany

© 1994 State University of New York

All rights reserved

Production by Susan Geraghty
Marketing by Terry Swierzowski

Printed in the United States of America

For information, address State University of New York
Press, State University Plaza, Albany, N.Y., 12246

Library of Congress Cataloging in Publication Data

Literacy across languages and cultures / edited by Bernardo M.
   Ferdman, Rose-Marie Weber, and Arnulfo G. Ramírez.
      p.   cm. — (SUNY series, literacy, culture, and learning)
   Includes bibliographical references (p.) and index.
   ISBN 0-7914-1815-4. — ISBN 0-7914-1816-2 (pbk.)
   1. Literacy—Social aspects. 2. Sociolinguistics. I. Ferdman,
Bernardo M., 1959–   II. Weber, Rose-Marie, 1938–   III. Ramírez,
Arnulfo G., 1943–   . IV. Series.
LC149.L4955   1994
302.2'244—dc20   93-750
                                                                  CIP

10 9 8 7 6 5 4 3 2 1

CONTENTS

PART 1

Introduction

CHAPTER 1

Literacy Across Languages and Cultures

Bernardo M. Ferdman and Rose-Marie Weber

Popular conceptions tend to portray literacy as a basic vehicle for social and economic advancement as well as a means of enhancing individual lives and fostering equal opportunity. Scholars and academics, while debating the accuracy or limitations of this image and even the very definition of literacy, at the very least seem to agree that more literacy among more people is desirable. Extending access to literacy for both children and adults has become a widespread goal in the United States and throughout the world. Business leaders maintain that the workforce is insufficiently proficient in the skills that will be increasingly necessary in the future. Educators struggle to meet the needs of a changing population that has a variety of values, backgrounds, and preparations. The focus has been broadening from one on illiteracy, then, to the larger problem of how to provide diverse people with the specific and expanded literacy skills they require for full participation in a variety of social contexts, including work, school, and home. Beyond these functional needs, the linkage of literacy with personal empowerment, social status, and individual growth also drives a variety of literacy efforts.

Members of linguistic and cultural minorities in the United States, as in other multiethnic societies, often face special challenges in having these needs addressed. This is especially so given the predominant and largely unexamined tendency in the United

States to equate literacy with English literacy. The premise of this book is that focusing on such people—people whose languages and cultures are not the dominant ones in the society—is crucial if we are to learn enough about becoming and being literate to permit truly accomplishing the goal of extending literacy as broadly in society as possible. Literacy has too often been portrayed primarily in functional terms and from a monolingual framework. For members of linguistic and cultural minorities, this has meant acquiring literacy in the context of theories and practices that are incompatible with their realities and experiences or that force them into unfamiliar or undesirable molds.

Together with a growing number of literacy scholars and practitioners, we believe that changing this situation means not only concerning ourselves with diversity, but also rethinking many of our assumptions about literacy itself. Consideration of the needs of linguistically and culturally diverse people can shed new light on how to think about the many ways children and adults become (and do not become) literate and what this means for them. Thus, extending knowledge and theory about literacy is one of our goals. We are also concerned with doing so in a way that can help those who are most concerned with applications. With this volume, we would like to do our part to shift attention from limited conceptions of literacy development to perspectives that permit heterogeneity in approach and function.

LINGUISTIC AND CULTURAL DIVERSITY

Consistent with the goal of spreading and "fine-tuning" literacy, educators and researchers have focused on developing a better understanding of literacy, literacy acquisition, and related processes. Later in this chapter, we give an overview of several major streams of research and theory on issues of literacy. While these have produced a voluminous literature, most of it concentrates on first-language and mother-tongue literacy, and in the United States mainly on English literacy. We find that insufficient attention has been given in this scholarly literature to the particular issues facing people who are immigrants, members of ethnolinguistic minorities, or cross-nationals. For many such individuals the language and culture of the educational system and the surrounding society differ from those of the home. Many such persons develop literacy in English while already having literacy skills in their native language. Scholars are only recently beginning to consider the implications for learners of becoming literate in the context of an educational system based on a second language or an unfamiliar culture.

At the same time, growing awareness of the changing demographics of the United States and calls for broader social equity are placing pressure on educational institutions to become more responsive to the needs of diverse ethnic groups. According to the Census Bureau, the Hispanic population in 1990 numbered 22.4 million, an increase of 53 percent from the 1980 count of 14.6 million. Thus, from 1980 to 1990 U.S. Hispanics grew from 6 to 9 percent of the total population. Similarly, the Asian and Pacific Islander group in 1990 numbered 7.3 million or 2.9 percent of the total population, having increased 107.8 percent since 1980. The African-American population numbered 30 million in 1990, 12.1 percent of the total, an increase of 13.2 percent since 1980. Finally, the American Indian group numbered 2 million or 0.8 percent of the total, having increased 37.9 percent since 1980. In contrast, the growth rate for the White group during the 1980s was only 6 percent. Thus, in 1990 members of non-European groups, including African-Americans, Latinos, Asians, and Native Americans, accounted for 25 percent of the U.S. population.

This diversity in the racial and ethnic make-up of the United States is reflected in the data on language. According to the 1990 Census, almost 32 million people in the United States (13.8 percent) over the age of 5 reported that they speak a language other than English at home (Waggoner, 1992a). Of these, approximately 14 million indicated that they have some difficulty with English or cannot speak it at all. An estimated additional 16 million persons who now speak English at home are originally from language-minority backgrounds, in that one or both of their parents spoke a non-English language at home. The majority (54 percent) of home speakers of non-English languages reported speaking Spanish, but substantial numbers speak French, German, Chinese, Italian, Polish, Korean, and Vietnamese (Waggoner, 1992b). Approximately 6.3 million children between the ages of 5 and 17 speak non-English languages at home, and 76 percent of them were reported to live in homes that are linguistically homogeneous (Waggoner, 1992b). In large urban areas, language diversity is even greater.

Thus, language and cultural heterogeneity in the United States are at the center of controversies regarding the role of differences in education and how these should be addressed by schools. Educators and researchers, though, cannot reach a consensus on whether there are more benefits to be gained by focusing on differences or by focusing on similarities. In large part, this is because such debates tap into value conflicts over the nature of U.S. society and the place of its component groups (Ferdman, 1990). While many argue that the role of the schools is to educate children into and by means of a common culture, others maintain that the best way to learn is by building on each child's own culture, language, and background. Still others insist that the educational system should help to attain a pluralistic society in which each group is permitted to maintain its own culture. Paralleling these debates are struggles by those groups seen as different from the historically dominant White majority to gain an equitable measure of power in education and in society at large. Because linguistic and cultural diversity in the United States typically has been associated with minority status, part of the struggle has involved attempts to eliminate the devaluation that often accompanies the perception of difference.

In recent years, language has been the focus of especially vigorous debate in the United States, as seen in controversy over English-only laws and conflicts in the area of bilingual education. Some groups, such as U.S. English and English First, actively work against the use and promotion of languages other than English in governmental and commercial spheres. Other groups, such as English Plus, oppose these efforts and support attempts to enhance bilingualism among both English speakers and linguistic minorities (Baron, 1991; Crawford, 1992a, 1992b; Horberger, 1990; Madrid, 1990; Padilla et al., 1991; Piatt, 1990). Historically, the language situation in the country has not been shaped by official language policies. Rather, the overwhelming turn to English as the national language has been accomplished by the linguistic choices of the citizenry and indirectly by the educational policy that led to the official requirement that one condition of citizenship be literacy in English (Heath, 1985). Today, political activity by U.S. English and similar linguistic interest groups has led almost a third of the states to enact constitutional amendments or resolutions legally making English the official state language (Hornberger, 1990; 1992). These measures are often motivated by such feelings as resentment of perceived privileges accorded minorities or unabashed prejudice against specific groups (see e.g., Padilla et al., 1991). They also may be driven, as Nunberg (1989) has argued, by a set of untenable beliefs about linguistic diversity. These include, for example, the view that retaining a native language and corresponding values is necessarily incompatible with learning English and assimilating to the majority culture, that if their first language is available people will not learn a second language, and that linguistic diversity is more threatening to national unity than other types of diversity, such as religious differences.

Bilingual education has been another major ground for vigorous language debates. Bilingual education has become especially controversial in those few cases where programs incorporate maintenance of the native language with the teaching of English. The values represented by maintenance programs challenge the idea of assimilation and Anglo-conformity and evoke for their opponents fears of uncontrollable divisions and loss of power. Transitional bilingual education programs, which are designed to phase in English slowly while educating children in their native language, have also been attacked, perhaps in part because they are often perceived as maintenance programs in disguise or are mistakenly thought to be ineffective. Although research results show the benefits of bilingual education programs over English immersion and English-as-a-second-language approaches for eventual learning of English and for the general academic progress of language-minority students (Hakuta & Gould, 1987; Imhoff, 1990; Medina & Escamilla, 1992; Mulhauser, 1990; Padilla et al., 1991; Ramirez, Yuen & Ramey, 1991; U.S. General Accounting Office, 1987b; Padilla, Fairchild & Valadez, 1990), controversy in this area continues. In part this may be because what is being debated is not so much the nature of the evidence but the proper role of non-English languages in an educational system largely geared towards assimilation. Huddy and Sears (1990), for example, report that opposition toward bilingual education increases among those with "antiminority sentiments, anti-Hispanic feelings, and nationalistic feelings . . . and . . . [is] even further exacerbated by a description of bilingual education as cultural and linguistic maintenance" (133).

Researchers have participated in the language debate, in part, through extensive work in the area of second-language learning and teaching (e.g., Bernhardt, 1991; Gardner, 1985; Kaplan,

1988; Ramírez, this volume). Although this work has explored variables at all levels, ranging from the individual cognitive to the macrosocietal (Hakuta, Ferdman & Diaz, 1987), it has concentrated on language and communication in general, rarely considering reading and writing in their own right (Carrell, 1988; Valdés, 1992; Weber, 1991) and tending, instead, to take them for granted. Because researchers focusing on the social, cultural, and social psychological aspects of bilingualism have tended to confound issues of literacy with other aspects of second-language acquisition and usage, it is only recently that researchers and educators focusing on literacy have begun to recognize the importance of these variables to their work.

Beyond language per se, culture and ethnicity are also gaining wider recognition as critical ingredients to any consideration of literacy (e.g., Applebee, 1991; Ferdman, 1990; Goldenberg, Reese & Gallimore, 1992; Langer, 1987; McCollum, 1991; Minami & Kennedy, 1991; Purves, 1988) and of schooling more generally (e.g., Bernal, Saenz & Knight, 1991; Fordham, 1988; Gibson & Ogbu, 1991; Heath, 1985; Matute-Bianchi, 1986; Ogbu, 1990). One aspect of this has to do with the implications of how different ethnic groups and their members are treated in society and its schools. John Ogbu, for example, has described the connections between the status of an ethnic group in society and the outcomes of schooling for its members. Ogbu argues that castelike minorities (those ethnic groups who were incorporated into the society involuntarily) tend to display lower achievement in school than "voluntary" minorities (those arising primarily from immigration) because the castelike groups are more likely to view the schools' demands as representing the oppressive dominant group. Another important aspect of the role of culture and ethnicity has to do with the nature and implications of ethnic and cultural diversity (Ferdman, 1992; Ferdman & Cortes, 1992). Ferdman (1990), for example, has argued that individuals' representations of "the behaviors, beliefs, values, and norms—in short, of the culture—appropriate to members of the ethnic group(s) to which [they] belong" (182) will play an important role in literacy acquisition and activity. By seeing *becoming* and *being* literate as processes that are very much culturally framed, we can begin to consider their transactional and fluid nature. Yet in spite of this and other work, a great deal of theoretical and empirical terrain remains unexplored.

We believe that by juxtaposing and linking those approaches that focus on the study of literacy and those that accent second-language acquisition and/or cultural transitions, we can move toward a more complete understanding of literacy among diverse populations and in multicultural societies. Given the goal of developing further knowledge of how to improve the educational process that has relevance beyond members of majority cultures and linguistic groups, more cross-fertilization between these areas of study will be required. In the process of forging this link, both researchers and educators can gain new insights into basic and applied aspects of literacy. This collection takes a special look at cross-language and cross-cultural literacy to introduce and to encourage research and theory that simultaneously consider and integrate literacy, language, and culture.

The authors of the chapters in this volume focus on the social and cultural contexts in which literacy develops and is enacted, with an emphasis on the North American situation. More and more educators and researchers are discovering that cognitive approaches, while very valuable, are insufficient by themselves to answer important questions about literacy in heterogeneous societies. There has been a movement in research from an exclusive focus on individual mastery to a recognition that it is the social context that gives mastery its impetus and meaning (e.g., de Castell & Luke, 1983; de Castell, Luke & Egan, 1986; Cook-Gumperz, 1986; Dyson, 1992; Edelsky, 1991; Hiebert, 1991; Jennings & Purves, 1991; Reder, 1987; Scribner & Cole, 1981; Snow et al., 1991; Street, 1984; Wallace, 1986; Willinsky, 1990). By considering the implications of family, school, culture, society, and nation for literacy processes, the chapters in this book help raise such questions as:

- In a multiethnic context, what does it mean to be literate?
- What are the processes involved in becoming and being literate in a second language?
- In what ways is literacy in a second language similar and in what ways is it different from mother-tongue literacy?
- What factors must be understood to better describe and facilitate literacy acquisition among members of ethnic and linguistic minorities?

- What are some current approaches that are being used to accomplish this?

We believe that these are vital questions for researchers and educators in a world that has a large number of immigrants, a variety of multiethnic and multilingual societies, and an increasing degree of multinational activity. In the next section, we discuss the various types of groups affected by issues of literacy across languages and cultures.

POPULATIONS OF INTEREST

The question of literacy across languages and cultures encompasses quite a broad set of populations and areas of study. Although the authors represented in this volume have each interpreted this theme in light of his or her own particular interests, here we attempt to provide a broader view of the groups and research questions relevant to cross-language and cross-cultural literacy. All the groups discussed include both children and adults, each with their own special needs in addition to those they share.

Immigrants

Many *immigrants* to the United States, whether or not they are literate in their native language, face the task of learning not only to speak but also to read and write in English. Indeed, one prerequisite for acquiring citizenship in the United States is demonstrating basic literacy in English. Certainly, the nature and the fluency of the literacy skills that immigrants bring with them should be an important factor in the process of acquiring English literacy. Although some newcomers to this country could be considered illiterate altogether, a good proportion have varying degrees of literacy skills in one or more languages other than English. From a purely monolingual perspective, it is difficult to know the implications of such skills for English literacy development.

We can expect that a number of other factors will also influence the experience of immigrants in acquiring or improving English literacy. These factors include the availability of resources in the native language(s), the status of the language(s) in the United States and in the person's immediate social environment, the relationship of prior literacy skills to those now required, and the perceived utility of English literacy. Also important should be the type and extent of educational facilities and the social standing and resources that are available to the immigrant (e.g., Fishman, 1966). For example, we might expect differences in the English literacy acquisition experiences of a trained engineer from Brazil who moves alone to a metropolitan community where there is a broad range of both job opportunities and educational options, and the experiences of a Cambodian farmer with no formal schooling who arrives accompanied by his and four other families to a semi-rural village that has little experience with immigrants and a limited set of job possibilities. Similarly, immigrant children who have been in school in their native country can be expected to be different in terms of literacy acquisition than children without prior schooling. Finally, we might expect that immigrants' experiences will vary depending on their motivations for coming to and staying in the United States (e.g., Ogbu, 1990) and on their current and previous social roles.

Ethnic and Cultural Minorities

Members of *ethnic and cultural minority groups* often face special obstacles on the path to literacy (e.g., Ogbu, 1990; Trueba, 1989). Among many such groups in the United States, the primary language of the home is not English. Traditional languages are maintained even though the surrounding society does not support maintenance or development of literacy with the same materials and infrastructure given to English literacy. Even in those cases in which bilingual education is offered, the school system is based on the primacy of English literacy.

Because children from linguistic minorities who start formal schooling have had different backgrounds and experiences than their peers from dominant groups, we might expect implications of these differences for the process of literacy development. Once the child is in school, the language differences between home and school can limit the ability of both to provide support for English literacy. Beyond the cross-linguistic considerations involved in becoming English literate, there are the additional issues involved in becoming literate in the home language (see, e.g., Goldenberg, Reese & Gallimore, 1992).

For adults and children from non-English backgrounds, clearly cross-language and cross-cultural literacy are relevant. Because members of some ethnic and cultural minorities, such as African-Americans, often share the dominant language and writing system, however, it can be easy to ignore these issues and treat the process of literacy acquisition as equivalent in all individuals, regardless of group membership. Research, however, including some reported in this volume, has shown that there is extensive variation not only in the features of literacy and language within various groups, but also in what mainstream literacy as defined within the society can represent to group members (e.g., Fordham, 1988; Gibson & Ogbu, 1991; Marsiglia & Halasa, 1992; Ogbu, 1990). For members of subordinated groups, reaction to oppression may take the form of resistance to literacy as defined by the dominant society. As mentioned above, Ferdman (1990) has argued that culture and cultural identity play an important role in becoming and being literate. To the extent that this is the case, it means that we must pay closer attention to the role of cultural and ethnic variation as they relate to literacy processes.

Foreign-Language Learners

A third type of group for which cross-language and cross-cultural literacy issues are also important is comprised by *learners of foreign languages,* including those for whom English is the native language and who are members of the dominant culture. Valdés (1992) refers to such individuals as "elective bilinguals," because they choose to learn a second language and "continue to spend the greater part of their time in a society in which their first language is the majority or societal language" (93). Indeed, a good deal of work in second-language acquisition has focused on members of this group, such as college and high-school students learning French, Spanish, and other languages (e.g., Bernhardt, 1991). Learners of English as a second language, especially those who are usually literate in another tongue (such as international students in the United States), have also been the subject of much research in the United States and are often included in this group (e.g., Carrell, Devine & Eskey, 1988). This work has tended to look at reading processes and, increasingly, at writing. Finally, temporary immigrants, people who reside temporarily in another country (for example, to work or study), also can be considered part of this group.

Such learners of foreign languages are usually motivated by different factors and otherwise vary in important ways (for example, in socioeconomic class) from immigrants or minorities, whom Valdés (1992) refers to as "circumstantial bilinguals." She points out that they, in contrast to elective bilinguals, "find that they must learn another language in order to survive" (94). We should expect that the process of developing literacy will not be the same for each of these groups.

Within and across each population described above, researchers can focus on a broad set of variables relevant to cross-language or cross-cultural literacy and literacy education. These factors can span across various levels of analysis, ranging from writing system variations to the contrasts among languages and cultures in what concepts they incorporate, what roles they assign to reading and writing, and what assumptions they make about how people learn.

RESEARCH STREAMS ON LITERACY ACROSS LANGUAGES AND CULTURES

Literacy, as a central activity in our modern society, has generated a flood of research. The large volume of extant research on literacy has followed a number of streams. Each of these considers different aspects of literacy and asks different types of questions. Here, we identify three major currents in literacy research. Language diversity in the United States has also commanded lively but largely independent scholarship. From this work, we mention four distinct approaches.

Currents in Literacy Research

The first important stream, one that draws on and contributes to cognitive psychology, focuses on the psychology of skilled reading as a visual, linguistic, and reasoning process. This perspective regards becoming literate as a developing skill of individuals, a skill that is shaped by cognitive constraints and constructive strategies emanating from or based in each learner. For example, the intricate, split-second maneuvers that take readers along at a rate of hundreds of words a minute, twice as fast as the usual comprehension of speech, are studied as a manifestation of the mind's complexities (e.g., Rayner & Pollatsek, 1989). In this stream, the individual learner is the basic unit of analysis, and considerations of environment, culture, and society are seen as relevant only insofar as they influence individual features or cognitive structures and processes. Whether or not this is explicitly recognized, the parameters of this line of research are culturally shaped.

A second stream of research, one that has been especially broad and turbulent, focuses on the teaching, understanding, and assessment of literacy as an educational objective in schools, essential to acquiring the knowledge and the world view represented there. Much of this research has been undertaken to answer questions about the best way to foster students' proficiency as readers and writers. For example, a current issue within this approach concerns the extent to which reading and writing, from preschool through college levels, should be taught as independent subjects through direct instruction or fostered through purposeful and authentic reading and writing from the outset (Adams, 1990; Willinsky, 1990). This question is being played out within the larger context of the social interactions that take place in school settings, the ways that schools and classrooms are organized, and the dimensions of public policy that impinge on daily activities (Barr et al., 1991). Thus, although research within this perspective is often done at an individual level of analysis, it is not restricted to it. The unit of analysis can also be the classroom, the school, or instructional approaches. In this stream, sociocultural considerations are important to the extent that they can help to clarify and improve educational practices. Much of this work, however, does not explicitly consider the role of culture in literacy acquisition.

The last stream of research, and the one most closely linked to this volume, examines literacy in society. In this perspective, reading and writing are viewed as practices occurring in a social context, guided by intention, laden with values, and taking on forms and functions that differ according to time and place. To use Scribner's (1984) terms, literacy has been variously conceived of as adaptation to the requirements of modern technological society, as the means to power in the structure of societies, and as a state of grace that societies endow to the accomplished. Some scholars taking this direction describe it as a "constructivist" approach (Hiebert, 1991) and often cite the work of Vygotsky (1978). Historians, anthropologists, and comparative educators working in this stream have cultivated an expansive view that reveals the diversity of conceptions of literacy, of the significance it may hold, and of its relationship to social, economic, and political factors. This broader stream has been paralleled by research that recognizes the differing routes to becoming literate and to achieving different states of literacy for different social ends (e.g., Schiefflin & Gilmore, 1986; Wagner, 1987). It presents challenges to the cognitive view, which seeks, if not assumes, a universal view of reading and writing. It also runs counter to the strong current that advocates a monolithic store of knowledge that should be provided by our educational systems. This research perspective is the one that permits most clearly asking questions about literacy across languages and cultures, because it addresses most directly issues of policy, settings such as the workplace, and aspects of societal variation and complexity. Choosing a language or dialect to read and write, learning to read more than one language, and using different languages for different purposes and with different levels of proficiency are all acts that have significance of wide range and subtlety over cultural contexts.

These three streams of literacy research—cognitive, educational, and social—have not been well integrated with each other or with other approaches. Yet at some junctures they flow into one another. In particular, the social context of reading and writing has in recent times taken on greater weight, so that their status as private processes, internal to the mind, are continually under review. For example, emergent literacy, the acquisition of reading and writing skills by young children as they engage with print at home and at school, is currently being studied as an extension of language development in the social context of family and child care, with important implications for teaching in the schools. Learning to read and write is not viewed as simply knowing the letters or accumulating a stock of words but also as purposefully engaging with print over talk and using strategies that shift with expanding knowledge (Sulzby & Teale, 1991).

Currents in Research on Language Diversity

As with literacy, research on language and multilingualism has been approached from a number of perspectives. These include linguistic, psycholinguistic, and sociolinguistic currents. The sociolinguistic current can be further subdivided into social and societal approaches.

The first important stream of research on linguistic diversity, that of linguistics proper, concentrates on the form of American languages themselves, both indigenous and transplanted, ranging from the intricacies of the sounds, syntax, and vocabularies of the native American languages like Mohawk, to the characteristics of African-influenced English such as Gullah, to the dialects of German in America. Furthermore, this stream has examined how vocabularies, sounds, and grammar have shifted historically through contact with one another in society, as well as how these language forms influence one another in the speech of bilingual individuals (Ferguson & Heath, 1981; Turner, 1982).

A second stream of research—psycholinguistics—concerns the cognitive aspects of bilingual abilities, focusing on how individuals acquire, organize, and activate their knowledge of more than one language or dialect to greater or lesser degrees over a range of settings (Grosjean, 1982; Ramírez, 1985). An important aspect of this work has considered, in defiance of research earlier in this century, how bilingual ability may be positively related to cognitive capacities in young children (Hakuta, 1986; Hakuta, Ferdman & Diaz, 1987).

The third stream of work falls within the sociolinguistic tradition that concentrates on social psychological factors. This perspective examines how individuals put their linguistic knowledge to use in social encounters—exploring in what settings, on what occasions, to whom, and to what immediate purpose this is done, thereby giving and taking meaning from the choice of language itself (e.g., Forgas, 1985; Ryan & Giles, 1982). Closely related to this dynamic is the value that speakers place on the variation within and across languages. This area of research has also explored how such values about a language may serve to sustain cultural solidarity among its speakers and invite others to learn it or neglect it (Fishman, 1966; Fishman, Cooper & Ma, 1971; Giles & Coupland, 1991; Giles & Johnson, 1987).

Finally, the fourth stream of language research, while also following a sociolinguistic tradition, is more focused on a societal level of analysis. This perspective addresses the distribution of languages and dialects in larger society and the social forces and institutions that have contributed to their maintenance or loss through the generations (Fishman, 1989; McKay & Wong, 1988;

Sagarin & Kelly, 1985). How nations and their constituent institutions orient themselves with regards to language planning (e.g., Foster, 1991) is encompassed by this approach.

Integrating the Study of Literacy and Language

When language differences are taken into account, the questions that might be asked in literacy research proliferate. Expanded consideration of diversity can be a vibrant source of important and broader research questions for each of the currents of literacy research discussed above.

In the cognitive stream such questions include:

- How do skilled bilingual readers and writers call on their knowledge of more than one language, pass back and forth between them, keep them separate, and yet use one language to reinforce the other?
- How does learning to read a language contribute to learning to speak a language, and vice versa?
- How do people come to know more than one written language?
- How do they learn to read and write through a language they do not speak and thus learn the language?
- Are there differences between children, adolescents, and adults as their abilities mature?

In the educational stream some questions include:

- How do children construct their knowledge of spoken and written second languages even as they are developing their first?
- How can specific instructional strategies contribute to their advancement?
- In what ways do the findings of researchers lend support to the common practice of educators in guiding students toward constructing their knowledge, values, and activities with written language?
- What is the place of reading and writing when teaching a second language?

In the social stream, the following questions arise:

- How do readers from different cultures value the knowledge of one or more written languages?
- To what ends do they choose one over another?
- To what extent do they take pleasure and take pains in learning and using them? What kinds of resistance are possible?
- In what ways do they give meaning to texts and to the activities of reading and writing themselves?

The extensive research on linguistic diversity in individuals, in classrooms, and in society has not contributed as much as might be expected to answering such questions. In part, this may be because in a large proportion of studies about bilingualism, literacy is taken for granted. With respect to individual abilities, for instance, researchers ask subjects to carry out reading and writing tasks in experimental settings and draw conclusions about linguistic abilities in general. In academic settings, research on the effects of instruction in foreign languages, classical languages, and English as a second language is done through the written language, presupposing students' knowledge of how to read and write with ease. In analyses of language use in communities, where an individual's choice of language for different purposes is traced in relation to topic, listeners, setting, and other such variables, the focus has often been on the spoken language. In broadly gauged descriptions of the number and uses of the various languages in a society, the respective place of written and spoken varieties, apart from the dominant language, rarely receives more than secondary attention.

Thus, as deep as the research streams are in the many aspects of literacy, they afford relatively few insights into questions concerning literacy across languages and cultures. A good deal of research on the gap between school language and children's knowledge of it in the schools has addressed the question of achievement through bilingual education and programs in English as a second language, in order to establish a basis for policy (Collier, 1987; Imhoff, 1990). In contrast, little attention has been given to looking at the ways that learners accomplish such academic achievement or how they in fact understand and create specific written texts.

Recently, however, interest has been accelerating with respect to a range of issues (Bernhardt, 1991; Weber, 1991). In school settings, for instance, specific studies have been undertaken on such topics as the development of word recognition across languages in early learners (Kendall, et al., 1987), the course of free-writing ability in Hispanic children (Edelsky, 1986), and the relevance of culturally specific background knowledge to the understanding of discourse (Barnitz, 1986). The particular challenge that students at the university level face when they need to be able to read English for academic purposes has gained attention (Carrell, Devine & Eskey, 1988). With respect to literacy in social context, the complexities of written language use and meaning have been examined in diverse settings that reveal informal as well as formal literacy learning, varying routes of socialization into reading and writing, collaborative literacy practices, and varying knowledge of the forms, uses, and significance attached to literacy (Reder, 1987). The possibility that such social factors influence the very skill of reading has also been considered (Devine, 1988). Furthermore, the place of the written language as an expression of cultural identity has been explored (Ferdman, 1990; Fishman, 1989).

THE PRESENT VOLUME

This collection is designed to continue and to elaborate some of the new directions described above. The chapters in this volume review and fill in gaps in previous work and provide examples of innovative approaches to the issues of literacy across languages and cultures. We hope that this will add to the growing interest in linking previously unrelated areas of research and creating knowledge applicable to the experience and situation of more diverse groups. By considering at once issues relevant to a number of groups that must approach literacy cross-linguistically or cross-culturally, we believe that we can broaden the terms for conceptualization, research, and practice. The authors of the chapters come from a variety of disciplines and perspectives. It is the interdisciplinary and complex view that results from the juxtaposition of their work that we would like to suggest is the way in which the study of literacy will be most fruitful and rich.

Stephen Reder, Arnulfo Ramírez, and Nancy Hornberger, in chapters 2, 3, and 4 respectively, each take a broad perspective in reviewing and synthesizing theoretical and empirical work relevant to understanding cross-language and cross-cultural literacy and literacy acquisition. Their chapters provide a substantial basis for framing future research, theory, and application in this area. In his chapter, Stephen Reder takes a social psychological perspective, describing literacy as a social and cultural process comprised by a set of culturally defined practices. He summarizes research showing how literacy practices vary across cultural groups within a society. Most importantly, Reder also develops a theory of literacy transmission and development that emphasizes the roles of practice and engagement and discusses the implications of this research and theory for education.

Arnulfo Ramírez focuses on learning to read and write in a second language for academic purposes by students already literate in a first language. He explores the implications for literacy of learner differences in second-language acquisition and of the characteristics of written texts. Ramírez also reviews the bearing on second-language literacy of current theories of second-language acquisition and conceptions of language proficiency. This chapter examines research and theory about the *technology of reading,* to use Reder's (1987) term; second-language reading is discussed as being done in the context of the classroom and from textbooks, as in Street's (1984) autonomous model of reading. Thus Ramírez's contribution represents an overview of an approach that is now shifting as it begins to incorporate consideration of the sociocultural contexts of literate activities that Reder discusses.

In her chapter, Nancy Hornberger offers an integrated theoretical framework for understanding biliterate contexts, development, and media. She posits the significance of thinking about these as continua rather than as polar opposites. As contexts for biliteracy, she includes micro-macro, oral-literate, and monolingual-bilingual continua. Continua of reception-production, oral-written, and L_1–L_2 transfer are important in understanding the development of the individual's communicative repertoire. Finally, she explains how biliterates can communicate using a variety of media, ranging from simultaneous to successive exposure, similar to dissimilar structures, and convergent to divergent scripts. Hornberger's chapter provides a useful conceptual structure for linking the various approaches to language and literacy and seeing how they relate to each other.

Chapters 5–10, by Concha Delgado-Gaitan, Virginia Vogel Zanger, Barbara McCaskill, Joanne Devine, Mark Zuss, and Alison d'Anglejan, respectively, each exemplify the application of a sociocultural perspective to aspects of cross-language and/or cross-cultural literacy. The authors adopt the lenses of their particular disciplines to discuss their research programs or to develop new theoretical positions. Seen as a group, these chapters provide strong arguments for the importance of considering the unique aspects of literacy across languages or cultures.

In her contribution, Concha Delgado-Gaitan links literacy activities within ethnic- and language-minority families, in this case Hispanics in California, to empowerment in the larger community. She presents a theoretical discussion on the process of empowerment and summarizes practical experience in the steps leading toward family empowerment with an eye toward the potential of family literacy. In her sociocultural view, family literacy is not simply a tool for fostering school achievement, but is also important for internalizing new ways of social engagement. Delgado-Gaitan describes an effort to guide Hispanic parents to interact with their children over storybooks and their ensuing involvement in community activities. She links this participation in the community to the parents' experience of shaping new patterns of interaction within the family.

Virginia Vogel Zanger's chapter explores the relationship between members of an important linguistic minority—Hispanic youth—and the dominant culture (as represented by the school), as well as the role of these relations in the youths' development of English literacy. Zanger shows vividly how Hispanic high school students experience their educational environment. She portrays conditions that include the school's failure to incorporate the students' language and culture, a racist and exclusionary school climate, and a breakdown in trust between Hispanic students and Anglo teachers, and she connects these to the Hispanic students' limited access to the conditions that facilitate literacy development.

Barbara McCaskill, as a scholar of English specializing in African-American literature, takes a different approach from the other authors to shed more light on the implications of cultural differences and the experience of oppression for the role of literacy in individuals and society. McCaskill analyses Harriet Jacobs's nineteenth-century narrative to show the interplay of minority—in this case slave—status and literacy. The slave is forced to adopt "mainstream" symbols of literacy to prove herself, yet these are inadequate and must be refashioned. Jacobs's ability to do this successfully speaks to the experience of those that find the odds insurmountable. The mainstream literacy Jacobs seems to adopt cannot do justice to her vision of life and the world around her, and so she must resolve the paradox of only being able to use a language that has no words for what she needs to say. The way she ultimately does this has important implications for today, when similar patterns continue to exist and affect members of marginalized and oppressed groups. Dominant views of literacy ensure that alternative experiences can only be described by exceptional individuals able to transcend the limitations of the images and symbols to which the dominant culture gives them access. McCaskill's chapter also speaks to the uses of literacy and the definitions of literacy in intergroup and interpersonal relations.

In her chapter, Joanne Devine analyzes the role that power differences have in influencing the access to literacy available to groups and individuals. Using muted group theory, she shows how groups with less power have been held to different standards and must use a different voice to be heard. Such power relationships have important implications for the differential transmission of literacy in society. Building on Zanger's and McCaskill's contributions, Devine articulates a perspective that highlights the importance of group-level societal phenomena for individuals' experiences as they acquire and use literacy skills.

Mark Zuss takes a theoretical view as he analyzes the role that ideology, as represented by values and subjectivity, has in influencing linguistic practices and approaches to literacy in culturally diverse classrooms. As members of different cultural groups come in contact with each other in educational contexts, the power relations between them and the roles they occupy are crucial determinants of the values that will be emphasized and enacted in teaching and learning. Zuss uses economic metaphors to show how the practices of some discourse communities dominate those of others, thus influencing the possibilities for learning available to members of minority groups.

In her chapter on current language and literacy issues in Quebec, Alison d'Anglejan takes a wide-angled view that links a number of factors usually considered separately. She examines the place of literacy in the French language policy of Quebec in light of demographic changes, recent surveys on literacy levels, and work-place requirements, revealing the ways in which literacy has been obscured in language policy and the principles that guide it. As she discusses educational efforts in second language and literacy, d'Anglejan gives special attention to the challenges presented by recent immigrants with low educational levels and their families. This chapter also affords readers the opportunity for comparison with the situation in the United States.

The final chapter is written by Jim Cummins, who is a noted researcher and writer on aspects of bilingualism and bilingual education, and is based on his reflections of the preceding chapters. Cummins takes a forceful and wide-ranging approach in arguing for the importance of considering literacy acquisition and development across languages and cultures in the sociopolitical context of public discourse on literacy. He provides a framework for integrating functional, cultural, and critical literacies that at once considers both the micro-interactions that occur in schools between students and teachers and the macro relations of power between groups in society. Cummins advances the notion that solving the "literacy crisis" and achieving true success in literacy instruction for linguistic and cultural minorities will only happen to the extent that currently coercive power relations among groups and between teachers and students are replaced with collaborative relations of power. Cummins's chapter represents a potent call to researchers, educators, and policy makers to keep in mind the full complexity of the issues as they seek to address the challenges of literacy across languages and cultures.

REFERENCES

Adams, M.J. (1990). *Beginning to read: Thinking and learning about print*. Cambridge: MIT Press.

Applebee, A.N. (1991). Literature: Whose heritage? In E.H. Hiebert (Ed.), *Literacy for a diverse society: Perspectives, practices, and policies*, (pp. 228–236). New York: Teachers College Press.

Barnitz, J.G. (1986). Toward understanding the effects of cross-cultural schemata and discourse structure on second language comprehension. *Journal of Reading Behavior, 18*, 95–116.

Baron, D. (1991). *The English-only question*. New Haven: Yale University Press.

Barr, R., Kamil, M.L., Mosenthal, P. & Pearson, P.D. (Eds.) (1991). *Handbook of reading research, Vol. 2*. New York: Longman.

Bernal, M.E., Saenz, D.S. & Knight, G.P. (1991). Ethnic identity and adaptation of Mexican American youths in school settings. *Hispanic Journal of Behavioral Sciences, 13,* 135–154.

Bernhardt, E.B. (1991). *Reading development in a second language: Theoretical, empirical, and classroom perspectives.* Norwood, NJ: Ablex.

Carrell, P.L. (1988). SLA and classroom instruction: Reading. *Annual Review of Applied Linguistics, 9,* 223–242.

Carrell, P.L., Devine, J. & Eskey, D. (1988). *Interactive approaches to second language reading.* New York: Cambridge University Press.

Collier, V.P. (1987). Age and acquisition of second language for academic purposes. *TESOL Quarterly, 21,* 617–641.

Cook-Gumperz, J. (Ed.) (1986). *The social construction of literacy.* New York: Cambridge University Press.

Crawford, J. (1992a). *Hold your tongue: Bilingualism and the politics of English only.* Reading, MA: Addison-Wesley.

———. (Ed.). (1992b). *Language loyalties: A source book on the official English controversy.* Chicago: University of Chicago Press.

de Castell, S. & Luke, A. (1983). Defining 'literacy' in North American schools: Social and historical conditions and consequences. *Journal of Curriculum Studies, 15,* 373–389.

de Castell, S., Luke, A. & Egan, K. (Ed.). (1986). *Literacy, society, and schooling: A reader.* Cambridge: Cambridge University Press.

Devine, J. (1988). A case study of two readers: Models of reading and reading performance. In P.L. Carrell, J. Devine & D.E. Eskey (Eds.), *Interactive approaches to second language reading* (pp. 127–139). New York: Cambridge University Press.

Dyson, A.H. (1992). *Whistle for Willie,* lost puppies, and cartoon dogs: The sociocultural dimensions of young children's composing. *Journal of Reading Behavior, 24,* 433–462.

Edelsky, C. (1986). *Writing in a bilingual program: Habia una vez.* Norwood, NJ: Ablex.

———. (1991). *With literacy and justice for all: Rethinking the social in language and education.* London: Falmer Press.

Ferdman, B.M. (1990). Literacy and cultural identity. *Harvard Educational Review, 60,* 181–204.

———. (1992). The dynamics of ethnic diversity in organizations: Toward integrative models. In K. Kelley (Ed.), *Issues, theory and research in industrial/organizational psychology* (pp. 339–384). Amsterdam: North Holland.

Ferdman, B.M. & Cortes, A. (1992). Culture and identity among Hispanic managers in an Anglo business. In S.B. Knouse, P. Rosenfeld & A. Culbertson (Eds.), *Hispanics in the workplace* (pp. 246–277). Newbury Park, CA: Sage.

Ferguson, C.A. & Heath, S.B. (Eds.) (1981). *Language in the USA.* New York: Cambridge University Press.

Fishman, J.A. (Ed.). (1966). *Language loyalty in the United States: The maintenance and perpetuation of non-English mother tongues by American ethnic and religious groups.* The Hague: Mouton.

———. (1989). *Language and ethnicity in minority sociolinguistic perspective.* Clevedon: Multilingual Matters.

Fishman, J.A., Cooper, R.L. & Ma, R. (1971). *Bilingualism in the barrio.* Bloomington: Indiana University.

Fordham, S. (1988). Racelessness as a factor in Black students' school success: Pragmatic strategy or pyrrhic victory? *Harvard Educational Review, 58,* 54–84.

Forgas, J.P. (Ed.) (1985). *Language and social situations.* New York: Springer-Verlag.

Foster, P. (1991). Literacy and the politics of language. In E.M. Jennings & A.C. Purves (Eds.), *Literate systems and individual lives: Perspectives on literacy and schooling* (pp. 37–50). Albany: State University of New York Press.

Gardner, R.C. (1985). *Social psychology and second language learning: The role of attitudes and motivation.* London: Edward Arnold.

Gibson, M.A. & Ogbu, J.U. (Eds.) (1991). *Minority status and schooling: A comparative study of immigrant and involuntary minorities.* New York: Garland.

Giles, H. & Coupland, N. (1991). *Language: Contexts and consequences.* Pacific Grove, CA: Brooks/Cole.

Giles, H. & Johnson, P. (1987). Ethnolinguistic identity theory: A social psychological approach to language maintenance. *International Journal of the Sociology of Language, 68,* 66–99.

Goldenberg, C., Reese, L. & Gallimore, R. (1992). Effects of literacy materials from school on Latino children's home experiences and early reading achievement. *American Journal of Education, 100,* 497–536.

Grosjean, F. (1982). *Life with two languages.* Cambridge: Harvard University Press.

Hakuta, K. (1986). *Mirror of language: The debate on bilingualism.* New York: Basic.

Hakuta, K., Ferdman, B.M. & Diaz, R.M. (1987). Bilingualism and cognitive development: Three perspectives. In S. Rosenberg (Ed.), *Advances in applied psycholinguistics. Vol. 2: Reading, writing and language learning* (pp. 284–319). New York: Cambridge University Press.

Hakuta, K. & Gould, L.J. (1987, Mar.). Synthesis of research on bilingual education. *Educational Leadership, 45,* 38–45.

Heath, S.B. (1985). Bilingual education and a national language policy. In J.E. Alatis & J.J. Staczek (Eds.), *Perspectives on bilingualism and bilin-*

gual education (pp. 75–88). Washington, DC: Georgetown University Press.

Hiebert, E.H. (Ed.) (1991). *Literacy for a diverse society: Perspectives, practices, and policies.* New York: Teachers College Press.

Hornberger, N.H. (1990). Bilingual education and English-only: A language planning framework. *Annals of the American Academy of Political and Social Science, 508,* 12–26.

———. (1992). Biliteracy contexts, continua, and contrasts: Policy and curriculum for Cambodian and Puerto Rican students in Philadelphia. *Education and Urban Society, 24,* 196–211.

Huddy, L. & Sears, D.O. (1990). Qualified public support for bilingual education: Some policy implications. *Annals of the American Academy of Political and Social Science, 508,* 119–134.

Imhoff, G. (Ed.) (1990). *Learning in two languages: From conflict to consensus in the reorganization of schools.* New Brunswick, NJ: Transaction Publishers.

Jennings, E.M. & Purves, A.C. (Eds.) (1991). *Literate systems and individual lives: Perspectives on literacy and schooling.* Albany: State University of New York Press.

Kaplan, R.B. (Ed.) (1988). Second language acquisition research. *Annual Review of Applied Linguistics, 9* [complete volume].

Kendall, J.R., Lajeunesse, G., Chmilar, P., Shapson, L.R. & Shapson, S.M. (1987). English reading skills of French immersion students in kindergarten and Grades 1 and 2. *Reading Research Quarterly, 22,* 135–160.

Langer, J.A. (Ed.) (1987). *Language, literacy, and culture: Issues of society and schooling.* Norwood, NJ: Ablex.

Madrid, A. (1990). Official English: A false policy issue. *Annals of the American Academy of Political and Social Science, 508,* 62–65.

Marsiglia, F.F. & Halasa, O. (1992, April). *Ethnic identity and school achievement as perceived by a group of selected mainland Puerto Rican students.* Paper presented at the meetings of the American Educational Research Association, San Francisco.

McCollum, P. (1991). Cross-cultural perspectives on classroom discourse and literacy. In E.H. Hiebert (Ed.), *Literacy for a diverse society: Perspectives, practices, and policies,* (pp. 108–121). New York: Teachers College Press.

McKay, S.L. & Wong, S.C. (Eds.) (1988). *Language diversity: Problem or resource?* New York: Newbury House.

Medina, M.J. & Escamilla, K. (1992). Evaluation of transitional and maintenance bilingual programs. *Urban Education, 27,* 263–290.

Minami, M. & Kennedy, B.P. (Eds.). (1991). *Language issues in literacy and bilingual/multicultural education.* Cambridge, MA: Harvard Educational Review.

Molesky, J. (1988). Understanding the American linguistic mosaic: A historical overview of language maintenance and language shift. In S.L. McKay & S.C. Wong (Eds.), *Language diversity: Problem or resource?* (pp. 29–68). New York: Newbury House.

Mulhauser, F. (1990). Reviewing bilingual-education research for Congress. *Annals of the American Academy of Political and Social Science, 508,* 107–118.

Nunberg, G. (1989). Linguists and the official language movement. *Language, 65,* 579–587.

Ogbu, J.U. (1990). Minority status and literacy in comparative perspective. *Daedalus, 119,* 141–168.

Padilla, A.M., Fairchild, H.H. & Valadez, C.M. (Eds.) (1990). *Bilingual education: Issues and strategies.* Newbury Park: Sage.

Padilla, A.M., Lindholm, K.J., Chen, A., Durán, R., Hakuta, K., Lambert, W. & Tucker, G.R. (1991). The English-only movement: Myths, reality, and implications for psychology. *American Psychologist, 46,* 120–30.

Pearson, P.D. & Cole, J. (1987). Explicit comprehension instruction: A review of research and a new conceptualization of instruction. *Elementary School Journal, 88,* 151–165.

Piatt, B. (1990). *Only English? Law and language policy in the United States.* Albuquerque: University of New Mexico Press.

Purves, A. (Ed.) (1988). *Writing across languages and cultures: Issues in contrastive rhetoric.* Newbury Park, CA: Sage.

Ramírez, A.G. (1985). *Bilingualism through schooling: Cross-cultural education for minority and majority students.* Albany: State University of New York Press.

Ramirez, J.D., Yuen, S.D. & Ramey, D.R. (1991). *Final report: Longitudinal study of structured English immersion strategy, early-exit and late-exit transitional bilingual education programs for language-minority children* (Executive Summary). San Mateo, CA: Aguirre International.

Rayner, K. & Pollatsek, A. (1989). *Psychology of reading.* Englewood Cliffs, NJ: Prentice-Hall.

Reder, S. (1987). Comparative aspects of functional literacy development: Three ethnic American communities. In D. Wagner (Ed.), *The future of literacy in a changing world.* Oxford: Pergamon.

Romaine, S. (1989). *Bilingualism.* Oxford: Basil Blackwell.

Rossell, C. & Ross, J.M. (1986). The social science evidence on bilingual education. *Journal of Law and Education, 15,* 385–419.

Ryan, E.B. & Giles, H. (Eds.) (1982). *Attitudes towards language variation: Social and applied contexts.* London: Edward Arnold.

Sagarin, E. & Kelly, R.J. (1985). Polylingualism in the United States of America: A multitude of tongues and a monolingual majority. In W. Beer and J.E. Jacob (Eds.), *Language policy and language unity* (pp. 20–44). Totowa, NJ: Rowman and Allenheld.

Schiefflin, B. & Gilmore, P. (1986). *The acquisition of literacy: Ethnographic perspectives.* Norwood, NJ: Ablex.

Scribner, S. (1984). Literacy in three metaphors. *American Journal of Education, 93,* 7–22.

Snow, C.E., Barnes, W.S., Chandler, J., Goodman, I.F. & Hemphill, L. (1991). *Unfulfilled expectations: Home and school influences on literacy.* Cambridge: Harvard University Press.

Street, B.V. (1984). *Literacy in theory and practice.* Cambridge: Cambridge University Press.

Sulzby, E. & Teale, W. (1991). Emergent literacy. In R. Barr, M.L. Kamil, P. Mosenthal & P.D. Pearson (Eds.), *Handbook of reading research, Vol. 2* (pp. 727–757). New York: Longman.

Swaffar, J.K. (1985). Reading authentic texts in a foreign language: A cognitive model. *Modern Language Journal, 69,* 15–34.

Trueba, H.T. (1989). *Raising silent voices: Educating the linguistic minorities for the 21st century.* New York: Newbury House.

Turner, P.R. (1982). *Bilingualism in the southwest,* 2nd ed. Tucson: University of Arizona Press.

U.S. General Accounting Office. (1987a). *Bilingual education: Information on limited English proficient students* (GAO/HRD-87-85BR). Washington, D.C.: author.

U.S. General Accounting Office. (1987b). *Bilingual education: A new look at the research evidence* (GAO/PEMD-87-12BR). Washington, D.C.: author.

Valdés, G. (1992). Bilingual minorities and language issues in writing: Toward professionwide responses to a new challenge. *Written Communication, 9,* 85–136.

Vygotsky, L. (1978). *Mind in society: The development of higher psychological processes.* Cambridge: Harvard University Press.

Waggoner, D. (1992a). Census sample reveals increase in multilingual and foreign-born populations. *Numbers and Needs: Ethnic and Linguistic Minorities in the United States, 2*(4), 1 ff. [Available from Dorothy Waggoner, Editor, Box G1H/B, 3900 Watson Place N.W., Washington DC 20016.]

———. (1992b). Four in five home speakers of non-English languages in the U.S. speak one of eight languages. *Numbers and Needs: Ethnic and Linguistic Minorities in the United States, 2*(5), 1 ff. [Available from

Dorothy Waggoner, Editor, Box G1H/B, 3900 Watson Place N.W., Washington DC 20016.]

Wagner, D.A. (Ed.). (1983). Literacy and ethnicity. *International Journal of the Sociology of Language, 42* (complete).

———. (Ed.) (1987). *The future of literacy in a changing world.* Oxford: Pergamon Press.

Wallace, C. (1986). *Learning to read in a multicultural society: The social context of second language literacy.* Oxford: Pergamon Press.

Weber, R.-M. (1991). Linguistic diversity and reading in American society. In R. Barr, M.L. Kamil, P. Mosenthal & P.D. Pearson (Eds.), *Handbook of reading research, Vol. 2* (pp. 97–119). New York: Longman.

Willinsky, J. (1990). *The new literacy: Redefining reading and writing in the schools.* New York: Routledge.

PART 2

Theoretical and Research Perspectives

CHAPTER 2

Practice-Engagement Theory: A Sociocultural Approach to Literacy Across Languages and Cultures

Stephen Reder

INTRODUCTION

A critical debate among literacy researchers, practitioners, and policymakers concerns whether to view literacy within a paradigm of *individual skills* or one of *cultural practices*. The individual skills paradigm, the older and more established of the two, emphasizes the mental processes underlying reading and writing. Considerable progress has been made by educators, psychologists, and cognitive scientists identifying the basic nature and organization of these hypothetical processes. But researchers and practitioners working within the paradigm have assumed such processes to be only marginally affected by the social contexts in which they occur. Literacy is thought of as something people carry around in their heads from setting to setting, from task to task. This skills orientation is often expressed as a "dipstick" model of literacy assessment and instruction, in which the individual's head can be opened up, a linear instrument inserted (the dipstick), and a measurement taken (the individual's literacy "level"). If there is not "enough" literacy inside, it is assumed more can be added through additional formal instruction.

An alternative paradigm for literacy has developed in recent years. Within this framework, literacy is conceived as a set of social or cultural *practices* and its participants as a *community of prac-*

tice. As a set of socially patterned activities, literacy develops and spread through a process of *socialization,* the means of which may include but are not necessarily limited to formal instruction (Reder & Green, 1985; Resnick, 1990). Indeed, these formal instructional activities are seen as just another—albeit often highly valued—set of literacy practices themselves.

It is not that one of these paradigms is right and therefore the other is wrong; in fact, they are not seen as being contrary to one another. Instead, each is seen as being more or less useful for particular explanatory and practical purposes. Each seems better able to highlight certain issues and account for certain kinds of empirical relationships. For example, the cultural practices paradigm better addresses issues of how the characteristics of literacy behaviors vary with and are closely fitted to the features of the contexts in which they occur. The individual skills paradigm overlooks the ways in which the details of reading, writing, and communicative activities are systematically fitted to the characteristics of the social situations in which such activities occur.

To illustrate the ways in which literacy articulates with social context, consider the following event taken from my own recent experience. On a recent visit to Washington, D.C., I stopped for lunch on Capitol Hill at a "Chinese-American Cafe." Bustling with the workday noon hour rush, the service and kitchen staff passed information among themselves in a good-natured, multilingual banter that could be heard above the din of the customers' conversations and rattling of utensils and plates. Not being as familiar with the restaurant's culinary offerings as were its regular patrons, I scanned the English-language menu on the wall. When I asked my waitress a question about how a certain dish was prepared, it was quickly apparent her command of English (ever so much better than my grasp of Cantonese) was not going to support the needed conversation. She called another waitress over to answer my question. The first waitress then took my order in English, wrote it down in Chinese, passed it to the kitchen, and later returned with my lunch. After finishing the meal, I called for my check. My waitress gestured towards the cash register. As I walked over there, she called out my order in Cantonese to the cashier, who added up the items manually on his abacus and finally entered a total on the electronic cash register.

In this example, the restaurant staff has incorporated the use of written materials into their activities in complex ways. Details of literacy use depend on complex interactions among task characteristics, allocations of functional roles, and oral and written language proficiencies among group members. In this setting, as well as in numerous others in the United States which others have described (Ferguson & Heath, 1981; Weber, 1991), there are complex relationships between the cultural and linguistic diversity of those in the group and the ways in which the various oral and written languages are functionally deployed to accomplish specific tasks.

Although multicultural and multilingual phenomena such as these certainly display task-specific patterning in the use of written language, literacy appears to be patterned into units of social practices regardless of the number of oral or written languages normally available or in use. Although the cultural practices paradigm is quite useful for understanding the societal distribution of literacy among multilingual and multicultural populations, it can also deepen our understanding of literacy in general. By helping to deepen our understanding of the scientific and educational issues of literacy in general, the nation's multicultural and multilingual diversity will once again serve as a valuable resource.

The remainder of this chapter is organized into three sections. The next section reviews research on literacy within the cultural practices paradigm, with particular attention to both multicultural and multilingual contexts. A particular version of the cultural practices approach, termed *practice-engagement theory*, is developed in the subsequent section. The final section discusses some implications of practice-engagement theory for education practice and policy and indicates some priority topics for further research and development.

LITERACY AS CULTURAL PRACTICE

Within the last decade, research on the nature and development of literacy in its social context has burgeoned. Although these issues have been explored within distinct disciplinary traditions, a shared view of *literacy as the use of written materials in cultural activities* has emerged. In this view, the critical issues for understanding the acquisition and development of literacy are (1) how the use of writing is incorporated into existing activities, (2) how writing is used to innovate new cultural practices, and (3) what processes underlie the *cultural transmission* or socialization of the practices. Cutting across these concerns is the fundamental issue of how individuals in their day-to-day interactions create and recreate the contexts in which written materials are used, how those interactions influence and are influenced by the use of written materials, and how participants interpret and give meaning to the texts and actions involved. These are important questions for literacy development in general, regardless of whether the written language in question represents a native or a second language, or whether the individuals are members of minority or mainstream groups.

Cross-cultural studies of literacy in different societies (e.g., Goody, 1968, 1986; Wagner, 1987) as well as in our society (e.g., Heath, 1983; Reder, 1987; Schieffelin & Gilmore, 1986; Scollon & Scollon, 1981) demonstrate sharp cultural variation in the ways in which literacy is incorporated into everyday life. These ethnographic studies carefully observe and analyze the occurrence of *literacy events,* interactions in which individuals use written materials. Many naturally occurring literacy events involve social interactions among cooperating individuals as well as interactions between individuals and written materials (Fingeret, 1983; Heath, 1983; Reder & Green, 1983; Shuman, 1983).

These literacy events are culturally patterned into recurring units, which Scribner and Cole (1981) have termed *literacy practices.* Cultural groups are said to have specific literacy practices in the same sense they are said to have specific religious practices, house-building practices, medicinal practices, and so forth. Examples of literacy practices are as varied as sending an office memorandum, mail-ordering from a catalog, reading the newspaper at the family breakfast table, having group reading lessons in a school classroom, filling out an unemployment form, reading bedtime stories to young children, reading responsively in a church service, and so forth.

Studies of literacy practices among varied ethnolinguistic groups have been increasing in recent years. In order to understand the ways in which the practices of various groups may be structured differently, systematic comparative studies of the full repertoire of literacy practices in specific communities are especially revealing. Examples of such comparative studies are Heath's (1983) study of three rural communities in the Piedmont (one working-class Black, one working-class White, one middle class); Schieffelin and Cochran-Smith's (1984) comparison of literacy development among a tribe in Papua, New Guinea, an urban Sino-Vietnamese immigrant community in the United States, and a middle class suburban community in the United States; Purves's (1987) analysis of cross-national studies of school-oriented literacy practices; and Reder's (1987) comparative analysis of literacy development in three ethnic communities in the United States—an Eskimo fishing village, a Hmong immigrant community, and a Hispanic community in the migrant stream.

In addition to these systematic comparative studies of literacy among nonmainstream groups, numerous detailed accounts of the repertoire of literacy practices within particular communities, families, and settings have been developed (e.g., Anderson & Stokes, 1984; Delgado-Gaitan, 1987; Fingeret, 1983; Mangubhai, 1984; Philips, 1972; Reder & Green, 1983; Scollon & Scollon, 1981; Scribner & Cole, 1981; Shuman, 1983; Taylor & Dorsey-Gaines, 1988; Weinstein, 1986). Detailed contextual analyses of single literacy practices have also been conducted (e.g., Gilmore, 1983; Heath, 1982; Teale, 1984).

These findings of literacy practices in their social contexts have produced several key findings that are relevant to our present purposes. These are reviewed below.

Literacy is Constitutive of Diverse Communicative Activities

The use of written materials is incorporated into a wide range of social and communicative practices. To be sure, literacy practices such as essay composition, newspaper reading, and taking written examinations are often accomplished at considerable distance from other communicative modalities such as conversation or gesture. But in the everyday accomplishment of many other communicative practices, frequent close contact, transposition, and interdependence among these modalities has been reported by Dyson (1990), Gee (1986), Heath (1983), and others. These studies have accrued considerable evidence that the "great divide" once believed to exist between oral and written language has been considerably exaggerated and distorted. As Tannen (1982) and Chafe (1982) pointed out, speech and writing do not represent the polar opposites characterized by Goody and Watt (1963), Olson (1977), and Ong (1982), but are instead comprised of multiple genres or practices, each of which has distinct characteristics located at different points along linguistic and interactional continua. Although the written essay (as an exemplar of a literacy practice) and informal conversation (as an exemplar of an "orality" practice) may lie at opposite ends of some continua (e.g., the dimensions of audience *involvement* and textual *fragmentation* described by Chafe, 1982), not all literacy and orality practices are differentiated to this degree. There are "orality" practices similar to essays (e.g., academic lectures) and literacy practices similar to informal conversation (e.g., short personal notes). When a range of practices is

> [L]ooked at in this way, the speech/writing, or orality/literacy, distinction begins to become problematic: What seems to be involved are different cultural practices that in certain contexts call for certain uses of language . . . (Gee, 1986:727–28)

Two points need to be clear here: (1) there is significant overlap among the functions and features of speech and writing across a much wider range of cultural activities than was once believed; and (2) many culturally patterned communicative practices draw *jointly* on speech and writing in their routine accomplishment. This has been found among young children learning to read and write (e.g., Dyson, 1990; Gundlach, Farr & Cook-Gumperz, 1989), urban adolescents' vernacular communications (Shuman, 1983), professional and technical workers on the job (Reder & Schwab, 1989), and in the informal activities of a variety of family and community networks across a wide range of settings (e.g., Fingeret, 1983; Heath, 1983; Taylor & Dorsey-Gaines, 1988).

The implications here are far-reaching for both the theory and the practice of literacy development. Rather than conceptualizing literacy development as inherently derivative from oral language, these findings suggest researchers and educators look towards a broader range of cultural activities as contexts for the development of literacy. A powerful approach to literacy development in a multilingual and multicultural society can be adapted from the work of Uriel Weinreich, a pioneer in the study of bilingualism, who defined *languages in contact* in terms of an individual speaker's alternation between the two languages (Weinreich, 1974). His framework had a profound influence on subsequent research on bilingualism by adding a focus on the characteristics of the social situations in which such alternations occur.

Weinreich's approach can be extended to the analysis of literacy development: Investigate the features of the social situations in which individuals alternately use oral and written language. Research on the development of writing in young children, for example, has convincingly demonstrated a close affinity and temporal alternation among speech, gesture, and drawing in the emergent uses of writing in young children (Dyson, 1990). A similar focus on situational patterns of contact and alternation between spoken and written languages may also clarify the development of literacy in multilingual and multicultural settings. Fishman, Riedler-Berger, Koling, and Steele (1985) investigated and compared the development and retention of multilingualism and multiliteracy among various ethnic communities in New York City. They concluded that stable patterns of multiliteracy in a community depend upon the allocation of each written language to noncompeting and complementary social functions, such as written Hebrew for religious purposes and written English for scientific purposes.

Although Fishman's findings are parallel to patterns of oral language choice found elsewhere, the parallel should *not* be construed as evidence of a simple derivative relationship between the development of spoken and written languages. The occurrence and use of spoken and written languages may be patterned differently. Spolsky (1981) provides an important illustration in his description of bilingualism and biliteracy among the Navajo in the Southwestern United States. The Navajo Tribal Council, a group whose activities were closely analyzed by Spolsky, normally conducts its business orally in the Navajo language, although most of its members are bilingual in English and speak it among themselves in certain situations. The Council keeps minutes and other records of their meetings in written English, although many Council members are also literate in the Navajo language and use written Navajo for certain purposes. When these records are read aloud back to the Council, it is in the Navajo language. These activities of the Tribal Council exemplify a general pattern observed on this reservation: Despite the bilingual and biliterate capabilities of many individuals, Navajo is the language normally spoken within the group, whereas English is the written language normally used within the group.

Literacy Development is Practice-Specific

The individual skills and cultural practices paradigms make different assumptions about the way in which literacy development "spreads out" through the activities of the individual. The skills approach sees literacy as a set of decontextualized information processing (e.g., encoding and decoding) skills, which the individual learns and then contextualizes by applying them to a progressively wider range of activities. The cultural practices perspective sees literacy skills and knowledge developing directly within specific contexts of practice that usually vary across languages and cultures. Current research on literacy development at both the individual and societal levels demonstrates the utility of the cultural practices paradigm for understanding how cultural factors impinge on literacy development.

At the level of individual development, a number of detailed studies of young children's emergent literacy (Chall & Snow, 1982; Dyson, 1990; Gundlach et al., 1989; Schieffelin & Cochran-Smith, 1984; Taylor and Dorsey-Gaines, 1988; Teale, 1986; Wertsch, 1984) report that young children directly acquire knowledge, skills, and values associated with the specific literacy practices of their home and other early social environments. Teale (1986) characterizes the literacy development of young children in Vygotskian terms: Children internalize the structure of the activities in which literacy is used in the world around them. Gundlach et al. (1989), in a comprehensive review of recent research on young children's literacy development, come to much the same conclusion, modeling the young child as a "literacy apprentice" whose literacy develops through learning the particular literacy practices of those with whom he or she comes into contact.

Studies of the societal development of literacy also report practice-specific development. For example, in a detailed sociohistorical analysis of literacy in an Eskimo fishing village, Reder and Green (1983) found literacy to be organized in terms of multiple underlying systems of values and socialization processes. The observed pattern of incorporation and use of written materials in everyday activities varied with the domain of activity (e.g., fishing, village governance, formal education, church affairs), the details of which depended on many historical and cultural factors. The literacy skills evident in some individuals' oral reading of liturgical materials in Church services, for example, were not deployed in their village governance activities (even though others might use written materials in those governance activities). In general, culturally transmitted, domain-specific values and meanings attached to the use of written materials shaped the nature and extent of individuals' use of literacy and thereby influenced the literacy skills and knowledge that developed in particular domains.

Similar context-specificity of literacy development and use has also been reported by other researchers in a wide range of other settings, including Scribner and Cole (1981), among the Vai of Liberia; Heath (1983), among rural communities in the Piedmont of South Carolina; Delgado-Gaitan (this volume), in a Hispanic community in the western United States; Schieffelin and Cochran-Smith (1984), among Asian immigrants in the United States; Fingeret (1983), among undereducated urban adults in the northeastern United States; and Taylor and Dorsey-Gaines (1988), among inner-city families.

Failure to recognize its practice-specificity can result in misleading or counterproductive views of literacy development. As Auerbach (1989) has pointed out, many "family-centered" or "intergenerational" literacy programs that have been developed to serve poor, minority, and immigrant families in the United States are based on erroneous assumptions about the literacy environments of their homes. Large-scale surveys of literacy that include self-reported information about materials in the home report differences among major social and economic groups in the prevalence of books, magazines, and newspapers in the home (e.g., Foertsch, 1992; Kirsch & Jungeblut, 1986). Since there is abundant evidence that parental interest in reading and reading habits influence the literacy development process (Neuman, 1986; Taylor, 1983), the implication is often drawn that homes with few books, magazines, and newspapers are therefore "deficient" environments for supporting literacy development.

Careful observational research, however, indicates such assumptions to be misfounded. Taylor and Dorsey-Gaines (1988), Anderson and Stokes (1984), Delgado-Gaitan (1987), and others have studied literacy practices in the homes of families from a range of ethnic and linguistic backgrounds. They find a rich array of literacy practices and literacy-related knowledge and values. Whereas White, middle-class families tend to own and read more books and magazines, other families are frequently engaged in a range of literacy practices involving such materials as lists, forms, notes, and letters. These results should induce educators to attend to these diverse literacy activities as potential contexts for literacy development rather than to the lack of book reading as a family "deficit," indicative of a family's low capacity or desire for supporting the children's education or literacy development (Auerbach, 1989; Moll, Amanti, Neff & Gonzalez, 1992).

Parents' effective support of their children's literacy development need not necessarily be linked to parental literacy use at all. Schieffelin and Cochran-Smith (1984) and Weinstein (1986) describe ways in which Asian refugee or immigrant families in the United States support their children's literacy development and education even though the parents themselves are not literate. The high values placed by the parents on literacy and education apparently can provide sufficient developmental support for their children's literacy. Providing a quiet place for reading and schoolwork in the home and asking children—and their teachers—about school progress are examples of the ways in which parents can provide effective support for their children's literacy development without being literate themselves. The theoretical significance of this will be considered below.

Literacy Practices Develop through Collaborative Activity

In moving from the individual skills to the cultural practices paradigm of literacy, there is a shift away from seeing literacy development as primarily a matter of advancing *individual* proficiency. Chaytor's (1945) study of the development of reading practices in the Middle Ages concluded that "silent reading" historically emerged from interactive oral reading practices, much as children's silent reading develops from collaborative oral reading practices. Careful studies of young children's reading practices (e.g., Teale, 1986) have detailed how these practices grow out of culturally shaped, collaborative interactions. In reading bedtime stories, for example, parents provide an intricate, negotiated process of task collaboration and support, variously called "scaffolding," "guided participation," or "respectful engagement" (Damon & Colby, 1987; Rogoff, 1986). Despite these minor variations of terminology, the essential point is that the process enables young children to acquire knowledge and skill for participating in the activity while, over time, assuming progressively more and more of the "functional load" needed to accomplish an initially collaborative activity.

Far from being an exception to the process through which

literacy practices are culturally transmitted, such collaborative activities are increasingly being identified as critical contexts for literacy development across a wide variety of cultural settings and age groups. Fingeret (1983), Shuman (1983), Heath (1982), Reder (1987), and Taylor and Dorsey-Gaines (1988) describe a wide range of collaborative literacy practices in immigrant and minority populations in the United States. Within those social settings in which adults sometimes engage in a narrow range of individual literacy practices, many essential reading and writing tasks are accomplished by others collaboratively; individuals share their literacy-related knowledge and skills just as they share other kinds of knowledge and skills, often on a reciprocal basis (Fingeret, 1983). In studying the development of literacy among Hmong immigrants in the United States, for example, Weinstein (1986) reports extensive collaboration both between and within generations in order to accomplish essential literacy tasks. Levin (1990) reported culturally specific values and socialization patterns associated with household and school-oriented collaborative task accomplishment and learning among native Hawaiian families. Watson-Gegeo (1990) found culturally specific models for collaboration and apprenticeship-like socialization processes among the Kwara'ae in the Pacific. Such cultural diversity in the interactional patterns for socializing children into the collaborative accomplishment of literacy practices has been widely reported in studies of family childrearing and communication patterns (e.g., Heath, 1983; Taylor & Dorsey-Gaines, 1988).

Participation Structures are Contexts for Literacy Development

If collaborative activities are critical contexts for literacy development, then the social structure of those situations is likely to have a substantial influence on the developmental process. Techniques developed by ethnographers of communication for the study and analysis of communicative activities in general (e.g., Hymes, 1968) have been very productively applied to the study of literacy practices in particular (Gilmore & Glatthorn, 1982; Schieffelin & Gilmore, 1986). Careful analysis of naturally occurring activities indicates that, as for communicative practices in general, literacy practices have characteristic interactional contexts termed *participation structures*. Participation structures may be conceptualized as constraints on interactions that embody consensually recognized and negotiated roles and role-based expectations among interactants for the accomplishment of some task. These structures constitute a context in which participants jointly accomplish and make sense of one another's behavior (McDermott, 1977).

Microbehavioral analysis of the social interactions within literacy practices shows that they are, like all communicative activities, shaped by a specific participation structure. Diverse participation structures for literacy practices have been described for a range of social situations and cultural groups. Individuals' skills and knowledge are engaged in varying ways in the accomplishment of a task, depending on the distribution of expertise among group members and the participation structure involved. Some participation structures encourage everyone to add their knowledge and skills to the process in more or less a democratic way; the process focuses more on the content of the contribution than on the social status of the contributor. Other participation structures tend to focus on the status of the contributor rather than on the content of his or her contribution. The participation structures of Native American groups are often contrasted with those of White, middle class groups in such terms (Scollon & Scollon, 1981). Heath (1983), in her landmark study of cultural variations in literacy practices across rural communities, also found differences in literacy use to be intimately associated with wider differences among participant structures evident in the communities' childrearing and socialization processes.

The significance of these participation structures for literacy activities cannot be represented only in terms of the distribution of literacy "skills" among members of the participant group; the varying social roles and attendant expectations for interaction are also crucial. This becomes particularly important for analyzing communicative activities, including ones related to literacy, involving members of diverse cultural groups. Profound cultural differences have been found in the normative structure, roles, and modes of interaction within everyday communicative activities, including ones in which literacy is imbedded (Heath, 1983; Philips, 1972; Scollon & Scollon, 1981). In the United States, individuals from minority families often bring culturally specific expectations about how communicative activities are to be conducted and interpreted in institutionalized settings such as schools and workplaces. When their expectations and understandings conflict with those of participants from socially dominant groups, cultural conflicts with attendant miscommunications often result; too often these communicative conflicts are the very contexts in which literacy practices are expected to develop (Michaels, 1981; Philips, 1972; Scollon & Scollon, 1981; Street, 1984).

Participation structures associated with literacy practices may overlap significantly with those supporting more general communicative activities. This seems to be particularly the case within social networks in which there is wide variation in individuals' communicative capabilities, for example, among immigrant families and communities. Studies of immigrants' literacy development, for example, have pointed out close relationships between the role of a literate "scribe" and that of an oral interpreter within participant groups collaborating to deal with their new society (Wagner, 1986).

Social Meanings Shape Literacy Development

In the analysis of communicative choice, sociolinguists such as Fishman (1972) have used the concept of *social meaning* to describe the social motivations underlying individuals' preferences for using particular languages in given multilingual contexts. In a bilingual setting, individuals' use of and alternation between languages can be understood in terms of their social motivations to display greater or lesser affinities to social groups in which use of one language or the other is preferred. A language-choice situation arises in communicative contexts in which participants have multiple roles and statuses as members of multiple social groups in which different languages are normally used or preferred. The language choices made closely reflect participants' definition of the situation, i.e., which of their multiple statuses is most pertinent or appropriate. In consensually foregrounding one particular set of statuses in this way, participants dynamically establish and recreate the social meanings of language choice in the given situation.

There have been some recent attempts to extend and apply this concept of social meaning to literacy (Fishman, 1972; Reder & Green, 1983; Spolsky, 1981; Stubbs, 1980; Szwed, 1981). In contexts in which multiple writing systems are in use—such as those described in Spolsky's study of Navajo-English biliteracy on an

Indian reservation in the Southwest or in Reder and Green's comparative study of Cyrillic-English, Hmong-English, and Spanish-English biliteracies among ethnic minority communities in the United States—the social meanings associated with literacy choices may be understood in the same way as those associated with language choices. We need only think of the image of the two immigrant brothers—one nostalgically reading the native language newspaper from the "old country" while the other eagerly reads the English language newspaper from his newly adopted country—to appreciate the depth and richness of these contrasting social meanings. But social meanings for literacy may also be generated by communicative choices to use *writing* in particular contexts rather than other media of communication. In the study of literacy in the Eskimo village, for example, choices and alternations between use of writing and oral communication in various activities carried specific social meanings for the villagers regardless of the language involved. In some contexts, the use of writing carried positive social meanings ("village"), whereas in other contexts it carried negative meanings ("outside").

Another source of social meanings for literacy practices may come from the larger societal or institutional contexts in which they are imbedded. Goody (1968, 1987), Street (1984), and others have illustrated, for example, how literacy is often constitutive of a society's power structure. When literacy practices entail participation in that power structure, as so often is the case, literacy and nonliteracy tend to carry the strong social meanings associated with access and nonaccess to that power structure and thereby impact the social distribution of literacy in the society (Edelsky, 1991; Gee, 1990; Lemke, 1989; Ogbu, 1990).

Literacy Develops Primarily through Acquisition

A major distinction made in research on second-language development is between *learning* and *acquisition* (Krashen, 1976). Second-language acquisition is an informal developmental process driven by immersion and social interactions in settings in which the language is used. Second-language learning, on the other hand, is a developmental process driven by formal instruction and study.

In these terms, the individual skills paradigm has traditionally assumed literacy development to be a learning rather than an acquisition process. Reading pedagogies have been structured around highly formalized instructional scopes and sequences. The reading "readiness" and later the reading "stage" of a child is seen in terms of a point on a unidimensional, context-independent scale of development. However, recent studies of literacy in the homes of preschool children (many of which are cited above) cast serious doubt on the validity of this conception. There is clear evidence in diverse societies and in numerous cultural groups within North America that literacy development has a strong acquisitional component. Children acquire the literacy practices of their home, both in situations in which parents actively encourage (if not teach) literacy (Snow & Ninio, 1986) and in situations where such explicit parental elicitation does not occur (Heath, 1982; Schieffelin & Cochran-Smith, 1984). An important finding in these studies, missing from previous accounts of "early readers" (e.g., Durkin, 1966), is that the child is acquiring much more than knowledge of the alphabet or sound-letter correspondences: Knowledge about the social and functional structure of the literacy practices themselves is being acquired (Teale, 1986), as well as the related values and expectations of the readers and writers with whom the child interacts (Gundlach et al., 1989).

There have been suggestions that the formal reading instruction in elementary schools, rather than effecting literacy learning (the formal instructional goal), actually provides opportunities for children to practice and thereby further develop the literacy that they have already acquired in nonclassroom contexts (Dyson, 1990; Gee, 1990; Wells, 1985, 1986). In addition to participation in the literacy practices of older siblings and adults in their homes, young children's play activities have all the earmarks of being significant contexts for literacy acquisition (Jacob, 1984). And among older children, a wide variety of peer-group literacy practices within schools occur *outside of classrooms,* few of which practices have much to do with the literacy activities formally structured in the classroom (Bloome, 1987; Gilmore, 1983; Griffin, 1977; Shuman, 1983). Recent large scale reading surveys and assessments of fourth, eighth, and twelfth graders in the United States have found clear relationships between literacy development and out-of-school activities as well as between literacy-development and classroom activities (Foertsch, 1992).

Literacy issues are central to learning and using English as a second language, both for formal learning in schools (Moll & Diaz, 1985, 1987) and for informal out-of-school learning (Delgado-Gaitan, 1987). Given the practical importance of these literacy issues, it is surprising that so little research has been conducted on literacy and second-language development. In reviewing the research on interactions between reading and linguistic diversity in the United States, Weber (1991) concluded that the lack of research enabled simplistic assumptions to retain currency in educational practice: "The assumption seems to be that reading will follow from knowing the structure of the language and knowing how to read in the first language" (108). Weber's review finds a somewhat contradictory research literature (with contradictory instructional implications) on how first-language literacy influences or should influence the instructional process for literacy in English as a second language.

Literacy development for adults, regardless of whether it is in a first or second language, also appears to have a strong acquisitional component (Reder & Green, 1985). Careful longitudinal studies of individual adults' literacy development are relatively rare, and further study of individual adult literacy development is clearly needed, especially outside of formal instructional programs.

A PRACTICE-ENGAGEMENT THEORY OF LITERACY DEVELOPMENT

The research findings outlined in the previous section call for an *acquisitional* theory of literacy development. Such a theory holds that individuals acquire literacy through participating in various literacy practices. As with general social-origins theories of cognitive development (e.g., Rogoff & Wertsch, 1984), the theory offered here, termed *practice-engagement theory,* assumes that the development and organizational properties of an individual's literacy are shaped by the structure and organization of the social situations in which literacy is encountered and practiced. Literacy development, according to this theoretical position, is driven by qualities of individuals' *engagement* in particular literacy practices. Factors or circumstances that affect such engagement (e.g., access to particular participant roles such as the "child" in a family's practice of reading bedtime stories) will correspondingly facilitate or hinder acquisition.

Practice-Engagement Theory and Cultural Differences

Such an approach is especially relevant to placing literacy development within the cross-cultural, cross-linguistic framework of this volume. The approach brings into focus issues of cultural and linguistic differences in the occurrence of particular literacy practices as well as in the qualities of individuals' engagement in those practices. Cultural influences on literacy development are examined not only in terms of patterned differences in the societal occurrence of various literacy practices, but also in terms of cultural and linguistic factors that organize the ways individuals participate in given literacy practices. Michaels (1981) examined the discourse features of young schoolchildren's oral "sharing time" activities, features she argued overlapped substantially with those of later-emerging school-based literacy activities. She found substantial differences among the ways in which children from varying cultural backgrounds participated in sharing time activities within a given classroom, differences that she argues reflect differential access to the literacy practices of the school. Scollon and Scollon (1981) reported cultural differences between the ways in which White and Athabascan children in Alaska tend to organize and participate in verbal activities. Like Michaels, Scollon and Scollon concur with Heath (1983) in suggesting that such differences are rooted in cultural variations among the prevailing informal discourse patterns of the children's homes and communities. These discourse differences, when brought to the school, quickly result in differential patterns of participation in school-based literacy practices, producing differences in literacy development itself.

Schooling and Practice-Engagement Theory

It is important to note that formal literacy instruction is not *assumed* to have a special role in literacy development. School literacy instruction is taken to be a set of literacy practices, albeit ones for which very strong social meanings exist in many societies. Practice-engagement theory considers school-based literacy practices the same way it does other literacy practices, examining the pattern of learners' engagements in specific practices as well as the association of cultural and sociolinguistic variables with variations in those engagements. As Damon has stated:

> Schooling is nothing more than nor less than a set of engagements between the child and a formal program of instruction. The quality of these engagements is all-important in determining what the child learns from them. Some school engagements generate learning and others do not. (1990:45)

The practice-engagement approach is not intended to denigrate the importance of schooling in literacy development, but rather to facilitate a better understanding of the impact diverse literacy practices have on literacy development. The relative contribution of various engagements in literacy practices in and out of schools thus becomes an empirical matter of some importance.

Approaches to Practice-Engagement

A critical issue in practice-engagement theory, whether in or out of school contexts, concerns what it *is* about a set of engagements that produces (or fails to produce) literacy development. There have been several approaches to this question, although most have been primarily focused on school-based literacy practices. Smith (1983), for example, considered *demonstrations* to be the critical component of interactions that produce learning; he defined demonstrations as "opportunities to see how something is done." In Smith's account, every act is a cluster of demonstrations: A teacher standing before a class, for example, demonstrates how a teacher talks, dresses, stands before a class, feels about the material being taught, and so on. A teacher reading aloud demonstrates how books are to be read, how a reader interprets and enlivens a text, and so forth. According to Smith, learning occurs when learners *engage* with a demonstration and, in so doing, assimilate the demonstration of another (present in either an act or an artifact) and transform it into actions of their own.

Seeing engagement as a prerequisite to learning from demonstrations, Smith then considered why individuals engage in some particular demonstrations but not in others. After dismissing several possible explanations, including ones based on motivation and conscious expectations, Smith concluded that the *sensitivity* of a demonstration is crucial for learner engagement; Smith defined sensitivity as the absence of expectations that learning will be difficult or will not occur. Smith concluded that sensitivity and hence engagement is naturally present in many situations, so that learning progresses naturally. Often it is unintended demonstrations (e.g., ones that lead students to believe that learning will be difficult, boring, or impossible) that block engagement and thus learning.

Engagement-oriented conceptions of literacy development related to Smith's ideas have been advanced by several theorists, including Holdaway (1979), Teale (1984), and Cambourne (1988). Holdaway identifies four processes underlying children's literacy acquisition: *observation* of literacy behaviors (literacy demonstrations in Smith's terms); *collaboration* with others who provide motivation, encouragement, and assistance; individual *practice* of literacy activities the learner has previously observed and tried collaboratively; and *performance* of learned activities with supportive feedback.

Teale also sees literacy developing through a child's engagement in reading and writing activities. The critical features of engagement in his theory pertain to *social interactions* (primarily with adults) that *mediate* the intellectual development underlying the acquisition of literacy. Following Vygotsky's (1978) theory, Teale sees these intellectual capacities as internalizations of social interactions. In Teale's view, it is children's participation in specific literacy practices such as collaborative storybook reading that is critical for literacy development; both *access* to such activities and the *mediation* that participation in them brings are crucial for literacy development (Teale & Sulzby, 1987).

Cambourne theorizes that literacy development depends on learners being *immersed* in various types of texts (cf. engaged in practices that use those texts); having *demonstrations* of how texts are constructed and used; interacting with others who have high positive *expectations* that they will learn (cf. Smith's sensitivity); taking *responsibility* for literacy learning; having opportunities to *use* what they are learning in "authentic" situations; and having opportunities to *approximate* (i.e., make mistakes) and get supportive *feedback* in collaborating on literacy activities with more knowledgeable others.

There is considerable overlap among these theories concerning the crucial role that social interactions, collaboration, and supportive relationships play in literacy acquisition. Edelsky (1991) advances another view of engagement and learning. In her view, it is the *meaningfulness* of an activity to the participants that creates engagement and, ultimately, learning. Edelsky's focus is on empowering culturally and linguistically diverse schoolchildren to control written language so it can serve their personal and group interests. In her conception of how meaningfulness relates to literacy engagement and learning, Edelsky points to the importance of school literacy practices that are wholes rather than analytical parts of the learner's language and experience:

> In this conception, the bits of written language that children read and write are not analytical parts stripped of pragmatic or other cues . . . they are functional wholes (stories read for entertainment, recipes written for cooking, . . . etc.). (1991:68)

In making an eloquent case for a meaning-based approach to literacy education (especially for ethnolinguistic minority children in the United States), Edelsky commends the teachers who

> write letters to the children; they discuss literature with them, listen to children's responses to the books they are reading and suggest others; they encourage children to focus on meaning as they read and to reflect on what they write. . . . And the children grow into reading and writing the way they did into talking— with the intense effort and great satisfaction that comes from doing worthwhile, honest, socio-psycho-linguistic work as members of a literate community. (69)

Practice-Engagement Beyond the School

Smith, Edelsky, Teale, and others propose features of engagement within school-based literacy activities that are critical for literacy learning. Their respective emphases on sensitivity, meaningfulness, and social interactions seem extensible to settings and social situations beyond the classroom. To broaden the range of settings, practices, and participatory roles beyond those of the school, however, requires a broader approach and perhaps additional theory. In particular, there is a need to systematize the notion of meaning and to integrate it with explicit characteristics of literacy activities that may vary across situations, tasks, and participatory roles. There are many ways this might be done, of course. One approach will be considered here in some detail, one that builds on the earlier work of Reder (1987; in press), which attempts to systematize a typology of engagements in literacy practices and consider the ways in which each impacts literacy development.

Modes of Engagement

The guiding assumption underlying this particular practice-engagement model is that various participation structures offer different opportunities to individuals for engagement in activities in which written language is constructed and used. This model characterizes the social roles and interaction patterns underlying literacy practices according to individuals' *modes of engagement* in the practices. Three distinct modes of engagement may be identified—*technological, functional,* and *social*:

> Individuals participate in these collaborative literacy practices in varied ways. Some persons directly manipulate written materials, reading and/or writing as part of performing the task at hand—these individuals are here said to be *technologically engaged* in the literacy practice. The term technologically engaged refers to the particular technology of writing involved in the practice. Other individuals may not be technologically engaged in the practice but nevertheless interact closely in performing the task with others who are technologically engaged—these individuals are said to be *functionally engaged* in the collaborative literacy practice. They may provide specialized knowledge and expertise as vital to the performance of the collaborative practice as the literacy skills of the technologically engaged participants. Other individuals may be neither technologically nor functionally engaged in the practice, but nevertheless have knowledge of the nature of the practice and its implications for the life of the community, and must routinely take others' technological and functional engagement into account. Individuals in such positions are here said to be *socially engaged* in the practice. (Reder, 1987:257)

A given individual may be engaged in a literacy practice in various combinations of these three modes; they are not mutually exclusive. Nearly all combinations are possible and in fact occur frequently across diverse settings. For example, an individual may be technologically engaged but not functionally engaged, as often happens when immigrants with little prior contact with written language come to the United States and are required to perform the technological act of signing their names on documents without understanding the legal or bureaucratic ramifications of so doing. Young schoolchildren frequently have been instructed initially in the technology of literacy before being taught how written language is used for social purposes. Conversely, in Elizabethan England, many individuals did not have the technological capacity to sign their names yet nevertheless were functionally engaged when they marked crucial documents with an X (e.g., their marriage licenses). Similarly, a business executive would be functionally but not technologically engaged in the practice of writing a business letter when she or he dictates it to a secretary who writes it down. Such distinctions are important in practice-engagement theory, of course, because it assumes that what individuals know and learn about literacy practices is directly related to their modes of engagement in them.

Engagement-Associated Knowledge

Three distinct types of knowledge about literacy practices are associated with these modes of engagement: *technological knowledge, functional knowledge,* and *knowledge of social meanings.* Technological knowledge pertains to a particular technology of reading and writing used in literacy practices, and usually includes knowledge of a script and the correspondence between its units and those of the spoken language, as well as knowledge of how to apply those correspondences in the context of the particular practice. Functional knowledge about a literacy practice refers to knowledge of how the technology is used for specific social purposes. Functional knowledge also encompasses knowledge of the specific kinds and sources of information needed to accomplish the task and of which individuals have the requisite technological skills for performing the task. The third system of knowledge, shared by all who are socially engaged in a literacy practice, concerns the social meanings associated with the literacy practice.

The technological, functional, and social modes of engagement in a literacy practice are the contexts in which individuals acquire the corresponding technological, functional, and social meaning knowledge about the literacy practice. Acquisition of particular kinds of knowledge thus depends on access to corresponding modes of engagement in the practice. This has several crucial implications. One implication is that inequities of access to critical participatory roles and modes of engagement in literacy practices may result in corresponding inequalities of socialization and development. If access to "academic" literacy practices, for example, is limited in some children's home environments (while other literacy practices may be prevalent), the children may be at a distinct disadvantage for initially engaging in the academic literacy practices of the school.

Another implication is that knowledge of the technological, functional, and social meaning components of literacy in some contexts may be socialized somewhat independently. Individuals whose engagement in literacy practices is for some reason restricted to one mode may acquire one type of knowledge pertaining to a literacy practice but not another. Functional knowledge of some literacy practices, for example, may develop well before the pertinent technological knowledge. A young child may acquire much functional knowledge about story reading (e.g., books have pages to be turned; consist of beginnings, endings, pictures, and words; can be used to get a parent's attention) well before developing the technological encoding and decoding skills for reading those stories independently. Similarly, a mechanic may have extensive functional knowledge of small engine repair before developing the technological skills needed to read technical materials that others use to make repairs.

Contrast these situations with those in which technological knowledge pertaining to literacy practices develops ahead of functional knowledge. Western schooling, as a prime example, often uses a decontextualized pedagogy of literacy, that is, the technological components of literacy are taught in school before students use them in functional contexts, that is, before functional knowledge develops. Olson (1977), Cook-Gumperz and Gumperz (1981), Snow (1983), and others have suggested that this "context independence" makes literacy development problematic for some students. Edelsky (1991) makes an eloquent case that such approaches may pose particular difficulties for ethnolinguistic minority children.

Social meanings associated with literacy practices may also be acquired without functional and technological knowledge. In the Eskimo fishing village studied by Reder and Green (1983), the entire community shared a system of social meanings governing literacy practices that were socialized among individuals having a broad range (including none!) of technological and functional knowledge about the literacy practices. For example, all villagers—regardless of their level of functional and technological knowledge—shared a negative view of outside government agencies' attempts to regulate village affairs through the use of written reports. Village elders were occasionally at the forefront of discussions about whether and how to resist such invasive literacy practices even though they were not able to engage in them in a technological or functional sense.

Practice-Engagement and Social Meanings

Access to participatory roles and modes of engagement in literacy practices may be severely impaired in the context of negative social meanings, whether in school or other environments. In some schools, for example, minority children's biggest educational problem may not be that they are behind in acquiring the technological knowledge of literacy but that they are acquiring negative social meanings for literacy as practiced in the classroom (DeStefano et al., 1982; McDermott, 1976; Zanger, this volume). Where such cultural conflicts exist, literacy development may encounter other problems as well. Heath (1983) and Gilmore (1983) offer powerful examples of how educators inadvertently but systematically misevaluate student literacy capabilities because of the ways in which the participation structures of the classroom limit students' displays of competence at performing literacy tasks. The limited repertoire of literacy practices acceptable in the classroom may prevent students from displaying (and teachers from observing) competencies that are routinely displayed in informal peer activities in home and community settings. In Gilmore's (1983) powerful example of "Steps," a verbal game played by urban Black children, youngsters demonstrate sophisticated communication and literacy skills on the playground, skills their teachers never see in the classroom.

The Persistence of Social Meanings: Literacy and Identity

Although the social meanings associated with literacy shape individuals' engagement—and nonengagement—in literacy practices, the social meanings involved are often deeply rooted in cultural history and resistant to change. Although to date there has been only a little relevant historical research on the topic, social meanings seem to change much more slowly than the technological and functional knowledge associated with literacy practices. In Reder and Green's (1983) sociohistorical study of an Eskimo fishing village, for example, the system of "village" versus "outside" social meanings associated with various literacy practices in the school, church, and other domains survived over hundreds of years and wholesale changes in the languages and alphabets associated with particular literacy practices. Ogbu's (1987, 1990) analysis of literacy development and minority status in the United States also suggests that some social meanings are highly resistant to change.

Ogbu acknowledges the contribution of cultural differences and conflicts to the difficulties minority children have in school and thus in becoming literate. But he argues that such explanations fail to account for why some minority groups (e.g., African-Americans, American Indians) have persistent disproportionate school failure rates whereas other minority groups (e.g., the Chinese in the Central Valley of California or the Punjabi in Valleyside, California) do not. Ogbu argues that too much research on minority children's educational issues is narrowly focused on

> the microsetting events of the classroom, school, or home and sometimes on the biographies of minority children. . . . Such events are rarely analyzed in the context of the minority group's history or its position in society. My view is that what goes on inside the classroom or school is greatly affected by the minority group's perceptions of and responses to schooling, and that is related to its historical and structural experiences in the larger society. (1990:144)

Ogbu's essential claim is that by comparing the historical, structural, and psychological factors influencing school-adjustment problems of various minority groups, one can show why one group is plagued by persistent poor performance while the other is not. He argues that the language and cultural differences of various minorities vis-à-vis the socially and economically dominant group are not qualitatively the same. The language and cultural patterns of some minority groups have been shaped by the history of the group's social and economic position in the United States. Although all minority groups display differences in language and culture at the time of their initial contact with the dominant group (Ogbu terms these *primary cultural and language differences*), additional differences develop over time (which Ogbu terms *secondary language and cultural differences*) that reflect the way the minorities are treated by the dominant group and the ways in which the minority group has come to perceive, understand, and react to that treatment. Ogbu contends that minority groups with histories of slavery, conquest, or colonization (glossed by Ogbu as *involuntary minorities*) tend to develop secondary cultural differences that discourage rather than encourage success in schooling and literacy:

> For example, when slavery was common, white Americans used legal and extralegal means to discourage black Americans from acquiring literacy and the associated behaviors and benefits. After the abolition of slavery, whites created barriers in employment and in other areas of life, effectively denying blacks certain economic and social benefits, but also the incentives associated with the education whites made available to them. . . . In a plural society like the United States, the various segments of the society—the dominant whites and the minority groups—tend to have specific cultural models, understandings of their status, of how American society works and their place in that working order. . . . The cultural models of minorities are shaped by the initial terms of their incorporation in American society, and their subsequent treatment by white Americans. (1990:148–149)

Ogbu's notion of a cultural model is much broader than the concept of social meaning. But it is clear that the group's cultural model specifies the social meanings that a minority group ascribes to literacy. For Ogbu, the cultural model (and thus the social meanings it engenders) become part of the group's sense of identity. Reder and Green (1983) argued that the persistence of social meanings for literacy helped to maintain the Eskimo villagers' sense of ethnic identity. Ferdman (1990) provided several examples of how literacy can become part of a group's cultural identity.

Summary

What seems missing from Ogbu's account is that only the school is seen as a means for the socialization and acquisition of literacy. This no doubt is a matter of emphasis rather than omission, but it nevertheless creates an impression of there being only one social meaning for literacy within a cultural group. Reder and Green (1983) found domain-specific social meanings and socialization patterns for literacy in the Eskimo village; McCaskill (this volume) similarly identifies multiple contexts, each likely carrying its own social meaning, for the historical development of literacy among African-Americans. Despite the importance of Ogbu's analysis and its implications for social and educational policy, it is essential to retain a focus on multiple meanings and domains for literacy development, and thus a theoretical connection between social meanings and patterns of social interaction, if literacy development is to be well understood and broadly facilitated.

By striving to integrate multiple social meanings with patterns of social interaction, practice-engagement theory provides a conceptual framework that can be particularly useful in addressing the development and expression of literacy in multicultural contexts and societies. By focusing on the relationship between individuals' orientation to multiple systems of social meanings and choices they make regarding the development and use of literacy, the framework is applicable to varieties of cross-cultural and intercultural contexts. These sociolinguistic relationships between expressed literacy choices/preferences and perceived social meanings align this theoretical position with other accounts of the relationship between literacy and cultural identity (cf. Ferdman, 1990).

Practice-engagement theory, however, attempts to specify these relationships in a more detailed, practice-specific way than do accounts such as Ferdman's or Ogbu's. By emphasizing the patterns of individuals' access to and participation in various roles within specific literacy practices, engagement theory seeks to account for the rich variety and patterning of literacy within as well as across cultural groups. The same constructs may be used to describe both the limiting of literacy development in an Eskimo village to certain domains of activity, as well as the relationships between Southeast Asian immigrants' literacy practices in their countries of origin and those emerging in their newly adopted homes in North America. The framework thus can address the rich variety of social circumstances in which literacy develops in a complex multicultural, multilingual society.

Related to practice-engagement theory is an emerging theoretical perspective in second-language learning called *second-language acquisition* (e.g., Beebe, 1987). The two perspectives share some important assumptions. Each assumes that the characteristics of the situations in which learners interact with others are critical for acquiring new communicative capacities. Differences in learning outcomes are seen as reflecting differences in exposure to (engagement in) the situations that foster the natural acquisition process. As Weber (1991) points out, there has been little systematic consideration of the ways in which literacy and second-language development may interact, although there is abundant evidence that they do interact. There is potential for the overlapping perspective between practice-engagement and second-language acquisition theories to facilitate the integration of literacy and second-language development in both theory and practice.

Finally, a relationship between practice-engagement theory and Soviet *activity theory* (Leont'ev, 1981) should be noted. A detailed discussion of the similarities and differences between the two is not possible in the space available here, but the intellectual debt is nevertheless worth acknowledging.

IMPLICATIONS FOR RESEARCH AND EDUCATIONAL PRACTICE

With acquisition occurring in the context of multiple literacy practices, it is important to look beyond formally organized teaching and learning activities as the only or even the principal settings for stimulating literacy development. Resnick has suggested that

> to 'bootstrap' ourselves into new levels of literacy participation, I believe we must actively develop other institutions for literacy practice. . . . We need multiple apprenticeship sites where children and youth can spend significant amounts of time working among people who are using the written word for practical, informational and pleasurable purposes. (1990:183)

Resnick's metaphor of apprenticeships for the acquisition of literacy skills in multiple contexts and activities is an appealing one. But the large-scale, systemic provision of new institutional arrangements for such activity may not effect increased literacy among diverse cultural and linguistic groups in pluralistic societies like the United States. Lacking in the conception is the recognition that social meanings for literacy are neither uniform nor positive across cultural groups. To be sure, some of the literacy acquisition problems facing minority children in Ogbu's analysis may be lessened by moving learning away from school-like settings. But there is no guarantee that these additional learning contexts (even if they are "informal" compared to schools) will not themselves be constructed to serve the interests of the socially and economically dominant groups rather than those of various minority groups. The recontextualization of literacy learning suggested by Resnick and other cognitive scientists may not be particularly effective unless and until literacy development, however and wherever acquired, brings with it expanded social and economic opportunities and rewards for all learners.

In choosing literacy practices as contexts for development, it is important to consider that not all literacy practices an individual comes into contact with are equally promising for acquisition. It is critical to understand the dynamics of the participation structure and social meaning for the individual; practices or situations that carry negative social meanings for an individual, or ones for which appropriate modes of engagement are relatively inaccessible, are not promising contexts for enhancing literacy development. At the same time, practices and situations that carry positive social meanings and to whose participant roles the individual has ready access are excellent candidates for stimulating literacy development.

There are many ways in which literacy development might be facilitated within the context of naturally occurring literacy practices. Three approaches or perspectives will be briefly described here—each encompasses a set of priorities for further research and an agenda for stimulating literacy development. The three perspectives are: (1) Modify existing literacy practices to provide literacy scaffolding to those in the process of acquiring literacy; (2) Introduce the use of written materials into existing communicative practices; and (3) Use the technology of writing to innovate new cultural practices. Each will be briefly considered.

Modifying Existing Literacy Practices

The first perspective focuses on the role of individuals who participate in literacy practices as "helpers"—that is, those who assist others with needed reading and writing tasks. Such literacy helpers are ubiquitous within the social networks and task-participation structures of undereducated or marginally skilled adults, especially individuals from minority groups (Fingeret, 1983). Reder and

Green (1985) suggest some strategies for increasing the informal pedagogical capacity of these networks, that is, to "give literacy away" by expanding literacy practices in ways that broaden the role of the natural helper to function in certain contexts as an informal tutor, one who could provide a literacy scaffolding for the learner, much as effective parents and teachers do.

As an illustrative application, Reder and Green suggested an alternative design for volunteer literacy tutoring programs. These programs typically first recruit learners and volunteer tutors independently, then train the tutors, and finally attempt to pair learners and tutors for instruction. Often learners and tutors paired in this way have little in common and encounter many logistical problems in trying to work together regularly; as a result, learner-tutor relationships are difficult to maintain and have high attrition rates. Reder and Green suggest trying to recruit tutors from the ranks of literacy helpers; by training helpers to provide instructional support to the individuals they are *already* helping with literacy tasks, it is anticipated that many of the logistical problems and cultural differences hindering haphazardly paired tutors and learners will be minimized.

Bennett (1992) reports some confirmatory data. Informal experiments with such "helper-based" tutoring programs in public libraries have shown considerable promise in ethnic and linguistic minority communities in urban areas in California. According to Bennett, traditional approaches to recruiting, training, and matching of tutors with learners have proved problematic in these communities because the preponderance of learners are from minority groups while the majority of volunteer tutors are not. This results in the aforementioned logistical problems and cultural conflicts. The very concepts of "volunteer" and "help" seem to carry strong cultural assumptions that have not been well addressed in the design of culturally diverse tutoring programs. The expansion of existing patterns of collaboration and assistance within naturally occurring literacy tasks seems to offer a promising new basis for designing more effective programs. For such modifications of literacy practices to be effective, of course, the social meanings of the changes involved must be acceptable to those involved, and this will not always be the case (cf. Fingeret, 1983). But where feasible, the contexts of naturally occurring collaborative literacy practices have many advantages over other types of instructional situations (Reder & Green, 1985).

In multilingual contexts, additional complexity may arise, since roles and social meanings must be understood with respect to both language choices and literacy choices. In the partially migrant bilingual (Spanish and English) community that my colleague Karen Wikelund has been studying, for example, very different social meanings are attached to use of literacy in the two languages—and are distinct from those attached to the speaking the two languages. For many individuals, becoming literate in their native Spanish language carries negative meanings (in contrast with the positive meanings attached to becoming literate in English), even though spoken use of Spanish is preferred in most situations. Among Hmong refugees in the United States, on the other hand, there are positive social meanings associated with developing literacy initially in the native language (Weinstein, 1986). Such differences in cultural patterns, of course, have enormous impact on how multilingual participant groups organize themselves to accomplish collaborative literacy practices. These factors will affect the feasibility and the optimal design of this approach in given contexts.

Add Writing to Existing Cultural Practices

The second approach involves introducing the use of writing into existing communicative and cultural practices. Once again, a critical design feature is making sure that the context carries positive rather than negative social meanings. Reder and Green (1985) describe an example from a rural, minority community in the Southeast of the United States. A retired schoolteacher, who grew up but did not teach in the community, developed a curriculum and materials that were delivered on playing cards. Small groups of individuals gathered on their front porches during the evenings to "play" with these special cards, just as their neighbors gathered on other porches to play their games. Others walked up and down the streets of the town, exchanging greetings with folks sitting or playing cards on their porches. This technique, in which the use of writing was introduced into familiar participant groups, settings, and cultural practices, endowed literacy development with positive social meanings for the participants and succeeded in stimulating literacy development after many other formalized approaches had failed.

Use Writing to Innovate New Literacy Practices

The third approach or perspective uses writing to innovate new cultural practices. Inventive uses of writing develop naturally in many individuals and groups, ranging from young children (Dyson, 1990; Gundlach et al., 1989) to children and adults in immigrant and refugee groups (Schieffelin & Cochran-Smith, 1984; Weinstein, 1986). Among immigrant and multinational populations, many apparently new literacy practices that arise in a given setting may actually be adapted from literacy practices in a different language or cultural setting. Schieffelin and Cochran-Smith (1984), for example, describe a young Sino-Vietnamese boy who uses his newly developed literacy in English to send all kinds of notes and cards to teachers, school officials, and other American acquaintances. In my own work with Hmong immigrants, writing was also observed being used extensively for such purposes among Hmong refugees throughout the United States. What seems to be involved in both cases is the use of writing to narrow social distance between the writer and his or her friends and acquaintances in the new country. What is particularly interesting is that Hmong individuals who had no technical knowledge of writing (either in English or often in their native language) also sent such cards and letters, using the skills of others to actually write them. This functional and social meaning knowledge, at least in the case of the Hmong, can be traced back to their native Laos, where such cards and letters were routinely sent, even by nonliterates. Such practices, of course, are natural contexts for stimulating the further development of literacy.

What Does This Have to Do with Schooling, Anyway?

These strategies for using naturally occurring cultural activities as contexts for stimulating literacy acquisition are of course also applicable to institutional contexts such as schools. Purves (1987) demonstrates, through cross-national studies of school reading and writing, that as they mature students bring extensive culturally specific knowledge and values to bear on their school literacy behaviors. Once again, the relationship between literacy acquisition and formal literacy instruction should be taken as problematic and challenging for both researchers and practitioners. School literacy practices can be effectively analyzed from a practice-engagement perspective.

The research reviewed in this chapter indicates that conflicts between the students' school, home, and community environments can have devastating educational consequences. At the same time, of course, it is possible for well-designed school literacy programs not only to avoid attaching negative social meanings to literacy but actually to endow literacy with positive social meanings (e.g., Edelsky, 1991). If students have access to positively valued literacy-related interactions in schools, their literacy development should be facilitated. This is exactly what Au's (1980) research demonstrates. Au describes the social organization of reading lessons in an exemplary program at Kamehameha School in Honolulu, designed to meet the educational needs of Native Hawaiian children. The participation structures of the reading lessons are designed to harmonize rather than conflict with those the young children brought to the classroom from their home and community environments. Marked facilitation of literacy development has resulted from this innovative approach, one that is clearly applicable to literacy development across other cultures and languages.

Besides utilizing culturally appropriate participation structures, what elements of culture should teachers draw on in their instruction? Too often a "culture-sensitive" curriculum is provided narrowly through reliance on folklore, arts, and crafts. Moll et al. (1992) attempt to innovate a new approach by systematizing the ways in which teachers can effectively utilize cultural features of their students' home environments to improve instruction. They use the term *funds of knowledge* to represent the ample cultural and cognitive resources of working-class households (from culturally diverse groups) that offer great potential for incorporation into classroom instruction. In arguing that teachers need to draw on funds of knowledge from their students' home environments, Moll et al. distinguish funds of knowledge from a more general concept of "culture":

> Although the term 'funds of knowledge' is not meant to replace the anthropological concept of culture, it is more precise for our purposes because of its emphasis on strategic knowledge and

related activities essential in households' functioning, development and well-being. It is specific funds of knowledge pertaining to the social, economic and productive activities of people in a local region, not 'culture' in its broader, anthropological sense, that we seek to incorporate strategically into classrooms. (1992:139)

Other researchers believe that equal access to literacy in a culturally and linguistically plural society such as the United States cannot be achieved simply through appropriate cultural diversification of classrooms and schools (no matter how well the cultural routines and materials from students' homes and communities are incorporated into instruction). They feel that the inequitable distribution of social and economic power in the society is strongly associated with differential access to particular literacy practices and genres of discourse. These power-associated practices and discourses are not taught explicitly in schools, which serves to maintain differential and inequitable access to what has been variously called "genre literacy" or "power literacy" (Delpit, 1987; Edelsky, 1991; Gee, 1990; Lemke, 1989). In this view, children who come from families and communities that do not share in the power wielded by the dominant social groups require explicit instruction about the conventions and strategies of these powerful literacies and discourses in order to gain full access to them. Delpit, in particular, contrasts process-oriented literacy instruction that encourages students to incorporate their own experience, culture, and language into instructional activities (which she terms "personal literacy") with explicit instruction in "power literacy"; she contends that "power literacy" instruction better serves the educational, social, and economic needs of children from ethnic and linguistic minority groups.

There is no simple way to resolve these contrasting views about how school literacy instruction can best serve the needs of culturally and linguistically diverse children. It seems likely that schools alone will not be able to remove the social and economic inequities present in the larger society. Whatever approach is taken and whatever innovations are made by the schools in literacy instruction will be most effective if complemented by expansion of the social and economic opportunities and rewards for all students to acquire societally valued skills and knowledge.

Need for Further Research and Development

A point of agreement among the various perspectives is that adequate access to a range of literacy practices both within and outside of the school underlies literacy development. Practice-engagement theory offers a framework for the analysis of how individuals participate in and learn from a variety of literacy practices. But this framework is as yet quite incomplete and needs further empirical validation and theoretical elaboration.

One research priority is the collection and analysis of longitudinal data sets that provide detailed information about individuals' access to and participation in a variety of literacy practices as well as their emerging literacy capabilities. Such research is needed for all age groups, from young children to school-aged children to adults. Such studies in the past have generally been limited to young children and focused on in-depth observation of relatively small numbers of individuals. These small-scale "micro" studies of young children need to be extended in two ways: (1) Conduct parallel studies of adolescent and adult literacy learners, and (2) Use small-scale qualitative studies to develop instrumentation and assessment methods that can be used in large-scale longitudinal surveys to gain needed data about individuals' engagement in various literacy practices and their related literacy capabilities.

Although there has been a flurry of recent statewide and national surveys of adult literacy conducted by the National Assessment of Educational Progress (NAEP), the type of research survey called for here is markedly different than the recent NAEP surveys. The NAEP surveys have utilized the psychometrically sophisticated measurement and assessment technology described by Kirsch and Jungeblut (1986). But the assessment instruments and interview procedures were designed for the purpose of comparing individuals along linear scales at a fixed point in time rather than for the purpose of advancing our understanding of the dynamic relationships among individuals' literacy development and the contingencies they perceive and experience between literacy development and social and economic opportunities and rewards. It is essential to develop and implement longitudinal survey and assessment methodologies appropriate to this research purpose if we are to understand better how to augment literacy development and make it more equitable in pluralistic societies such as the United States.

The hope here is that such large-scale research can eventually be driven by needs for better understanding of the interplay among the many influences on literacy development and of how best to facilitate and democratize literacy acquisition. When both macro- and microlevel literacy research can address this common core of concern, the long and arduous shift from the individual skills to the cultural practices paradigm will have tremendous impact on educational practice and literacy development.

REFERENCES

Anderson, A.B. & Stokes, S.J. (1984). Social and institutional influences on the development and practice of literacy. In H. Goelman, A. Oberg, & F. Smith (Eds.), *Awakening to literacy* (pp. 24–37). Portsmouth, NH: Heinemann.

Au, K. (1980). Participation structures in a reading lesson with Hawaiian children. *Anthropology & Education Quarterly, 11*, 91–115.

Auerbach, E.R. (1989). Toward a social-contextual approach to family literacy. *Harvard Educational Review, 59*, 165–181.

Beebe, L.M. (Ed.). (1987). *Issues in second language acquisition.* New York: Newbury House.

Bennett, A. (1992). Personal communication.

Bloome, D. (Ed.). (1987). *Literacy and schooling.* Norwood, NJ: Ablex.

Cambourne, B. (1988). *The whole story: Natural learning and the acquisition of literacy in the classroom.* New York: Ashton Scholastic.

Chafe, W.L. (1982). Integration and involvement in speaking, writing and oral literature. In D. Tannen (Ed.), *Spoken and written language.* Norwood, NJ: Ablex.

Chall, J.S. & Snow, C. (1982). *Families and literacy: The contribution of out-of-school experiences to children's acquisition of literacy.* A final report to the National Institute of Education.

Chaytor, H.J. (1945). *From script to print: An introduction to medieval vernacular literature.* Cambridge: W. Heffer and Sons.

Cook-Gumperz, J. & Gumperz, J. (1981). From oral to written culture: The transition to literacy. In M.F. Whiteman (Ed.), *Variation in writing: Functional and linguistic-cultural differences.* Hillsdale, NJ: Erlbaum.

Damon, W. (1990). Reconciling the literacies of generations. *Daedalus, 119*, 33–53.

Damon, W. & Colby, A. (1987). Social influence and moral change. In W. Kurtines & J. Gewirtz (Eds.), *Moral development through social interaction.* New York: Wiley.

Delgado-Gaitan, C. (1987). Mexican adult literacy: New directions for immigrants. In S.R. Goldman & H. Trueba (Eds.), *Becoming literate in English as a second language* (pp. 9–32). Norwood, NJ: Ablex.

Delpit, L. (1987). The silenced dialogue: Power and pedagogy in educating other people's children. *Harvard Educational Review, 58,* 280–298.

DeStefano, J., Pepinsky, H. & Sanders, T. (1982). Discourse rules for literacy learning in a first grade classroom. In L.C. Wilkinson (Ed.), *Communicating in the classroom* (pp. 101–129). New York: Academic Press.

Durkin, D. (1966). *Children who read early.* New York: Teachers College Press.

Dyson, A.H. (1988). *Drawing, talking and writing: Rethinking writing development (Occasional Paper No. 3).* National Center for the Study of Writing and Literacy, Berkeley: University of California, Berkeley.

———. (1990). *The word and the world: Reconceptualizing written language development or do rainbows mean a lot to little girls? (Technical Report No. 42).* National Center for the Study of Writing and Literacy, Berkeley, CA: University of California, Berkeley.

Edelsky, C. (1991). *With literacy and justice for all: Rethinking the social in language and education.* London: The Falmer Press.

Ferdman, B.M. (1990). Literacy and cultural identity. *Harvard Educational Review, 60,* 181–204.

Ferguson, C.A. & Heath, S.B. (1981) (Eds.). *Language in the USA.* New York: Cambridge University Press.

Fingeret, A. (1983). Social network: A new perspective on independence and adult illiterates. *Adult Education Quarterly, 33,* 133–146.

Fishman, J.A. (1972). Domains and the relationship between micro and macrosociolinguistics. In J.J. Gumperz & D.H. Hymes (Eds.), *Directions in sociolinguistics* (pp. 435–453). New York: Holt, Rinehart & Winston.

Fishman, J.A., Riedler-Berger, C., Koling, P. & Steele, J.M. (1985). Ethnocultural dimensions in the acquisition and retention of biliteracy: A comparative ethnography of four New York City schools. In J. Fishman, M.H. Gertner, E.G. Lowy & W.G. Milan (Eds.). *The rise and fall of the ethnic revival: Perspectives on language and ethnicity* (pp. 377–441). New York: Mouton.

Foertsch, M.A. (1992). *Reading in and out of school: Factors influencing the literacy achievement of American students in grades 4, 8 and 12, in 1988 and 1990.* Washington, DC: National Center for Education Statistics.

Gee, J.P. (1986). Orality and literacy: From *The savage mind* to *Ways with words. TESOL Quarterly, 20,* 747–751.

———. (1990). *Social linguistics and literacies: Ideology in discourses.* London: The Falmer Press.

Gilmore, P. (1983). Spelling 'Mississippi': Recontextualizing a literacy-related speech event. *Anthropology & Education Quarterly, 14,* 235–255.

Gilmore, P. & Glatthorn, A. (Eds.). (1982). *Children in and out of school.* Washington, DC: Center for Applied Linguistics.

Goody, J. (Ed.). (1968). *Literacy in traditional societies.* London: Cambridge University Press.

———. (1986). *The logic of writing and the organization of society.* Cambridge: Cambridge University Press.

———. (1987). *The interface between the written and the oral.* Cambridge: Cambridge University Press.

Goody, J. & Watt, I. (1963). The consequences of literacy. *Comparative Studies in Society and History, 5,* 27–68.

Griffin, P. (1977). How and when does reading occur in the classroom. *Theory into Practice, 16*(5), 376–383.

Gundlach, R., Farr, M. & Cook-Gumperz, J. (1989). Writing and reading in the community. In A.H. Dyson (Ed.), *Writing and reading: Collaboration in the classroom.* Urbana: National Council of Teachers of English.

Heath, S.B. (1982). What no bedtime story means: Narrative skills at home and school. *Language in Society, 11,* 49–76.

———. (1983). *Ways with words: Language, life and work in communities and classrooms.* Cambridge: Cambridge University Press.

Holdaway, D. (1979). *The foundations of literacy.* Sydney: Ashton Scholastic.

Hymes, D.H. (1968). The ethnography of speaking. In J.A. Fishman (Ed.), *Readings in the sociology of language.* The Hague: Mouton.

Jacob, E. (1984). Learning literacy through play: Puerto Rican kindergarten children. In H. Goelman, A. Oberg & F. Smith (Eds.), *Awakening to literacy* (pp. 73–83). Exeter, NH: Heinemann.

Kirsch, I.S. & Jungeblut, A. (1986). *Literacy: Profiles of America's young adults.* Princeton, NJ: Educational Testing Service.

Krashen, S. (1976). Formal and informal linguistic environments in language acquisition and language learning. *TESOL Quarterly, 10,* 157–168.

Lemke, J. (1989). Social semiotics: A new model for literacy education. In D. Bloome (Ed.), *Classrooms and literacy* (pp. 289–309). Norwood, NJ: Ablex.

Leont'ev, A.N. (1981). The problem of activity in psychology. In J.V. Wertsch (Ed.), *The concept of activity in Soviet psychology.* Armonk, N.Y.: M.E. Sharpe.

Levin, P. (1990). Culturally contextualized apprenticeship: Teaching and learning through helping in Hawaiian families. *Quarterly Newsletter of the Laboratory of Comparative Human Cognition, 12,* 81–86.

Mangubhai, F. (1984). Fiji. In R.M. Thomas and T.N. Postlethwaite (Eds.), *Schooling in the Pacific Islands* (pp. 167–201). Oxford: Pergamon Press.

McCaskill, B.A. Literacy in the loophole of retreat: Harriet Jacobs's nineteenth-century narrative. This volume.

McDermott, R.P. (1976). *Kids make sense: An ethnographic account of the interactional management of success and failure in one first-grade classroom.* Unpublished doctoral dissertation, Stanford University.

———. (1977). Social relations as contexts for learning in school. *Harvard Educational Review, 47,* 198–213.

Michaels, S. (1981). "Sharing Time": Children's narrative styles and differential access to literacy. *Language in Society, 10,* 423–442.

Moll, L.C., Amanti, C., Neff, D. & Gonzalez, N. (1992). Funds of knowledge for teaching: Using a qualitative approach to connect homes and classrooms. *Theory into Practice, 31*(2), 132–141.

Moll, L.C. & Diaz, S. (1985). Ethnographic pedagogy: Promoting effective bilingual education. In E. Garcia & R.V. Padilla (Eds.), *Advances in bilingual education research.* Tucson: University of Arizona Press.

———. (1987). Change as the goal of educational research. *Anthropology and Education Quarterly, 18,* 300–311.

Neuman, S. (1986). The home environment and fifth-grade students' leisure reading. *Elementary School Journal, 83,* 333–343.

Ogbu, J.U. (1987). Opportunity structure, cultural boundaries and literacy. In J.A. Langer (Ed.), *Language, literacy and culture* (pp. 149–177). Norwood, NJ: Ablex.

———. (1990). Minority status and literacy in perspective. *Daedalus, 119,* 141–168.

Olson, D.R. (1977). From utterance to text: The bias of language in speech and writing. *Harvard Educational Review, 47,* 257–281.

Ong, W.J. (1982). *Orality and literacy.* New York: Methuen.

Philips, S.U. (1972). Participation structures and communicative competence: Warm Springs children in community and classroom. In C. Cazden, V. John & D.H. Hymes (Eds.), *Functions of language in the classroom* (pp. 370–394). New York: Teachers College Press.

Purves, A.C. (1987). Literacy, culture and community. In D. Wagner (Ed.), *The future of literacy in a changing world* (pp. 216–232). Oxford: Pergamon.

Reder, S. (1987). Comparative aspects of functional literacy development: Three ethnic American communities. In D. Wagner (Ed.), *The future of literacy in a changing world* (pp. 250–270). Oxford: Pergamon Press.

———. (in press). Getting the message across: Cultural factors in the intergenerational transfer of cognitive skills. In T.G. Sticht & B. McDonald (Eds.), *The intergenerational transfer of cognitive skills.* Norwood, NJ: Ablex.

Reder, S. & Green, K.R. (1983). Contrasting patterns of literacy in an Alaska fishing village. *International Journal of the Sociology of Language, 42,* 9–39.

———. (1985). *Giving literacy away: An alternative strategy for increasing adult literacy development.* Portland, OR: Northwest Regional Educational Laboratory.

Reder, S., & Schwab, R.G. (1989). The communicative economy of the workgroup: Multichannel genres of communication. *Office: Technology and People, 4,* 177–195.

Resnick, L.B. (1990). Literacy in school and out. *Daedalus, 119,* 169–185.

Rogoff, B. (1986). Adult assistance of children's learning. In T.E. Raphael (Ed.), *The contexts of school-based literacy* (pp. 27–42). New York: Random House.

Rogoff, B. & Wertsch, J.V. (Eds.) (1984). *Children's learning in the "zone of proximal development."* San Francisco: Jossey-Bass.

Schieffelin, B.B. & Cochran-Smith, M. (1984). Learning to read culturally: Literacy before schooling. In H. Goelman, A.A. Oberg & F. Smith (Eds.), *Awakening to literacy* (pp. 3–23). Portsmouth, NH: Heinemann.

Schieffelin, B. & Gilmore, P. (Eds.). (1986). *The acquisition of literacy: Ethnographic perspectives. (Advances in Discourse Processes, XXI).* Norwood, NJ: Ablex.

Scollon, R. & Scollon, S.B.K. (1981). *Narrative, literacy and face in interethnic communication.* Norwood, NJ: Ablex.

Scribner, S. & Cole, M. (1981). Unpacking literacy. In M.F. Whiteman (Ed.), *Variation in writing: Functional and linguistic-cultural differences* (pp. 71–87). Hillsdale, NJ: Lawrence Erlbaum Associates.

Shuman, A. (1983). Collaborative literacy in an urban multiethnic neighborhood. *International Journal of the Sociology of Language, 42,* 69–81.

Smith, F. (1983). *Essays into literacy.* Exeter, NH: Heinemann.

———. (1985). A metaphor for literacy: Creating worlds or shunting information? In D.R. Olson, N. Torrance & A. Hildyard (Eds.), *Literacy, language and learning: The nature and consequences of reading and writing.* Cambridge: Cambridge University Press.

Snow, C.E. (1983). Literacy and language: Relationships during the preschool years. *Harvard Educational Review, 53,* 165–189.

Snow, C.E. & Ninio, A. (1986). The contracts of literacy: What children learn from learning to read books. In W. Teale & E. Sulzby (Eds.), *Emergent literacy: Writing and reading* (pp. 116–138). Norwood, NJ: Ablex.

Spolsky, B. (1981). Bilingualism and biliteracy. *The Canadian Modern Language Review, 37,* 475–485.

Street, B. (1984). *Literacy in theory and practice.* Cambridge: Cambridge University Press.

———. (in press). *Discourse, context and ideology: Essays in literacy and anthropology.* Cambridge: Cambridge University Press.

Stubbs, H. (1980). *Language and literacy: The sociolinguistics of reading and writing.* London: Routledge & Kegan Paul.

Szwed, J. (1981). The ethnography of literacy. In M.F. Whiteman (Ed.), *Variation in writing: Functional and linguistic-cultural differences* (pp. 13–23). Hillsdale, NJ: Erlbaum.

Tannen, D. (1982). The oral/literate continuum in discourse. In D. Tannen (Ed.), *Spoken and written language: Exploring orality and literacy.* Norwood, NJ: Ablex.

Taylor, D. (1983). *Family literacy: Young children learning to read and write.* Exeter, NH: Heinemann.

Taylor, D. & Dorsey-Gaines, C. (1988). *Growing up literate: Learning from inner-city families.* Portsmouth, NH: Heinemann.

Teale, W.H. (1984). Reading to young children: Its significance for literacy development. In H. Goelman, A. Oberg & F. Smith (Eds.), *Awakening to literacy* (pp. 110–121). Exeter, NH: Heinemann.

———. (1986). Home background and children's literacy development. In W.H. Teale & E. Sulzby (Eds.), *Emergent literacy: Writing and reading* (pp. 173–206). Norwood, NJ: Ablex.

Teale, W.H. & Sulzby, E. (1987). Literacy acquisition in early childhood: The roles of access and mediation in storybook reading. In D.A. Wagner (Ed.), *The future of literacy in a changing world* (pp. 111–130). Oxford: Pergamon.

Vygotsky, L.S. (1978). *Mind in society: The development of higher psychological processes.* M. Cole, V. John-Steiner, S. Scribner & E. Souberman (Eds.). Cambridge: Harvard University Press.

Wagner, D.A. (1986). Personal Communication.

———. (1987). *The future of literacy in a changing world.* Oxford: Pergamon.

Watson-Gegeo, K.A. (1990). The social transfer of cognitive skills in Kwara'ae. *Quarterly Newsletter of Comparative Human Cognition, 12,* 86–89.

Weber, R. (1991). Linguistic diversity and reading in American society. In R. Barr, M. Kamil, P.B. Mosenthal, & P.D. Pearson (Eds.), *Handbook of reading research, Vol. 2* (pp. 97–119). New York: Longman.

Weinreich, U. (1974). *Languages in contact.* New York: Mouton de Gruyter.

Weinstein, G. (1986). *From mountaintops to city streets: An ethnographic investigation of literacy and social process among the Hmong of Philadelphia.* Unpublished doctoral dissertation, University of Pennsylvania.

Wells, G. (1985). Preschool literacy-related activities and success in school. In D.R. Olson, N. Torrance & A. Hildyard (Eds.), *Literacy, language, and learning: The nature and consequences of reading and writing* (pp. 229–255). Cambridge: Cambridge University Press.

_____. (1986). Styles of interaction and opportunities of learning. In A. Cashdan (Ed.), *Literacy: Teaching and learning languages skills* (pp. 17–31). Oxford: Basil Blackwell.

Wertsch, J.V. (1984). *Vygotsky and the social formation of mind.* Cambridge: Harvard University Press.

Zanger, V.V. "Not joined in": The social context of English literacy development for Hispanic youth. This volume.

CHAPTER 3

Literacy Acquisition Among Second-Language Learners

Arnulfo G. Ramírez

INTRODUCTION

The process of becoming literate in a second language (L2) has attracted considerable scholarly attention in the past decade. Numerous books have been published on the issues related to teaching and learning to read English as a second/foreign language (Alderson & Urquhart, 1984; Dubin, Eskey & Grabe, 1986; Mackay, Barkman & Jordan, 1979). Others have centered on the dynamics of L2 writing (Connor & Kaplan, 1987; Gaudiani, 1981; McKay, 1984). Some publications have approached literacy in terms of bilingual populations (Garcia & Flores, 1986; Goldman & Trueba, 1987; Wallace, 1986), while others conceive of written products as cultural artifacts representing particular organizational patterns (Kaplan, 1983; Purves, 1988; Smith, 1987).

Literacy acquisition among L2 learners involves a number of important questions. The first set of concerns relates to the conception of literacy itself. How are reading and writing abilities described in terms of language elements? How are reading and writing abilities characterized according to different models of language proficiency? To what extent are the two modalities interrelated? The second major question centers on the nature of literacy acts. Reading and writing activities can encompass a broad range of text types ranging from literary forms (short stories, essays, poems) to informative materials (instructions, notices, handbooks). What are the different types of reading and writing genres?

What are the main reasons for reading and writing? What types of cognitive operations are associated with different kinds of literacy activities?

The third significant area of concern focuses on the nature of literacy skills and the role of learner differences. Reading and writing activities can be seen from various perspectives. Seeing reading as an interactive process, for example, assumes that text comprehension is based on the notion that the reader constructs meaning on the basis of the text itself and the prior knowledge available to the reader (Barnett, 1989; Carrell, Devine & Eskey, 1988; Swaffar, Arens & Byrnes, 1991). In addition, the reader's level of language proficiency (Carrell, 1991) and the use of a variety of reading strategies (Barnett, 1988; Grabe, 1991) affect the comprehension process. Writing activities entail matters like content or topic, text structure, composing strategies, and reader's expectations (Raimes, 1991). How can one characterize the reading and writing processes? What strategies do learners use in text comprehension and text creation? To what extent are reading and writing activities interconnected? What role do learner differences play in L2 literacy acquisition? What relationships exist between literacy and the social context? This chapter will address the three major questions outlined above and will answer the specific queries noted for each area.

CONCEPTIONS OF L2 LITERACY

The concept of literacy in a second language has changed with our evolving views on the nature of what is language and how it should be taught. Second-language instruction has tended to separate oral language (listening and speaking) from the written modality (reading and writing). During the 1940s and 1950s structural linguistics exerted a major influence on L2 teaching by emphasizing the primacy of oral language, with writing as the visible means to record speech. Reading and writing activities served primarily as contexts for oral language drills. Texts were often utilized to reinforce grammatical patterns and vocabulary development in audiolingual language programs. The "natural" sequence of instruction that had to be followed was listening, speaking, reading, and finally writing. Since language was speech, not writing, texts provided the cultural

basis for contextualizing speech. This orientation was also reflected in language teaching methods—like the "natural
approach"—that were based on child-language-acquisition research and stressed the importance of oral language development
before literacy (reading and writing) instruction (Krashen & Terrell, 1983). L2 acquisition, at least the oral modality, was accomplished through subconscious processes similar to those involved
in mother-tongue acquisition (Krashen, 1982). Reading and writing abilities are developed through conscious learning activities
that involve complex cognitive processes, requiring practice opportunities until the various subtasks are automatized (McLaughlin,
1987).

Conceptions of L2 proficiency have also separated linguistic
abilities according to the oral and written modalities. Hernández-
Chávez, Burt, and Dulay (1978), for example, conceive of proficiency in terms of a behavioral-structural model that segments
language into sixty-four separate units involving four linguistic
categories (vocabulary, grammar, pronunciation, and semantics),
the oral and written modalities (comprehension and production
abilities associated with the written and oral mode), and sociolinguistic performance concerning questions of usage (speech style
and communicative functions) and language varieties (stan-
dard/nonstandard dialects and sociolinguistic domains). Reading
and writing abilities are seen as separate language skills rather
than connected discourse involving textual features beyond the
level of vocabulary, grammar, and semantics. Oller (1979), on the
other hand, argues for the existence of a global language proficiency factor that accounts for most of the performance difference in a
wide variety of language proficiency measures. This single-concept
expression of proficiency, described as "expectancy grammar," is
strongly related to cognitive variables and academic achievement
and appears to exist across all four language skills (listening,
speaking, reading, and writing). This global ability is attributed to
the fact that "in the meaningful use of language, some sort of
pragmatic expectancy grammar must function in all cases", and
this perceptual ability is "a psychologically real system that se-
quentially orders linguistic elements in time and in relation to
extralinguistic elements in meaningful ways" (1979, p. 25). This
position emphasizes the central role that expectation and predic-

tion play across language tasks and asserts that language itself cannot be meaningfully segmented into separate, discrete components.

Reading and writing acts are depicted by Cummins (1980, 1983) in terms of cognitive demands and contextual features. He relates listening/speaking abilities to interpersonal communication skills or context-embedded communication in which the participants can negotiate meaning through the use of gestures and feedback to indicate that the message has not been understood. This type of language proficiency is supported by a wide range of situational cues and a shared reality among the participants that make it unnecessary to elaborate explicitly the linguistic message. Reading and writing activities, on the other hand, occur as part of context-reduced communication that relies primarily on linguistic cues to establish meaning and in some cases may involve suspending knowledge of the "real" world so as to interpret or manipulate the logic of communication correctly. A text explaining a complicated process, for example, requires that the sender organize a considerable amount of information that must be stated explicitly in order for the receiver to understand and follow the directions needed to complete the activity successfully. Cognitively undemanding tasks such as filling out a form with personal information or locating the title of a chapter in a book appear to require little cognitive involvement since the linguistic behaviors usually have become automatized with practice for most learners. This cognitive orientation toward literacy skills considers reading and writing processes without paying special attention to textual features (e.g., syntactic elements, vocabulary, discourse structures) and extralinguistic aspects (e.g., the learner's familiarity with the topic and language proficiency).

Canale's (1984) conception of L2 proficiency does not separate language abilities in terms of the oral and written forms. Instead he characterizes linguistic communication with respect to various systems of knowledge and skills associated with four interesting factors:

1. Grammatical competence: mastery of the language code (verbal or nonverbal), concerned with such features as lexical items and rules of sentence formation, pronunciation, and literal meaning.

2. Sociolinguistic competence: mastery of appropriate language use in different sociolinguistic contexts, with emphasis on appropriateness of meanings (e.g., attitudes, speech acts, and propositions) and appropriateness of forms (e.g., register, non-verbal expression, and intonation).

3. Discourse competence: mastery of how to combine and interpret forms and meanings to achieve a unified spoken or written text in different genres by using (a) cohesion devices to relate utterance forms (e.g., pronouns, transition words, and parallel structures) and (b) coherence rules to organize meanings (e.g., repetition, progression, consistency, and relevance of ideas).

4. Strategic competence: mastery of verbal and non-verbal strategies (a) to compensate for breakdowns in communication due to insufficient competence or to performance limitations (e.g., strategies such as use of dictionaries, paraphrase, and gestures) and (b) to enhance the effectiveness of communication (e.g., deliberately slow and soft speech for rhetorical effect). (p. 112)

Reading and writing abilities here are seen as part of communicative competence. Sending and receiving written messages encompasses various systems of knowledge and skills that include extralinguistic aspects such as knowledge of the world, interpersonal communication strategies, and awareness of social conventions.

Functional language proficiency as reflected in American Council on the Teaching of Foreign Languages (ACTFL) Guidelines (1986) establishes hierarchical performance levels for listening, speaking, reading, and writing. For each language area, integrated descriptions of linguistic abilities are specified according to functions (informing, asking questions, narrating past/future activities, expressing agreement/disagreement), contexts (topics like everyday situations, family life, travel, professional interests), and accuracy levels (the degree to which the functions are accomplished and the extent to which the message is understood or found acceptable among native speakers). This tripart description of language proficiency (function, context, and accuracy) establishes reading and writing abilities by comparing individual performance levels with integrated descriptions of linguistic abilities. These descriptions, however, do not take into account how readers interact with different types of texts (Lee, 1988) and how reading competencies interact or influence writing abilities (Swaffar, 1988).

The view of L2 reading as an interactive, multidimensional process takes into account textual features such as topic familiarity, rhetorical structure, vocabulary, and grammar, as well as reader characteristics and comprehension strategies. L2 readers construct the meaning of a text by making use of both text-based and extra–text-based components (Bernhardt, 1986). The text-based elements include word recognition, phonemic/graphemic decoding, and syntactic feature recognition. Extra–text-based components encompass intratextual perception (the reconciliation of different segments of the text with what precedes and follows), prior knowledge (the reader's level of familiarity with the text's context), and metacognition (the extent to which the reader thinks about what she or he is reading).

Background knowledge is particularly significant for L2 readers. According to schema theory, readers can adequately comprehend a text if they have the preexisting knowledge structures to organize knowledge of language and the world. Carrell and Eisterhold (1983) note that efficient readers rely on information processing based on linguistic data from the text, which is then mapped against the readers' schemata. Nunan (1984), for example, found that among high school ESL readers, background knowledge about the topic was a more important factor in reading comprehension than the syntactic complexity of the text. Similarly, Hudson (1982) demonstrated the importance of schemata in the interpretation of texts by showing that relevant background knowledge can compensate for a student's level of language proficiency as a factor in reading comprehension.

With respect to writing, Bell and Burnaby (1984) point out that the composing process is an extremely complex activity involving the control of language both at the sentence level (grammatical structures, vocabulary, punctuation, spelling, and letter formation) and beyond the sentence rank (organizing and integrating information into cohesive and coherent paragraphs or texts). Meaningful writing requires attending to a number of constraints that can affect the reader's reconstruction of meaning. These constraints, according to Nystrand (1982), include the following:

1. graphic constraints—matters of orthography, legibility, punctuation, spacing, and layout;

2. syntactic constraints—sentence structure, homonym confusion, omission of punctuation marks, and in a few cases violations of prescribed usage;

3. semantic constraints—assumptions about what the reader brings to the text and the presentation of "new information" based on the reader's "given information";

4. textured constraints—the use of cohesive devices (reference, substitution, ellipsis and conjunction) that help to disambiguate or maintain text continuity;

5. contextual constraints—factors such as format, genre, mode, type and title that are relevant to the text's situation. (pp. 64–65)

Developments in the field of first-language (L1) writing among primary-school children (e.g., Graves, 1983) and reading instruction (e.g., Goodman, 1989) have given rise to the concept of "whole language". The term "whole language" incorporates a number of basic principles: (1) language is a whole, and any attempt to fragment it into parts—grammatical patterns, word lists, phonics classes—destroys it; (2) language must be kept "whole" or it's no longer language; (3) language cannot be split into oral and written language as is commonly done in traditional ESL texts and courses like listening, reading, or writing; (4) in a literate society, the use of written language is as natural as conversation among people; and (5) the uses of written language can be developed as naturally as the uses of oral language (Rigg, 1990). These principles used in native-language English classrooms have been incorporated to some extent in ESL instruction, particularly at the elementary school level. Mangelsdorf (1989) argues for the need to draw parallels between speaking and writing, thereby enhancing L2 acquisition by approaching (1) speaking and writing as communication, (2) speaking and writing as interaction, and (3) speaking and writing as dialogue. Enright and McCloskey (1988) point out, for instance, that the writing process can encourage collaboration among writers and provide numerous opportunities for the creation and use of meaningful discourse as students participate in full-group or small-group activities while prewriting, drafting, sharing their drafts, and responding to writing by revising, editing, and publishing their written products.

The reading-writing connections represented by current instructional approaches suggest that both processes influence each other in an interactive manner. Carson Eisterhold (1990) has pointed out that L2 reading and writing do influence each other in a reciprocal manner although the relationship between the two processes changes with different stages of language development. The interaction between both processes appears to be a complex phenomenon involving such variables as L2 language proficiency, educational experiences in L1 and L2, and differences in cultural literacy practices (Carson, Carrell, Silberstein, Kroll & Kuehn, 1990). Thus, L2 literacy acquisition cannot be conceived as separate, independent language modalities but instead must be conceived as interdependent language skills, cognitive processes, and means of learning (Grabe, 1991).

L2 READING AND WRITING ACTS

Reading and writing activities in a second language can involve a broad range of genres and require numerous linguistic competencies. L2 reading can include a broad range of text types such as plays, short stories, essays, poems, and novels. They may also involve informative materials (e.g., labels, warnings, recipes, handbooks, instructions, notices, rules and regulations), orientational texts (e.g., travel brochures, menus, plane and train schedules, catalogs, posters, signs, TV and radio guides, advertisements), evaluative reports (e.g., editorials, magazine articles, travel essays, reviews, biographies), and visuals with texts (e.g., comic strips, cartoons, maps, pictures with captions, charts, diagrams). The reader may only need to recognize the name and numbers on a street sign (i.e., understanding explicitly stated information) or may be required to go beyond the text, as in the case of having to judge the fairness in reporting found in a newspaper editorial.

At present there is no comprehensive taxonomy with which to classify the extensive variety of text types. Child (1987) has proposed a classification scheme based on the degree to which reader and writer share background information. These text types are organized hierarchically to correspond with ACTFL (1986) proficiency levels, and they include four basic categories based on the essential purpose of the text: orientational, instructive, evaluative, and projective. Lee and Musumeci (1988) have extended Child's system to include the reading skills that parallel the hierarchies of text types. Reading enumerative texts (e.g., signs, addresses, office designations) involves the recognition of memorized elements. Orientational texts (e.g., travel forms, schedules, program guides, menus, brief messages) require skimming and scanning reading strategies. Decoding and classifying processes are associated with instructive texts (e.g., ads, labels, instructions, directions, short narratives, factual reports). Reading skills such as inferring, hypothesizing, and interpreting are related to evaluative texts (e.g., editorials, analyses, literary texts, biography). Projective texts (e.g., art critiques, literary texts, technical papers, philosophical discourse, argumentation) require strategies such as the ability to analyze, verify, extend, and hypothesize. Lee (1988) argues that there are many factors that can affect text difficulty, thus making Child's hierarchy questionable. Text difficulties can be attributed to such areas as the topic reflected in the lexical items, passage density associated with the proportion of concepts or information units in the passage, or the cognitive strategies the reader needs to employ to accomplish particular comprehension tasks.

Written language has many forms (e.g., poems, directions, pamphlets, schedules, letters, reports, essays, novels) and performs numerous communicative functions (e.g., to inform, entertain, persuade, instruct, express personal feeling, warn, praise). There are at least two main reasons for reading texts: for pleasure and for obtaining information (Byrnes, 1985). When we read, we tend to approach written texts in four basic ways (Grellet, 1981:4):

1. Skimming: reading a text superficially and rapidly in order to obtain the gist or main idea

2. Scanning: reading a text quickly in order to locate a specific item of information

3. Extensive reading: reading longer texts, usually for one's own pleasure and for the purpose of global understanding and fluency development

4. Intensive reading: reading shorter texts to extract information and to develop accuracy in comprehension at the level of detail

Moreover, reading often involves the act of reconstructing meanings sent by a writer at a remote time and place. Much of the language of written texts is carefully "edited" (i.e., complete sentences, fewer redundancies, and conventional features such as paragraphing, spelling, rules, and punctuation marks). Since the meaning cannot be negotiated between the participants, as it can with speaking situations, a considerable amount of information will have to be made explicit to the reader in order to facilitate comprehension (Stubbs, 1980).

As with reading acts, writing demands can vary significantly—from filling out forms to corresponding with acquaintances through personal letters to the creation of short stories and poems. Britton et al. (1975) have suggested a scheme to describe writing by taking into account the role of the writer (spectator or participant in the composing process) and the three major functions of written language: expressive (personal writing similar to informal talk), transactional (information sharing, often intended for a specific audience, placing the writer as a participant as she or he informs, directs, persuades), and poetic (literary works such as poems, short stories, or plays, in which the writer adopts the role of spectator by distancing self from the immediate context in order to tell the story or create the poem). Kaplan (1983) on the other hand, points out that there are essentially four basic types of writing activities:

1. Writing without composing (e.g., filling blanks in writing exercises, completing forms, writing transcriptions/word lists)
2. Writing for informational purposes (e.g., note taking, writing reports, summarizing and outlining)
3. Writing for personal purposes (e.g., journals, diaries, memos, notes)
4. Writing for imaginative purposes (e.g., stories, plays, poems)

Kaplan adds that while the list appears to be hierarchical, it is difficult to establish an order of acquisition at this time since writing involves the control of four kinds of knowledge: of aspects of language, of writing conventions, of subject or topic, and of the intended audience. The text types provided in the ACTFL (1986) proficiency levels for writing, for example, relate content/topics, language functions, and accuracy levels to performance behaviors established on the basis of a hierarchy, ranging from novice to the superior level, with nine specific generic descriptions. The descriptions for the three types of "novice" writers and the two levels of "advanced" students are presented here:

Novice: The novice level is characterized by an ability to produce isolated words and phrases.

> *Novice-low:* able to form some letters in an alphabetic system. In languages whose writing systems use syllabaries or characters, writer is able to both copy and produce the basic strokes. Can produce romanization of isolated characters, where applicable.

> *Novice-Mid:* able to copy or transcribe familiar words or phrases and reproduce some from memory. No practical communicative writing skills

> *Novice-High:* able to write simple fixed expressions and limited memorized material and some recombinations thereof. Can supply information on simple forms and documents. Can write names, numbers, dates, own nationality, and other simple autobiographical information, as well as short phrases and simple lists, can write all the symbols in an alphabetic or syllabic system or 50–100 characters or compounds in a character writing system. Spelling and representation of symbols (letters, syllables, characters) may be partially correct.

Advanced: The advanced level is characterized by an ability to write narratives and descriptions of a factual nature of at least several paragraphs in length on familiar topics.

> *Advanced:* able to write routine social correspondence and join sentences in simple discourse of at least several paragraphs in length on familiar topics. Can write simple social correspondence, take notes, and write cohesive summaries and resumes as well as narratives and descriptions of a factual nature. Has sufficient writing vocabulary to express self simply with some circumlocution. May still make errors in punctuation, spelling, or the formation of nonalphabetic symbols. Good control of the morphology and the most frequently used syntactic structures, e.g., common word-order patterns, coordination, subordination, but makes frequent errors in producing complex sen-

tences. Uses a limited number of cohesive devices, such as pronouns, accurately. Writing may resemble literal translations from native language, but a sense of organization (rhetorical structure) is emerging. Writing is understandable to natives not used to the writing of nonnatives.

Advanced-plus: Able to write about a variety of topics with significant precision and in detail. Can write most social and informal business correspondence. Can describe and narrate personal experiences fully but has difficulty supporting points of view in written discourse. Can write about the concrete aspects of topics relating to particular interests and special fields of competence. Often shows remarkable fluency and ease of expression, but under time constraints and pressure writing may be inaccurate. Generally strong in either grammar or vocabulary, but not in both. Weakness and unevenness in one of the foregoing or in spelling or character-writing formation may result in occasional miscommunication. Some misuse of vocabulary may still be evident. Style may still be obviously foreign.

The trisectional descriptions of L2 writing proficiency according to context, function, and accuracy include a number of factors or dimensions that relate to such aspects as the writing system, length of the product, sequence of development (creativity versus memorization), organizational elements, and topic familiarity. These areas are not based on a coherent theory of L2 writing nor do they take into account the role of transfer from L1 writing or the cultural authenticity both in form and style of different writing tasks (Valdés, Haro & Echevarriarza, 1992). At the same time, the guidelines do not consider the series of complicated mental operations that are required to produce written discourse. Clark and Clark (1977) have stated that a writer has to consider such aspects as (1) the meaning that is to be conveyed, (2) the genre of the text (a narrative, a description, an explanation), (3) the style of the prose (e.g., casual vs. formal, neutral vs. personal), (4) the purpose of the text (e.g., to inform, to persuade, to invite), and (5) the amount of detail needed to accomplish the writer's intention. This perspective takes into account both textual considerations and communicative intent beyond Kaplan's (1983) types of writing activity and Britton's et al. (1975) role of the writer.

Writing activities comprise both content and particular types of discourse patterns. Genres such as narratives, directions, reports, and business letters follow specific discourse formats and patterns of organization. While there are universal rhetorical devices for organizing information according to such semantic structures as comparison/contrast, definition/classification, and analysis/synthesis, differences may exist between languages at the level of grammar, particularly in the manner available in which syntactic devices in a language are used to convey meaning (Kaplan, 1972). At the same time, writing in different languages appears to be associated with particular cultural patterns of communication (Purves, 1988). This variation can be appreciated in physical appearance of the text (e.g., indentation, margins, scripts, punctuation), and the macro-discourse structure of the paragraph (e.g., topic sentence supported by examples or details). In English for instance, the dominant paragraph pattern tends to be linear-like when compared to nonlinear organizational structures in languages like Arabic or Chinese (Kaplan, 1966). Ostler (1987), for example, has observed that the English compositions written by Arabic speakers tend to contain elaborate parallel structures. This cultural preference appears to have some relationship to Koranic writing style. Thus, composing in a second language may reflect a transfer of writing styles based on first-language discourse patterns.

LITERACY SKILLS AND LEARNER DIFFERENCES

Reading and writing activities in a second language have been seen from various perspectives. Reading has been viewed as a "bottom-up" process of decoding written symbols, starting from the smaller segments (individual letters, syllables, words) and working to the larger units (clauses, sentences, paragraphs). Reading comprehension involves various strategies that the reader uses to build progressively larger units of the language until meaning can be extracted. Reading has also been described as a "top-down" process in which the reader brings to the task an array of information, ideas, and beliefs about the text. The reader initiates the process by making predictions about the meaning of the text as she or he employs knowledge of vocabulary, syntax, discourse, and the world. Skill in reading depends on the efficient interaction between linguistic knowledge and background knowledge associated with the topic.

A third perspective assumes that readers use both text-based (bottom-up) and reader-based (top-down) strategies. Readers make guesses and those predictions, in turn, facilitate the decoding. As readers decode, they are able to relate the text to their own background knowledge. Thus, meaning is created through the interaction of text and reader. Stanovich (1980) has noted that efficient L2 reading may require the integration of both strategies.

It is important to note that there are many different types of strategies associated with reading a text. Van Parreren and Schouten–Van Parreren (1981) point out that students writing in their native language may need to acquire at least six crucial subskills and learn when to apply each subskill given the nature of the task:

1. Recognize the type of text (e.g., fictional, informative, persuasive)
2. Recognize different types of text structure (e.g., story schema, expository prose)
3. Predict and summarize the content of a text/passage
4. Make inferences with respect to information that is textually implicit
5. Determine the meaning of unknown from the context
6. Analyze the word morphology of unknown words

Studies of actual L2 reading strategies have shown that students are actively engaged in the process of constructing meaning. Hosenfeld et al. (1981) observed that successful adolescent readers (English speakers learning French) used a variety of strategies that involved both bottom-up and top-down processes. For example, they skipped unnecessary words and guessed contextually, relied on illustrations and titles to make inferences, kept meaning in mind, made use of their knowledge of the world, identified words according to grammatical category, looked up words, used margin glosses, evaluated guesses, and used context in preceding and succeeding sentences and paragraphs as they tried to make sense of the text. Block (1986) found that ESL college readers brought their knowledge of the reading process and approaches to the task. The use of various comprehension strategies did not seem to correspond to language-specific features. Readers who were aware of text structure and monitored their reading skills were able to learn more course content. Clarke (1980) concluded that "good" readers in both L1 and L2 tended to perform better than "poor" readers in both languages, in this case Spanish speakers learning English as adults. Nevertheless, text complexity caused some L2 readers to revert to poor reading strategies due to limited language proficiency. In the case of French, Hauptman (1979) noted that poor readers in English (L1) tended to use similar strategies when reading French texts. They tended to experience difficulty in both languages especially in the use of semantic information, contextual cues, and making guesses. Barnett (1988) established that students who considered and remembered "context" as they read understood more about the text than students who made less use of this strategy. The use of contexts as a reading strategy seems to have been associated with the students' own perception that it was effective in text comprehension and appears to have resulted in better reading scores among this group of college students learning French.

At present, there is considerable interest in the role of learner strategies. These strategies range from traditional reading skills like skimming and scanning, reading for meaning, and making inferences, to more recently recognized reading strategies like activating appropriate background knowledge and recognizing text structure. Chamot and Kupper (1989), for example, found in their case study of effective learners of Spanish that the students

1. read Spanish in ways similar to English (L1);
2. searched for meaning by reading according to phrases (constituent groups) rather than single words;
3. used a number of cognitive strategies to aid comprehension (e.g., translation, summarizing, self-evaluation);
4. employed self-monitoring procedures to minimize comprehension break-downs; and
5. utilized remediation strategies such as inferencing, elaboration (relating new information from the passage to prior knowledge), and deduction during comprehension break-downs.

Chamot and Kupper suggest the use of retrospective or think-aloud interviews as a means of identifying reading strategies during group activities, thereby making learners aware of their own thinking processes and those of their classmates.

Kern (1989) argues that most students can benefit from direct instruction in specific strategies that can assist them in word recognition, such as inferring word meaning through the use of context, or synthesizing meaning from larger segments of texts. Carrell (1989) further states that strategy training and practice need to go beyond task-specific considerations and include instruction in metacognitive awareness. Students need to be made aware of what types of reading strategies are involved; why they should learn; where, when, and how they should be used in different reading situations; and how they should evaluate or monitor their own strategy use. Presumably, such strategy training would help to minimize some of the differences between "good" and "poor" L2 readers.

The process of learning to write has been approached from Krashen's (1984) theory of language acquisition, which makes a distinction between two independent processes: *acquisition* and *learning*. Acquisition is primarily an unconscious process that occurs during the comprehension of language input within a meaningful context that favors learning under appropriate affective conditions. Learning, on the other hand, is a conscious process that usually results from formal grammar study or practice. From this perspective, writing competence is acquired through reading while fluency in writing performance is learned through extensive practice (Dvorak, 1986). The most effective writing practice is that which has a communicative orientation, such as asking students to inform, persuade, or describe their personal experiences. Grammar teaching and error-correction should be limited to simple, learnable rules.

Learning to write has also been seen as a developmental process. Emig (1988) argues that L1 writing skills emerge in predictable stages as children learn to separate and then to consolidate their speaking and writing abilities. Children move from expressive writing, which relies heavily on their oral language competence, to transactional writing, which involves a greater concern for the reader-audience. The third stage, which not all writers attain, is poetic writing, in which the focus is the writing itself (e.g., poem, short story, play) and the message the author/writer tries to convey. Some aspects of this perspective have been incorporated in L2 writing programs in recent years, particularly with young children who are taught through the "whole language" approach (Rigg, 1990; Enright & McCloskey, 1988).

Writing abilities in a second language parallel the development of certain composing abilities in the first language. For example, the development of syntactic complexity (e.g., simple sentences joined first by coordination, then subordination, and finally clause reduction) seems to follow a pattern similar to L1 learners (Gaies, 1980). The use of complex sentence structures in L2 can increase as in L1 composition by providing students with sentence-combining exercises (Cooper & Morain, 1980). Learners also appear to be sensitive to the mode of discourse, producing more complex structures in argumentation than in narration (Dvorak, 1987). Another parallel interest is that L2 learners respond more positively to teacher's feedback when the correction is related to content (Semke, 1980; Cordelle & Corno, 1981) rather than form (Hendrickson, 1980).

The concern for grammatical accuracy in written composition has been a topic of great concern. Semke (1980) found that error treatment among first-year college German students suggests that teachers' feedback on content produces higher gains in writing fluency than requiring learners to correct and rewrite their own compositions. Lalande's (1982) study comparing the effects of two methods of error correction (rewriting compositions based on teacher feedback verses self-correction of teacher-noted error types) shows that neither feedback on errors nor self-gains in grammatical accuracy were evident during the experimental period.

What learners actually do as they self-correct their written compositions indicates that students utilize a number of strategies to analyze and repair their language when they are informed of certain types of errors (Franzten & Russel, 1987). Learners, for instance, tend to correct their own errors according to a binary-option strategy: an error of x type needs a correction of y, where x and y are usually treated as instructional pairs (e.g., *ser/estar* in Spanish; much/many in English; *connaître/savoir* in French). Learners also seem to follow an "order of correctability," with individual correction rates higher for simpler errors (e.g., article-adjective agreement) than complex rules (e.g., aspectual distinctions that verb forms convey). Coombs (1986) notes that L2 writers in German are able to control the grammatical aspects of syntactic structures (e.g., word order and agreement) before they are able to use them effectively in discourse situations (e.g., infrequent use of discourse markers and text-structuring devices for the reader's benefit). More important, it appears that the correction of composition errors may produce only a low correlation between knowledge of grammar and writing abilities.

Approaching writing as a process may be potentially more beneficial to all students (Zamel, 1983). Assigning a letter grade, for example, can influence the length of compositions and the number of errors/type of errors (Chastain, 1990). Substantial writing practice may encourage students to write longer compositions with fewer errors and a higher level of creativity (Smith, 1990). Chamot and Kupper (1989), for instance, report that the writing strategies among effective students learning Spanish as L2 yield important insights about the writing process itself. These students engaged in the following behaviors while composing in high school Spanish classes:

1. Followed the same processes used for writing in English: planning, composing, and reviewing
2. Focused on the writing task without being distracted
3. Tried to think and generate ideas in Spanish while writing
4. Stayed within their vocabulary range instead of looking for translations of English words and phrases, often substituting alternate words and phrases when intended forms could not be recalled
5. Concentrated on integrating new ideas rather than focused on linguistic problems
6. Employed a number of cognitive strategies (deduction, substitution, and elaboration—relating parts of new information to each other)
7. Utilized metacognitive strategies such as planning and self-monitoring to check, verify, and correct the status of the written product in terms of a proposed writing plan

Other case studies of L2 writers reveal important insights about the writing process. It appears that L2 writers arrive at their final product through a series of stages, much as L1 writers do.

Zamel (1983) concluded that skilled ESL writers approached writing as a creative, generative process, not always based on a clear, linear direction. Writing involved integrating new ideas, revising those already recorded, and reconstructing the basic framework. Writing also required the ability to assess the clarity of thought and logic and the capacity to distance oneself from the text, in order to take into account the reader's point of view. Unskilled writers, on the other hand, were less concerned with the creation of meaning and tended to approach their writing as a series of linguistic elements—words, sentences, and paragraphs—that had to be organized in a linear fashion. Lapp (1984) compared the writing behaviors of skilled and unskilled ESL writers and noted significant differences during the prewriting and writing phases as well as the use of revising strategies among skilled writers. Skilled writers spent more time thinking about the writing task itself, organizing their ideas and information, reviewing sentence and paragraph structure while attending to meaning, and making frequent revisions to clarify meaning or to change the direction/focus of the text. Unskilled writers, on the other hand, spent little time in planning, were concerned primarily with the word choice and sentence formation, and used revisions for changes at the surface level, such as checking for correct grammar, spelling, and punctuation.

Learner differences extend beyond "successful" and "unsuccessful" literacy behaviors. Reading and writing activities are essentially social acts involving a relationship between the self and society (Santos, 1992). Individuals may become literate in L2 for instrumental purposes (occupational reasons, educational goals, immigration requirements) or integrative motives (personal desire to relate/interact with the people of the target culture). The particular type of motivational orientation may act as a powerful factor in determining the level of L2 proficiency attained by distinct groups of learners (Ely, 1986; Gardner, 1980; Gardner & Lambert, 1972). At the same time, levels of L2 literacy might be explained in terms of group membership. L2 literacy acquisition among members of the dominant, majority group can be seen as an "additive" kind of bilingualism, not affecting the loss of L1 skills nor creating identity problems associated with linguistic acculturation. Learners from language-minority groups (e.g., hyphenated citizens such as Mexican-Americans, Chinese-Americans, Turkish-

Germans, Moroccan-French) may encounter a "subtractive" form of bilingualism resulting in loss or erosion of L1 abilities (Lambert, 1980).

Members of ethnolinguistic minority groups may find themselves in a "biliteracy" world requiring different uses for L1 and L2. Reading and writing activities in L1 might serve to maintain a feeling of identity within the family, ethnic group, and the linguistic community. Literacy activities in L2 might relate to participation in the wider society in domains associated with work, government, health care, and social services. Literacy from this perspective can encompass such language needs as basic survival requirements (product labels, highway road signs), academic skills (textbooks, manuals, and essays), maintaining personal relationships (letters, telegrams), and personal uses (comics, magazines, newspapers, novels). Certain types of texts may be associated with one language (e.g., newspapers, magazines, warnings, reports, business correspondence) while other genres might be related with the other (e.g., personal letters, church bulletins, photo novels). This distributional pattern of text types might correspond to the "high" and "low" status of the two dialects within a diglossic language situation (Ferguson, 1959).

Literacy demands in L1 might be linked to intragroup needs (family, religion, and recreation), while L2 needs could revolve around intergroup uses (workplace, government services, education, mass media). The type of literacy—or biliteracy—that needs to be promoted would involve making decisions about the role different languages or dialects should play in society. Educators and literacy specialists will have to decide which broad types of literacy levels (functional, cultural, and critical) need to be promoted (Williams & Capizzi-Snipper, 1990). Functional literacy (basic writing and reading of simple texts) would encompass texts that enumerate (numbers, names, address), orient (travel forms and schedules, guides, menus, news headlines), and instruct (ads, labels, instructions, directions, short narratives and reports). Cultural literacy involves the use of "cultural schemata" necessary for fully comprehending texts (editorials, reviews, literary works) in a social sense. Critical literacy entails an understanding of the ideology of written texts (critiques, literary works, philosophical writing, technical reports). Adult learners may be able to provide L2 literacy planners with valuable insights about their reading/writing experiences and needs, motivations for literacy learning, and individual strategies for literacy acquisition (Cisneros & Leone, 1990).

CONCLUSION

Literacy acquisition in L2 has been conceived, until recently, in terms of separate linguistic abilities associated with the oral and written modalities. Second/foreign language instruction has tended to introduce written discourse after oral practice. L2 literacy has been conceptualized in terms of discrete language components, pragmatic notions of grammar, and communicative frameworks. Reading and writing acts can be described in relation to context-reduced communication, requiring specific cognitive processes and involving various systems of linguistic knowledge and skills. The current ACTFL guidelines establish reading and writing proficiency levels on the basis of hierarchical performance behaviors that incorporate a range of language functions, topics, and accuracy notions. The use of extra–text-based knowledge, reading and composing strategies, and metalinguistic awareness of literacy conventions also play an important role in L2 literacy acquisition.

Developments in L1 instructional theory have influenced approaches in L2 literacy, particularly the "whole" language perspective in ESL methodology. At the same time, reading and writing activities are described in the context of a broad range of text types or genres involving specific discourse structures, linguistic features, and cognitive processes. Some L2 genres may follow culturally bound patterns, which can differ significantly from L1 rhetorical styles.

Conceptions of L2 literacy activities have been greatly influenced by L1 theoretical perspectives. L2 reading has been viewed from "bottom-up", "top-down", schema theory, and learner strategies orientations. L2 writing has been described from an input (reading) and practice (writing) model, as a developmental sequence intimately connected with oral language growth, and as a creative, generative process. As would be expected, the acquisition of L2 literacy skills is influenced by learner characteristics as well as instructional practices. Skilled and unskilled L2 learners interact differentially with L2 texts. Classroom procedures such as teacher feedback, opportunity to practice, and task demands also influence literacy outcomes. Learners as members of social groups may have particular motivational orientations for attaining specific levels of L2 literacy skills. For some ethnolinguistic groups, L2 literacy should be examined in relation to L1 literacy levels and the social allocation of the two languages. Distinct types of L2 learners will pose special literacy problems, which will require particular solutions.

REFERENCES

ACTFL Provisional Proficiency Guidelines. (1986). Hastings-on-Hudson, NY: ACTFL Materials Center.

Alderson, J.C. & Urquhart, A.H. (Eds.). (1984). *Reading in a foreign language.* London: Longman.

Barnett, M.A. (1988). Reading through context: How real and perceived strategy use affects L2 comprehension. *Modern Language Journal, 72,* 150–162.

_____. (1989). *More than meets the eye. Foreign language reading: Theory and practice.* Englewood Cliffs, NJ: Prentice-Hall & Center for Applied Linguistics.

Bell, J. & Burnaby, B. (1984). *A handbook for ESL literacy.* Toronto: OISE.

Bernhardt, E. (1986). Reading in a foreign language. In B.H. Wing (Ed.), *Listening, reading, writing: Analysis and application* (pp. 93–115). Middlebury, VT: Northeast Conference on the Teaching of Foreign Languages.

Block, E. (1986). The comprehension strategies of second language readers. *TESOL Quarterly, 20,* 463–494.

Britton, J.L., Burgess, T., Martin, N., McLeod, A., & Rosen, H. (1975). *The development of writing abilities.* London: Macmillan Education.

Byrnes, H. (1985). Teaching toward proficiency: The receptive skills. In A.C. Omaggio (Ed.), *Proficiency, curriculum, articulation: The ties that bind* (pp. 77–107). Middlebury, VT: Northeast Conference on the Teaching of Foreign Languages.

Canale, M. (1984). A communicative approach to language proficiency assessment in a minority setting. In C. Rivera (Ed.), *Communicative competence to language proficiency assessment: Research and application* (pp. 107–122). Clevedon, England: Multilingual Matters.

Carrell, P.L. (1989). Metacognitive awareness and second language reading. *Modern Language Journal, 73,* 121–134.

_____. (1991). Second language reading: Reading ability or language proficiency? *Applied Linguistics, 12,* 159–179.

Carrell, P.L., Devine, J. & Eskey, D. (Eds.). (1988). *Interactive approaches to second language reading*. Cambridge: Cambridge University Press.

Carrell, P.L. & Eisterhold, J.C. (1983). Schema theory and ESL reading pedagogy. *TESOL Quarterly, 17,* 553–573.

Carson Eisterhold, J. (1990). Reading writing connections: Toward a description for second language learners. In B. Kroll (Ed.), *Second language writing: Research insights for the classroom* (pp. 88–101). New York: Cambridge University Press.

Carson, J., Carrell, P.L., Silberstein, S., Kroll, B. & Kuehn, P. (1990). Reading-writing relationships in first and second language. *TESOL Quarterly, 24,* 245–266.

Chamot, A.U. & Kupper, L. (1989). Learning strategies in foreign language instruction. *Foreign Language Annals, 22,* 13–24.

Chastain, K. (1990). Characteristics of graded and ungraded compositions. *Modern Language Journal, 74,* 10–14.

Child, J.R. (1987). Language proficiency levels and the typology of texts. In H. Byrnes & M. Canale (Eds.), *Defining and developing proficiency: Guidelines, implementations and concepts* (pp. 97–106). Lincolnwood, Il: National Textbooks.

Cisneros, R. & Leone, E. (1990). Becoming literate: Historias de San Antonio. In J.J. Bergen (Ed.), *Spanish in the United States: Sociolinguistic issues* (pp. 86–109). Washington, D.C.: Georgetown University Press.

Clark, H.H. & Clark, E.V. (1977). *Psychology and language*. New York: Harcourt Brace Jovanovich.

Clarke, M. (1980). The short circuit hypothesis of ESL reading—or when language competence interferes with reading performance. *Modern Language Journal, 64,* 203–209.

Connor, U. & Kaplan, R.B. (Eds.). (1987). *Writing across languages: Analysis of L2 text*. Reading, MA: Addison-Wesley.

Coombs, V.M. (1986). Syntax and communicative strategies in intermediate German composition. *Modern Language Journal, 70,* 114–124.

Cooper, T. & Morain, G. (1980). A study of sentence-combining techniques for developing written and oral fluency in French. *French Review, 53,* 411–423.

Cordelle, M. & Corno, L. (1981). Effects on second language learning of variations in written feedback on homework assignment. *TESOL Quarterly, 15,* 251–262.

Cummins, J. (1980). The cross-lingual dimensions of language proficiency: Implications for bilingual education and the optimal age issue. *TESOL Quarterly, 14,* 175–187.

————. (1983). Language proficiency and academic achievement. In J.W. Oller, Jr. (Ed.), *Issues in language testing research* (pp. 108–126). Rowley, MA: Newbury House.

Dubin, F., Eskey, D.E. & Grabe, W. (Eds.). (1986). *Teaching second language reading for academic purposes.* Reading, MA: Addison-Wesley.

Dvorak, T.R. (1986). Writing in a foreign language. In B.H. Wing (Ed.), *Listening, reading, writing: Analysis and application* (pp. 145–167). Middlebury, VT: Northeast Conference on the Teaching of Foreign Languages.

————. (1987). Is written FL like oral FL? In B. Van Patten, T.R. Dvorak & J.F. Lee (Eds.), *Foreign language learning: A research perspective* (pp. 79–91). Cambridge, MA: Newbury House.

Ely, C.M. (1986). Language learning motivation: A descriptive and causal analysis. *Modern Language Journal, 70,* 28–35.

Emig, J. (1988). Writing as a mode of learning. In G. Tate & E.P.J. Corbett (Eds.), *The writing teacher's sourcebook* (2nd ed.) (pp. 85–91). New York: Oxford University Press.

Enright, D.S. & McCloskey, M.L. (1988). *Integrating English: Developing English language and literacy in the multilingual classroom.* Reading, MA: Addison-Wesley.

Ferguson, C.A. (1959). Diglossia. *Word, 15,* 325–340.

Frantzen, D. & Russel, D. (1987). Learner self-correction of written compositions: What does it show us. In B. Van Patten, T.R. Dvorak & J.F. Lee (Eds.), *Foreign language learning: A research perspective* (pp. 92–107). Cambridge, MA: Newbury House.

Gaies, S.J. (1980). T-unit analysis in second language research: Applications, problems and limitations. *TESOL Quarterly, 14,* 53–60.

Garcia, E.E. & Flores, B. (Eds.). (1986). *Language and literacy research in bilingual education.* Tempe, AZ: Center for Bilingual Education.

Gardner, R. (1980). On the validity of affective variables in second language acquisition: conceptual, contextual and statistical considerations. *Language Learning, 30,* 255–270.

Gardner, R.C., & Lambert, W.E. (1972). *Attitudes and motivation in second language learning.* Rowley, MA: Newbury House.

Gaudiani, C. (1981). *Teaching writing in a foreign language curriculum.* Washington, DC: Center for Applied Linguistics.

Goldman, S.R. & Trueba, H.T. (Eds.). (1987). *Becoming literate in English as a second language.* Norwood, NJ: Ablex.

Goodman, Y. (1989). Roots of the whole language movement. *The Elementary School Journal,* Special Issue on Whole Language, *90,* 113–127.

Grabe, W. (1991). Current developments in second language reading research. *TESOL Quarterly, 25,* 375–406.

Graves, D. (1983). *Writing: Teachers and children at work.* Exeter, NH: Heinemann.

Grellet, F. (1981). *Developing reading skills.* Cambridge: Cambridge University Press.

Hauptman, P.C. (1979). A comparison of first and second language reading strategies among English-speaking university students. *Interlanguage Studies Bulletin* (Utrecht, The Netherlands), *4,* 173–201.

Hendrickson, J.M. (1980). The treatment of error in written work. *Modern Language Journal, 64,* 216–221.

Hernández-Chávez, E., Burt, M.K. & Dulay, H.C. (1978). Language dominance and proficiency testing: Some general considerations. *NABE Journal, 3,* 41–54.

Hosenfeld, C., Arnold, V., Kirchoffer, J., Laciura, J. & Wilson, L. (1981). Second language reading: A curricular sequence for teaching reading strategies. *Foreign Language Annals, 14,* 415–422.

Hudson, T. (1982). The effects of induced schemata on the "short-circuit" in L2 reading: Nondecoding factors in L2 reading performance. *Language Learning, 32,* 1–31.

Kaplan, R.B. (1966). Cultural thought patterns in intercultural education. *Language Learning, 16,* 1–20.

———. (1972). *The anatomy of rhetoric: Prolegomena to a functional theory of rhetoric.* Philadelphia: Center for Curriculum Development. (Distributed by Heinle & Heinle.)

———. (1983). An introduction to the study of written texts: The "discourse compact". In R.B. Kaplan, A. d'Anglejan, J.R. Cowan, B.B. Kachru, & G.R. Tucker (Eds.), *Annual Review of Applied Linguistics: 1982* (pp. 138–151). Rowley, MA: Newbury House.

Kern, R. (1989). Second language reading strategy instruction: Its effects on comprehension and word inference ability. *Modern Language Journal, 73,* 135–149.

Krashen, S.D. (1982). *Principles and practices in second language acquisition.* New York: Pergamon.

Krashen, S.D. and Terrell, T. (1983). *The natural approach.* New York: Pergamon.

Krashen, S. (1984). *Writing: Research, theory and applications.* Oxford: Pergamon.

Lalande, J. (1982). Reducing composition errors. *Modern Language Journal, 66,* 140–149.

Lambert, W.E. (1980). The two faces of bilingual education. *NCBE* (National Clearinghouse for Bilingual Education) *Forum, 3.*

Lapp, R.E. (1984). *The process approach to writing: Toward a curriculum for international students*. Unpublished master's thesis, University of Hawaii, Manoa, HI.

Lee, J.F. (1988). Toward a modification of the "proficiency" construct for reading in a foreign language. *Hispania, 71,* 941–953.

Lee, J.F. & Musumeci, D. (1988). On hierarchies of reading skills and text types. *Modern Language Journal, 72,* 173–187.

Mackay, R., Barkman, B. & Jordan, R.R. (Eds.). (1979). *Reading in a second language: Hypotheses, organization, and practice*. Rowley, MA: Newbury House.

Mangelsdorf, K. (1989). Parallels between speaking and writing in second language acquisition. In D.M. Johnson & D.H. Roen (Eds.), *Richness in Writing* (pp. 134–145). New York: Longman.

McKay, S. (1984). *Composing in a second language*. Rowley, MA: Newbury House.

McLaughlin, B. (1987). *Theories of second-language learning*. London: Edward Arnold.

Nunan, D. (1984). *Discourse processing by first language, second phase and second language learners*. Unpublished doctoral dissertation, The Flinders University of South Australia.

Nystrand, M. (1982). An analysis of errors in written communication. In M. Nystrand (Ed.), *What writers know* (pp. 57–74). New York: Academic Press.

Oller, J.W. (1979). *Language tests at school: A pragmatic approach*. New York: Longman.

Ostler, S.E. (1987). English in parallels: A comparison of English and Arabic prose. In U. Connor and R.B. Kaplan (Eds.), *Writing across languages: Analysis of L2 text* (pp. 169–185). Reading, MA: Addison-Wesley.

Purves, A.C. (Ed.). (1988). *Writing across languages and cultures: Issues in contrastive rhetoric*. Newbury Park, CA: Sage.

Raimes, A. (1991). Out of the woods: Emerging traditions in the teaching of writing. *TESOL Quarterly, 25,* 407–430.

Rigg, P. (1990). Whole language in adult ESL programs. *ERIC/CLL News Bulletin, 13*(2), 1,3,7.

Santos, T. (1992). Ideology in composition: L1 and ESL. *Journal of Second Language Writing, 1*(1), 1–15.

Semke, H. (1980). *The comparative effects of four methods of treating free writing assignments on the second language skills and attitudes in college level first year German*. Unpublished doctoral dissertation, University of Minnesota.

Smith, K.L. (1990). Collaborative and interactive writing for increasing communication skills. *Hispania, 73,* 77–87.

Smith, L.E. (Ed.). (1987). *Discourse across cultures: Strategies in world Englishes.* New York: Prentice Hall.

Stanovich, K. (1980). Toward an interactive-compensatory model of individual differences in the development of reading fluency. *Reading Research Quarterly, 16,* 32–71.

Stubbs, M. (1980). *Language and literacy: The sociolinguistics of reading and writing.* London: Routledge & Kegan Paul.

Swaffar, J.K. (1988). Readers, texts, and second languages: The interactive processes. *Modern Language Journal, 72,* 123–149.

Swaffar, J., Arens, K. & Byrnes, H. (1991). *Reading for meaning: An integrated approach to language learning.* Englewood Cliffs, NJ: Prentice Hall.

Valdés, G., Haro, P. & Echevarriarza, M.P. (1992). The development of writing abilities in a foreign language: Contributions toward a general theory of L2 writing. *Modern Language Journal, 76,* 333–352.

Van Parreren, C.F. & Schouten-Van Parreren, M.C. (1981). Contextual guessing: A trainable reader strategy. *System, 9,* 235–241.

Wallace, C. (1986). *Learning to read in a multicultural society: The social context of second language literacy.* Oxford: Pergamon.

Williams, J.D. & Capizzi-Snipper, G. (1990). *Literacy and bilingualism.* New York: Longman.

Zamel, V. (1983). The composing processes of advanced ESL students: Six case studies. *TESOL Quarterly, 17,* 165–187.

CHAPTER 4

Continua of Biliteracy

Nancy H. Hornberger

As public schools in the United States increasingly serve speakers of languages other than English in a predominantly English-speaking society, the need for an understanding of biliteracy becomes more pressing. Among the eighteen research priorities recently established by the U.S. Department of Education, the first listed is "the teaching and learning of reading, writing, or language skills particularly by non- or limited English speaking students" ("Department of Education," 1988).

It is not that such teaching and learning does not occur. Consider the following three narrative vignettes. In an urban fourth-grade class composed of eleven Asian and seventeen Black children, Sokhom,[1] age 10, has recently been promoted to the on-grade-level reading group and is doing well. She is no longer in the school's pull-out English for Speakers of Other Languages (ESOL) program and spends her whole day in the mainstream classroom. At home, she pulls out a well-worn English-Khmer dictionary that she says her father bought at great expense in the refugee camp in the Philippines. She recounts that when she first came to the United States and was in second grade, she used to look up English words there and ask her father or her brother to read the Cambodian word to her; then she would know what the English word was. Today, in addition to her intense motivation to know English ("I like to talk in English, I like to read in English, and I like to

This chapter originally appeared in 1989 in the *Review of Educational Research* 59(3), 271–296. Copyright 1989 by the American Educational Research Association. Reprinted by permission of the publisher.

write in English"), Sokhom wants to learn to read and write in Khmer, and in fact has taught herself a little via English.

In another urban public school across the city, Maria, a fifth grader who has been in a two-way maintenance bilingual education program since prekindergarten, has both Spanish and English reading every morning for 1¼ hours each, with Ms. Torres and Mrs. Dittmar, respectively. Today, Mrs. Dittmar is reviewing the vocabulary for the story the students are reading about Charles Drew, a Black American doctor. She explains that "influenza" is what Charles's little sister died of; Maria comments that "you say it [influenza] in Spanish the same way you write it [in English]."

In the same Puerto Rican community, in a new bilingual middle school a few blocks away, Elizabeth, a graduate of the two-way maintenance bilingual program mentioned above, hears a Career Day speaker from the community tell her that of two people applying for a job, one bilingual and one not, the bilingual has an advantage. Yet Elizabeth's daily program of classes provides little opportunity for her to continue to develop literacy in Spanish; the bilingual program at this school is primarily transitional.

All three of these girls are part of the biliterate population of the United States. The educational programs they are experiencing are vastly different with respect to attention to literacy in their first language, ranging from total absence to benign neglect to active development; and from mainstream with pull-out ESOL to transitional bilingual education to two-way maintenance bilingual education. Biliteracy exists, as do educational programs serving biliterate populations. Yet, provocative questions remain to be answered, primarily about the degree to which literacy knowledge and skills in one language aid or impede the learning of literacy knowledge and skills in the other.

A framework for understanding biliteracy is needed in which to situate research and teaching; this review attempts to address that need. Because biliteracy itself represents a conjunction of literacy and bilingualism, the logical place to begin to look is in those two fields. This seems particularly appropriate because the twin, and some suggest conflicting (Wong-Fillmore & Valadez, 1986:653), goals of bilingual education and ESOL programs in elementary public schools in the United States are for students to (a) learn the second language (English) and (b) keep up with their monolingual peers in academic content areas.

The fields of literacy and bilingualism each represent vast amounts of literature. There is a relatively small but increasing proportion of explicit attention to (a) bilingualism within the literature on literacy and literacy within the literature on bilingualism and (b) second or foreign languages within the literatures on the teaching of reading and writing and reading and writing within the literatures on second or foreign language teaching. Perhaps the reason for the relative lack of attention is that when one seeks to attend to both, already complex issues seem to become further muddled. For example, Alderson (1984:24) explored one such muddled area: If a student is having difficulty reading a text in a foreign language, should this be construed as a reading problem or a language problem? It turns out, however, as this review will show, that by focusing findings from the two fields on the common area of biliteracy, we elucidate not only biliteracy itself but also literacy and bilingualism. All the above literatures were considered for this review, with special focus on those studies and papers that explore the area of overlap, that is, biliteracy.

Neither a complete theory of literacy nor a complete theory of bilingualism yet exist. In both fields, the complexity of the subject; the multidisciplinary nature of the inquiry, including educators, linguists, psychologists, anthropologists, sociologists, and historians; and the interdependence between research, policy, and practice make unity and coherence elusive objectives (cf. Hakuta, 1986:x; Langer, 1988:43; Scribner, 1987:19).

This review proposes a framework for understanding biliteracy, using the notion of continuum to provide the overarching conceptual scheme for describing biliterate contexts, development, and media. Although we often characterize dimensions of bilingualism and literacy in terms of polar opposites such as first versus second languages (L1 vs. L2), monolingual versus bilingual individuals, or oral versus literate societies, it has become increasingly clear that in each case those opposites represent only theoretical endpoints on what is in reality a continuum of features (cf. Kelly, 1969:5). Furthermore, when we consider biliteracy in its turn, it becomes clear that these continua are interrelated dimensions of one highly complex whole.

Figures 4.1–4.3 schematically represent the framework by depicting both the continua and their interrelatedness. The figures show the nine continua characterizing contexts for biliteracy, the development of individual biliteracy, and the media of biliteracy, respectively. Not only is the three-dimensionality of any one figure representative of the interrelatedness of its constituent continua, but it should be emphasized that the interrelationships extend across the contexts, development, and media of biliteracy as well (see figures 4.1–4.3).

The notion of continuum is intended to convey that although one can identify (and name) points on the continuum, those points are not finite, static, or discrete. There are infinitely many points on the continuum; any single point is inevitably and inextricably related to all other points; and all the points have more in common than not with each other. The argument here is that for an understanding of biliteracy, it is equally elucidating to focus on the common features and on the distinguishing features along any one continuum.

In an attempt to disentangle the complexities of biliteracy, the sections that follow introduce the nine continua one at a time,

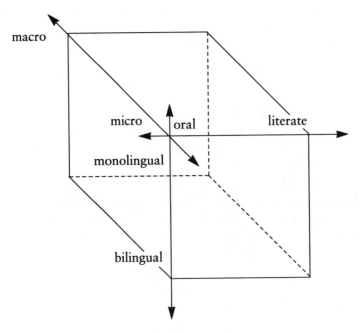

FIGURE 4.1
THE CONTINUA OF BILITERATE CONTEXTS

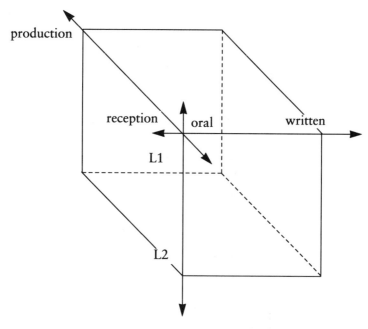

FIGURE 4.2
THE CONTINUA OF BILITERATE DEVELOPMENT IN THE
INDIVIDUAL

citing illustrative works from the literatures mentioned above in support of each one. In the first section, represented in figure 4.1, contexts for biliteracy are defined in terms of three continua: micro–macro, oral–literate, and monolingual–bilingual. The second section, represented in figure 4.2, introduces the continua that characterize the development of the biliterate individual's communicative repertoire: reception–production, oral language–written language, and L1-L2 transfer. The third section, represented in figure 4.3, describes three continua characterizing the relationships among the media through which the biliterate individual communicates: simultaneous–successive exposure, similar–dissimilar structures, and convergent–divergent scripts. Throughout the discussion of the nine continua, the interrelationships among them are also brought out. The paper concludes with comments on the implications of the continua for research in and teaching of biliteracy.

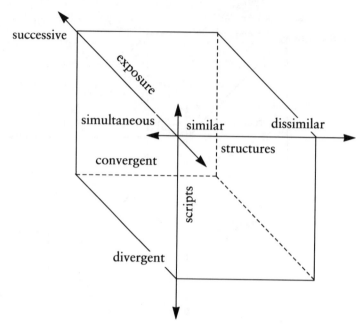

FIGURE 4.3
THE CONTINUA OF BILITERATE MEDIA

CONTEXTS OF BILITERACY

An interest in context as an important factor in all aspects of language use dates back at least to the early 1960s and the beginnings of sociolinguistics and the ethnography of communication (Fishman, 1968; Hymes, 1964; Pride & Holmes, 1972). Building from communicative theory and work by Roman Jakobson published in 1953 and 1960, Hymes suggested an array of components that might serve as a heuristic for the ethnographic study of speech events, or more generally, communicative events, where such events refer to activities or aspects of activities that are directly governed by rules or norms for the use of language and that consist of one or more speech acts.[2] This array of components included participants, settings, topics, goals, norms, forms, genres, and so forth and was later formulated by Hymes (1974:53–62) into the mnemonic SPEAKING (Setting, Participants, Ends, Act, Key, Instrumentalities, Norms, Genres).

From within the ethnography of communication have come

occasional calls for the ethnography of writing (Basso, 1974) and the ethnography of literacy (Szwed, 1981). In a recent paper Dubin (1989) assured those attending the Communicative Competence Revisited Seminar that the ethnography of communication is alive and well in the literacy field, and she went on to describe her own current study of what she termed the "mini-literacies" of three biliterate immigrants.

Indeed, in the last decade the literacy field has seen a series of persuasive arguments for the significance of context for under-standing literacy. Heath is one who has explicitly undertaken the study of literacy in context, within an ethnography of communica-tion framework. She noted that reading varies in its functions and uses across history, cultures, and "contexts of use as defined by particular communities" (1980:126) and went on to document this in her 1983 study. Scribner and Cole (1981) drew from their study of literacy in Liberia to argue that "literacy is not simply learning how to read and write a particular script but applying this knowledge for specific purposes in specific contexts of use" (236). Gee (1986) contended that literacy has no meaning "apart from particular cultural contexts in which it is used" (734). Also, Langer (1988) found one of three new emphases of books and articles on literacy in the 1980s to be "the effects of context and culture on literacy," and went on to suggest that all three literacy volumes she reviewed (Bloome, 1987; de Castell, Egan & Luke, 1986; Olson, Torrance & Hildyard, 1985) share a concern with literacy in con-text (or what Olson et al. called literacy as situational).

Street (1984) rejected what he labeled the autonomous model of literacy and argued for the ideological model, which assumes that the "meaning of literacy depends upon the social institutions in which it is embedded" (8). Therefore, he continued, it makes more sense to refer to multiple literacies than to any single literacy; he described such a case from his own fieldwork in Iran (cf. also Gee, 1986:719). Thus, he opted for a contextualized rather than a decontextualized view of literacy.

Biliteracy, like all literacies, can be taken to be "radically con-stituted by [its] context of use" (Erickson, 1984:529). What do the literatures on bilingualism, literacy, and biliteracy tell us about the contexts of biliteracy? This review suggests that there is an implicit, and at times explicit, understanding in the literatures that any particular context of biliteracy is defined by the intersection of at least three continua—the micro–macro continuum, the oral–literate continuum, and the monolingual–bilingual continuum—and that any attempt to understand an instance of biliteracy by attending to only one of these contextual continua produces at best an incomplete result.

The Micro–Macro Continuum

Sociolinguists have recognized a distinction between micro and macro levels of analysis from the beginning. Indeed, one can characterize areas of sociolinguistic inquiry in a quadrant model that distinguishes between micro and macro levels of analysis of social interaction and micro and macro levels of linguistic analysis (see figure 4.4). Such a model makes clear the range of contexts for the analysis of language use. Thus, generalizing broadly, at the micro-micro level of context a particular feature of language (e.g., cohesion, rhythm, or a phoneme) is examined in a particular piece of text or discourse; at the micro-macro level, patterns of language use are examined in the context of a situation or a speech event; at the macro-micro level, a particular feature of language is examined in the context of a society or a large social unit; and at the macro-macro level of context, patterns of language use are examined within or across societies or nations.

Insights from a consideration of bilingualism in context include, for example, at the micro-macro level, the recognition that the bilingual individual keys language choice to characteristics of the situation (e.g., Grosjean, 1982:127–145). At the macro-macro

LEVELS OF SOCIAL INTERACTION

		MICRO	MACRO
LEVELS OF LINGUISTIC ANALYSIS	MICRO	*Micro-Micro* Ethnomethodology Discourse Analysis Interactionist Sociolinguistics	*Macro-Micro* Variationist Sociolinguistics
	MACRO	*Micro-Macro* Ethnography of Communication	*Macro-Macro* Sociology of Language

FIGURE 4.4
MACRO AND MICRO SOCIOLINGUISTICS

level are the insights that there may exist domains[3] associated with one or another language in bilingual societies (e.g., Fishman, 1972; Grosjean, 1982:130–132), or that a language may fulfill one of a range of functions in the society. These functional roles include the high or low variety in a diglossic situation,[4] such as classical and colloquial Arabic in Arabic-speaking societies (Ferguson, 1959); a second language of widespread use, such as English in Singapore (Williams, 1987); a foreign language (e.g., Alderson & Urquhart, 1984); or a language of wider communication (LWC), such as Swahili in East Africa.

On the other hand, insights from a consideration of literacy in context include, for example, Bloome and Green's (1984) differentiation within the micro-micro context between the intrapersonal and interpersonal contexts of reading, where the former encompasses "the individual's background knowledge, skills, and general approach to reading" and the latter refers to "the organization of reading events, the interaction of participants involved in reading events, the influences that the interaction of participants had on the reading process, as well as how the reading process influenced the interaction of participants" (413). Lytle and Botel (1988:12) represented micro and macro levels of context schematically with successively larger concentric circles consisting of student; classroom; school as a community; home, neighborhood, town/city, state, and region; and national, cultural, and multicultural environment.

The point to be emphasized here is that micro and macro levels of context are perhaps best represented in neither a dichotomous nor a layered relationship, but as a continuum. Any particular instance of biliteracy is defined at one point along the continuum, whether it is a child using an L1–L2 dictionary to learn her L2 at the micro end or a language minority population making only minimal use of its L1 in written form at the macro end. This does not deny that other levels of context impinge on that instance; it was noted earlier, with respect to all the continua, that any one point is inevitably and inextricably related to all other points. Yet, if we are to begin to understand biliteracy we must be careful to define each instance by its particulars.

A number of studies of biliteracy make one or another end of the continuum salient while revealing the continuity between them. At the macro level, biliteracy often exists in a context of unequal power relations: One or another literacy becomes marginalized (Baynham, in press); or literacies become specialized by functions—Amharic, Arabic, and English literacy in Ethiopia (Ferguson, 1985:137) or English, Hindi, and Fijian literacy in Fiji (Mangubhai, 1987:190–193, 201–204). Changing societal contexts lead to changing biliteracy configurations: Whereas the literate minority among the Panjabi in Northern India used to learn literacy in either Hindi or Urdu, "the expansion of education, expanded roles of regional languages in education and public life, and the reluctance of Sikhs to be identified with either Hindus or Muslims" led many Panjabis to adopt literacy in their mother tongue (Ferguson, 1985:178).

At the micro level, situational factors such as the roles of public writers, the juxtaposition of traditional and modern uses of literacy in and outside of school, the use of the individual writing board, and memorization and oral recitation for learning lessons all bear on literacy in French, standard Arabic, and Moroccan Arabic in Morocco (Wagner, Messick & Spratt, 1986).

The Oral–Literate Continuum

The above studies point to the relevance of the micro–macro continuum for an understanding of biliterate contexts. They also suggest, however, that a complete picture of biliteracy necessarily entails the other two continua: the oral–literate and monolingual–bilingual continua. Consider the following series of contextual barriers to literacy for the Northern Ute people in northeastern Utah. The barriers to literacy range from the macro to micro level, across Ute and English, and from oral to literate uses.

Barriers to literacy in Ute include the implicit new model of social organization literacy brings—literates versus nonliterates as opposed to kinship ties and sodalities; the reversal of traditional leadership patterns ensuing from literacy acquisition by the younger generation; the limited "real world" usefulness of Ute literacy; the potential inappropriateness (in spiritual terms) of expressing Ute in writing; the relative drabness of print as compared to beadwork, basketry, ceremonial dress, and other visual communication already in use; and the relative lack of flexibility and potential for individual variation in response to different situations in written Ute as compared to oral Ute expression. On the other hand, contextual barriers to literacy in English include the pervasive influence of Ute patterns of discourse in students' written English, schooling as a painful experience for the Ute, and the limited usefulness of English literacy given high unemployment rates unaffected by literacy (Leap, 1987:18–48).

The example of Ute oral discourse patterns in English written by Utes is an example of the oral–literate continuum, which is the second of the defining continua for contexts of biliteracy. Any particular instance of biliteracy is located at a point on the oral–literate continuum, but there is also a close relationship between oral and literate uses of language, as exemplified in the Ute case.

Heath (1982) demonstrated how a familiar literacy event in mainstream U.S. culture, the bedtime story, is embedded in oral language use. In addition, her study (Heath, 1983) of the functions and uses of literacy in mainstream, Black working-class, and White working-class homes in the southeastern United States clearly reveals not only that speech and literacy are interrelated in each group, but that differences among the groups are not so much along the lines of oral versus literate cultures as along the lines of which literacies most closely resemble those of the school.

There may be, in any one society, many varieties of literacy, including uses of literacy "for storytelling and reading, . . . for immediate functional purposes in the home and work; for leisure and pleasure purposes; and for personal exploration as in diaries and private notebooks" (Street, in press). Yet all these literacies are not equally "powerful" in society. As Cook-Gumperz (1986) illustrated, there has been, in Western society, a shift from the eighteenth century onward from "a *pluralistic* idea about literacy as a composite of different skills related to reading and writing for many different purposes and sections of a society's population, to a twentieth-century notion of a single, standardised *schooled literacy*" (22).

Street (1988a) argued that "literacy practices are always embedded in oral uses, and the variations between cultures are generally variations in the *mix* of oral/literate channels" (5) and *not* due to a dichotomous difference between the oral and literate worlds, as Ong (1982), for example, proposed and many writers still accept (e.g., Parry, 1987:63). Street refuted the idea of the "great divide" between orality and literacy (cf. Scribner & Cole, 1981:4), where the oral world is characterized with terms such as "formulaic, conservative, [and] homeostatic" and the literate world with terms such as "abstract, analytic, [and] objective (1988a:1). He noted that the characteristics that Ong would attribute to literacy are, in fact, "those of the social *context* and specific culture in which the literacy being described is located" (Street, 1988a:5; cf. Gee, 1986:728).

Street further noted, as did Murray (1988:351, 370), that even some of the recent papers discussing the relation between orality and literacy as a continuum continue to reinforce the concept of the great divide. Street (1988b:64, 70) went on to examine and refute various "literacy myths" that divide literacy from orality on grounds of cohesion, connectedness, lexical versus paralinguistic features to encode meaning, and degree of situational embeddedness. Earlier, Tannen (1985) suggested that what many have called features of spoken versus written language (specifically, degrees of contextualization and devices of cohesion) are, in fact, features reflecting relatively more or less focus on interpersonal involvement, which may characterize either spoken *or* written language.

Both Street and Murray have argued for less emphasis on the supposed differences between written and oral language use and more on the contexts in which speakers choose between written and oral media in the same way they make other linguistic choices (Murray, 1988:352, 370). Murray (1988:353, 368–369) drew from Hymes's and Halliday's models and proposed a taxonomy of those aspects of the context of situation (field, speaker/hearer, setting) that contribute to choice of medium (face to face, telephone, paper, or computer) and mode (specific subtypes within medium) within the speech community of an IBM research laboratory.

In sum, orality and literacy share many common features and the features that have been identified with one or the other have more to do with the context in which language is used than with oral versus literate use.

The Monolingual–Bilingual Continuum

The same can be said for the third defining continuum for contexts of biliteracy, the monolingual–bilingual continuum. At the macro level, consider the specialization of functions for languages and varieties. In monolingual societies, different varieties of one language may be firmly identified with high and low functions (Ferguson, 1959; cf. also Duranti and Ochs, 1986:219, on Samoa). So, too, in bilingual societies, different languages may experience specialization of function (Fishman, 1967). The important distinction appears to be less the difference in languages than the differences in contexts, functions, and use (cf. also Gee, 1986:728).

Similarly, at the micro level, the difference between monolingual and bilingual individuals is not so much that bilinguals possess two complete sets of functions and uses of language, one for each language. Rather, bilinguals switch languages according to specific functions and uses, whereas monolinguals switch styles in the same contexts. "Bilingualism . . . is a special, salient case of the general phenomenon of linguistic repertoire. No normal person, and no normal community, is limited to a single way of speaking" (Hymes, 1986:38). Grosjean (1985) argued for a bilingual ("wholistic") rather than a monolingual (fractional) view of bilingualism. In the bilingual view, bilinguals are perceived to have unique and specific linguistic configurations that are different from those of monolinguals in either language, in the same way that a hurdler is neither a sprinter nor a high jumper but something completely different (cf. also Gumperz, 1969:244).

Zentella (1981) showed that code-switching,[5] stigmatized because it is believed to reflect the bilingual's lack of complete knowledge and control of the two languages, in fact reflects a highly sensitive response to contextual factors. In her study, she grouped contextual factors into three categories from the point of view of the observer: "on the spot" (factors of setting and participants), "in the head" (communicative factors such as style, functions, and conversational strategies), and "out of the mouth" (linguistic factors such as language of the switch, loans, and grammaticality). That is, code-switching represents highly competent, context-specific language use.

The argument here is that monolingualism and bilingualism are more alike than different. The functions and uses to which different varieties and styles are put in a monolingual individual or society are the same ones to which different languages are put in a bilingual individual or society.

Contexts of biliteracy are defined, then, by these three continua. Any particular instance of biliteracy is located at a point of intersection among the three. To return to our opening vignettes, Sokhom's use of the English-Khmer dictionary to learn L2 words represents an instance toward the micro, oral, and monolingual ends of the continua; the bilingual middle school's predominant use of written L2 represents an instance toward the macro, literate, and bilingual ends of the continua. With the wide range of possible biliterate contexts as defined by these three continua for background, we will now turn to a consideration of the biliterate individual's development of communicative competence in biliterate contexts.

BILITERATE DEVELOPMENT IN THE INDIVIDUAL

Within the ethnography of communication framework, the term *communicative competence* designates the knowledge and ability of individuals for appropriate language use in the communicative events in which they find themselves in any particular speech community. This competence is, by definition, variable within individuals (from event to event), across individuals, and across speech communities. Individuals draw on their communicative repertoire to participate appropriately in any given context. This review suggests that for the biliterate individual, that repertoire is crucially defined by at least three continua: reception-production, oral language-written language, and L1-L2 transfer (see Figure 4.2).

Further, the development of biliteracy in individuals occurs along the continua in direct response to the contextual demands placed on these individuals. "The environmental press that requires the successful interactant to use distinct subsets of linguistic and sociolinguistic knowledge can change from moment to moment in face-to-face interaction, and from one discourse unit to another in a written text with which ego is confronted. . . . Interaction with others in producing these diverse verbal and written texts constitutes practice in language use." (Erickson, 1991:342).

Finally, it should be clarified that the notion of continuum in development is not intended to suggest that development is necessarily continuous or gradual; it may, in fact, occur in spurts and with some backtracking. Rather, the argument is that development within any one continuum draws on features from the entire continuum (cf. Heath, 1986:150, on the "single developmental model").

The Reception-Production Continuum

One of the longstanding theories of language development in both the reading and the foreign language teaching literatures has involved a dichotomy between oral and written language and one between receptive and productive skills. The assumption has been that oral language development (listening and speaking) precedes written language development (reading and writing) and that receptive skills (listening and reading) precede productive ones (speaking and writing). Thus, the "logical sequence" of language development was believed to be listening, speaking, reading, and writing (e.g., Smith, 1967:54–57). Along with the other dichotomies presented in this review, the reception-production dichotomy (and the oral-written dichotomy discussed next) has been superseded by a view that recognizes that receptive and productive development occurs along a continuum, beginning at any point, and proceeding, cumulatively or in spurts, in either direction.

In second-language acquisition research, a decade or more of attention to "comprehensible input"[6] as crucial to the learner's acquisition of the second language has recently been extended to a recognition that learners must also have the opportunity to produce "comprehensible output"[7] (Pica, Holliday, Lewis & Morgenthaler, 1989; Swain, 1985). That is, speaking, as well as listening, contributes to the negotiation of meaning in interaction, which in turn is said to lead to language acquisition. In a review article exploring lessons from first-language acquisition for second-language acquisition, Gathercole (1988) argued that recent research shows that "the relationship between comprehension and production is not unidirectional—that progress in either may lead to progress in the other" (426).

In the reading field, Goodman and Goodman (1983) have argued that "people not only learn to read by reading and write by writing but they also learn to read by writing and write by reading" (592). Hudelson (1984:229) added that this is true for second as well as first languages.

A number of studies in biliterate settings have confirmed the interrelationship of skills along the reception-production continuum. In a study among immigrant children in Israel, Feitelson (1987:178–179) found that being read to in formal primary school settings prepared students for subsequent reading comprehension. In Fiji, Mangubhai (1987:200) found that as a result of the Book Flood Project, receptive skills in English (reading and listening comprehension) improved and apparently transferred to other related language skills. In highland Puno, Peru, Quechua-speaking children taught via their first language as medium of instruction showed not only improved oral participation but increased reading and writing performance in school (Hornberger, 1988:190–198).

The Oral Language–Written Language Continuum

As the research cited above already suggests, not only do listening-speaking and reading-writing development occur along a continuum, but so too does oral-written development. As noted above in the discussion of the oral–literate continuum, many literacy events occur embedded in oral language use (cf. Heath, 1982). The counterpart to this embeddedness in the development of literacy is that children learn to read and write through heavy reliance on spoken language. Goodman and Goodman have shown how oral miscues[8] provide clues as to the development of reading (Goodman, 1982:89–168; Grove, 1981:11–13). Similarly, Wilde (1988) argued that children's use of their own "invented" spellings, based at the beginning on children's knowledge of the sounds of the language (and later on patterns and meaning relationships), helps them in language development.

Bi- and multilingual readers provide evidence that, like listening-speaking and reading-writing development, development along the oral–written language continuum is not necessarily unidirectional. In the rote learning and memorization of the Koran in Muslim societies, emphasis is placed on "reading" a text that is of a "conceptual and linguistic complexity far beyond the understanding of the young children who memorize it" (Baynham, in press). The level of the reading outstrips the children's speaking knowledge of the language; yet they do read it.

Hudelson (1984:224, 231) pointed out that children learning English as a second language can and do both read and write English before they have mastered the oral and written systems of the language. Hudelson concluded:

> The processes of writing, reading, speaking, and listening in a second language are interrelated and interdependent. It is both useless and, ultimately, impossible to separate out the language processes in our teaching . . . or to try to present ESL [English as a second language] material in a linear sequence of listening, speaking, reading, and writing. (1984:234)

The L1–L2 Transfer Continuum

Biliterate development is defined not only by continuities between spoken and written language, between listening and speaking, and between reading and writing, but also by those between the first language (L1) and the second language (L2). Recognizing the close connections between development in one and the other language, researchers have attempted to determine to what extent knowledge of one language *transfers* to the other (and aids learning) and to what extent knowledge of the one *interferes* with the other (and impedes learning).

Researchers have approached the question of transfer versus interference in two general ways, both focused on the search for evidence of positive transfer. They have asked what kinds of *positive* effects reading instruction in one language might have on reading achievement in the other and what kinds of *negative* effects the *absence* of reading instruction in one language might have on reading achievement in the other. These questions have usually been framed in terms of transfer from L1 to L2, and occasionally in terms of transfer from L2 to L3 (see Wagner, Spratt & Ezzaki, 1989) or L2 to L1 (Canadian immersion studies).

Research on the question of negative effects has generally revealed that the absence of L1 reading instruction does not necessarily have a negative effect; however, in almost every case, researchers have been careful to note that whether or not direct L2 instruction will have a negative effect depends substantially on the context in which it occurs.

For example, a series of studies investigated whether initial instruction in L1 or L2 is more conducive to successful acquisition of L2 literacy skills. Engle (1975) and Dutcher (1982) reviewed a number of these studies and arrived at conclusions that buttress the view that the context of language use, rather than the language per se, is the deciding factor. In a review of eight studies in seven multilingual countries on the use of first and second languages in primary education, including Modiano's (1973) Mexico study, the Canadian immersion programs (Lambert & Tucker, 1972; Lambert, 1985), and the Rock Point Navajo School (Rosier & Holm, 1980), Dutcher (1982) concluded that there is no one answer to the question of what is the best choice of language as the initial language of instruction for children in primary school. Rather, the answer varies from case to case depending on micro and macro contextual factors such as the child's cognitive and linguistic development in L1 (cf. also Niyekawa, 1983:104–113), parental attitudes and support for the languages and the school, and the status of both languages in the wider community (Dutcher, 1982).

In an earlier review drawn on by Dutcher, Engle (1975) also found that neither what she called the "direct approach" (i.e., instruction in L2) nor the "native language approach" (i.e., instruction in L1) was clearly superior to the other for the teaching of initial reading and subject matter in multilingual contexts; rather, a series of contextual issues needed to be taken into account.

Tucker (1986:362–363) reiterated this point with reference to the transferability of the Canadian immersion model to U.S. settings. He listed the following as salient contextual attributes that contribute to the success of Canadian immersion programs: The children's L1 is a language of high social and economic status; the children come from families of middle socioeconomic status backgrounds; participation is voluntary; parents play a strong and catalytic role in the programs; formal L2 instruction occurs from the very beginning; teachers are native L2 speakers; an L1 language arts component is added to the curriculum by Grade 2; and L1 is used for content instruction beginning at Grade 3 or 4.

More recently, Wagner et al. (1989), who found that instruction in their second language did not necessarily put Berber monolingual children at a disadvantage with respect to their Arabic-speaking peers by the fifth year of primary school, offered a number of contextual explanations for this "counter-example" to the UNESCO (1953) mother tongue literacy axiom: lack of competing literacy in Berber, Arabic as the language of Islam, the ascendancy of spoken Moroccan Arabic in the small-town context of the study, and the usefulness of the Koranic preschool experience for promoting reading skills. The same study found that both Berber- and Arabic-speaking children's acquisition of their second literacy (French) was substantially dependent on their first literacy (Arabic) acquisition.

This last finding directly addresses the other of the two transfer questions (i.e., what kinds of positive effects literacy in one language might have on literacy in the other). The two general lines of findings in the research in this area are that (a) what appears to be interference from L1 in L2 is better construed as evidence for learning in that it represents the *application* of L1 knowledge to L2, and (b) the stronger the foundation and continuing development in L1, the greater the potential for enhanced learning of L2.

Consider the example of errors in oral second-language acquisition. In the audiolingual method of second-language teaching, popular in the 1940s to 1960s, errors in the second language were seen as the result of first-language habits *interfering* with the acquisition of second-language habits. Today, in contrast, with the advent of transformational grammar and first-language acquisition research, a new view has emerged. In this view, the learner is "credited with having an interlanguage . . . [incorporating] characteristics of both the native and target language of the learner,"[9] and errors are seen as clues to the nature of the interlanguage and the process of second-language acquisition (Hakuta & Cancino, 1977:297). That is, what was once seen as simply interference from the first language into the second is now recognized as evidence of the creative application of L1 knowledge to L2 learning. Just as miscues and invented spellings provide clues as to the development of reading and writing, interlanguage provides clues as to the development of the second language.

In studies of biliterate development, as well, the notion of interference has given way to that of transfer. Edelsky (1986) refuted the interference "myth," arguing that children in the bilingual program she studied *applied* what they knew about first-language writing to second-language writing:

> they were applying everything from specific hypotheses about segmentation, spelling, and endings to general strategies for literacy acquisition (e.g., use the input—Spanish print does not have k's; English print does not have tildes and accents), to high level knowledge (that texts are contextually constrained), to a crucial process (orchestration of cuing systems). (73, 117; see also Edelsky, 1982)

This accords with Thonis's (1981:150–154) and Hakuta's (1987) suggestions that most transfer of skills from L1 to L2 occurs in a global way, rather than point by point; that is, transfer is not word for word, but rather involves processes and strategies. Wald, too, found that both "English language skills (such as knowledge of syntactic devices for organizing information) and cross-language literacy skills (such as strategies for organizing in-

122 THEORETICAL AND RESEARCH PERSPECTIVES

formation in writing) interact in the acquisition of English literacy [for East Los Angeles Hispanic bilingual advanced high school students]" (1987:180). Research on Spanish and English reading lessons in a bilingual school in Philadelphia suggests that the strategy of "attacking" new words by identifying roots and suffixes may transfer between the two languages (Hornberger & Micheau, 1988). Finally, two studies using the Sentence Verification Technique in Spanish and English with sixth- and seventh-grade students in transitional bilingual education programs showed that (a) listening and reading skills transferred from L1 to L2, and (b) subject matter knowledge acquired by means of L1 transferred to L2 (Carlo, Sinatra & Royer, 1989).

Work in the field of contrastive rhetoric has shown that native language discourse patterns have an impact on writers' learning of a second language and its discourse patterns. Söter's (1988:202) study comparing one writing task (a simple bedtime story) carried out by Vietnamese, Arabic-speaking Lebanese, and native English-speaking students in Sydney, Australia, demonstrated the influence of the students' prior knowledge of literacy and literary experiences on their current experiences and writing performance. Indrasuta's (1988:222) comparison of writing by a group of Thai writers in Thai and English found that the writers brought L1 rhetorical style and appropriateness to their L2 writing.

Leap (1987) analyzed English compositions by Ute fourth graders and argued that Ute discourse strategies are at work in their English writing. Such strategies include "non-exhaustive presentation of detail, . . . active engagement of the reader as well as the writer in the construction and presentation of meaning," and choosing "to write a 'personal opinion' essay in . . . 'corporate terms'" (Leap, 1987:36, 38).

Influence of L1 on L2 along the L1–L2 writing development continuum can be seen as interference or transfer, depending on the writer's goals. The aim in contrastive rhetoric has generally been to make the biliterate's ESL writing more congruent with English rhetorical style (e.g., Kaplan, 1988:278), that is, eradicating interference. Leap (1987:44–46), on the other hand, noted that Ute students should be able to choose whether they will acquire the rhetorical patterns associated with written standard English or stay with Ute rhetorical patterns in writing English, and thus communicate Ute-centered perspectives more effectively (i.e., a choice between eradicating interference and making creative use of transfer).

As noted above, the second line of argument concerning L1–L2 transfer is that the potential and benefit for positive transfer of reading/writing skills to L2 increase with the greater development of L1 skills. Studies by Rosier and Holm (1980), Reyes (1987), and Roller (1988) point to cumulative effects of bilingual instruction with benefits for L2 literacy becoming more evident each year after the third grade (cf. also Genesee, 1987:43, 129). Moll and Díaz (1985) found that strong reading skills in Spanish could be drawn on to improve reading in English by fourth-grade bilingual students. In a study of second-, third-, and fourth-grade Spanish-speaking students in a transitional bilingual program, Zutell and Allen (1988:338–339) found that the more successful spellers differentiated between Spanish and English systems, whereas poorer spellers' English spellings were influenced by the effect of Spanish phonology on their pronunciation of English words.

Such results find theoretical support in Cummins's linguistic interdependence hypothesis[10] and in Lambert's notions of additive and subtractive bilingualism.[11] They also accord with Thonis's (1981) claims that "hasty, premature introduction to the second writing system may result in two weak sets of [reading/writing] skills" (178) and Niyekawa's (1983) assumption that "the higher the grade level at the time of transfer to an L2 school, the less time it should take the children to catch up because they have more knowledge to serve as context and more skills to transfer" (112).

Finally, a note about the question Alderson (1984:24) posed as to whether a learner's difficulties with reading a foreign text stem from a reading problem or a language problem. It is relevant here to note that he concluded that both are probably involved, but for low levels of foreign language competence the problem is likely one of language. Clarke (1981:78) had similar findings for adult ESL readers (see also Carrell, 1987:3). Edelsky (1982) also found that "the child's second language proficiency was the factor that most directly influenced the relative syntactic simplicity of the English texts [they wrote]" (226), even though the child's knowledge of more complex syntax in the first language might be high. Similarly, in a study that focused on the transfer of decoding skills from Spanish to English in beginning reading, Faltis (1986) found that in addition to the extent of mastery of decoding in Spanish, the students' "proficiency in English as a second language played a central role in affecting transfer" (156). In other words, highly efficient reading/writing ability in L1 does not make up altogether for lack of knowledge of L2.

That is, development along one continuum is crucially affected by development along the others. This is not to imply, however, that development occurs in one straight line along all three continua simultaneously from, say, oral receptive L1 competence to written productive L1–L2 competence. In fact, depending on the particular context, development is likely to zigzag across points within the three-dimensional space defined by the three continua. Thus, a more exact answer to Alderson's question might be: Both, either, or neither, depending on the context.

To return again to the initial vignettes, Sokhom's biliterate development could be characterized as beginning at a point near the L1 oral receptive ends of the continua, moving through a point near the L2 written receptive space and toward a point near the middle of all three continua. In contrast, Maria's biliterate development could be characterized as starting at a point near the L1 oral receptive ends of the continua, moving through a point near the middle of all three continua and toward a point midway along the reception–production and oral–written continua, near the L2 end.

In sum, the individual's biliterate development occurs along all three continua simultaneously and in relation with each other; this is why the notion of transfer has been such a tenacious and, at the same time, frustratingly elusive one. The potential for transfer along and across the continua is apparently infinite. Not only are the three continua of biliterate development related to each other, they are also related to the continua of biliterate contexts, as we have seen in the above discussion, and to the continua of biliterate media, as we will see below.

THE MEDIA OF BILITERACY

It is, after all, through the media of the two languages that the biliterate individual communicates in any particular context. Indeed, the media are a part of that context. The continua that define the relationship between the media are simultaneous–successive exposure, similar–dissimilar structures, and convergent–divergent scripts. Each of these continua is argued to have a bearing on the individual development of biliteracy, and especially on the potential for transfer in that development; however, research has not yet clarified which, if either, end of the continuum is the more conducive to positive transfer.

The Simultaneous–Successive Exposure Continuum

In the bilingualism field, a distinction is often made between simultaneous and successive bilingual language acquisition (McLaughlin, 1985) or early and late bilingualism (Lambert, 1985:120). Early bilinguals are those who become bilingual in infancy; late bilinguals do so in adolescence. Similarly, a child who acquires two languages before age 3 is doing so simultaneously; one who acquires one language before age 3 and the other after age 3 is doing so successively.

Differences are attributed to the two kinds of bilinguals; for example, it was suggested that early bilinguals have more compounded language systems and late bilinguals more coordinated ones (Lambert, 1985:120).[12] Nevertheless, there is increasing recognition that type and degree of bilingualism have more to do with systematic use of the two languages than with age of acquisition. Genesee (1989), for example, has recently refuted the hypothesis that children who learn two languages simultaneously have a unitary, undifferentiated language system, arguing instead that "bilingual children develop differentiated language systems from the beginning and are able to use their developing languages in *contextually sensitive ways*" (161; italics added).

It should be emphasized that the findings that a stronger first language leads to a stronger second language do not necessarily ✓ imply that the first language must be fully developed before the second language is introduced. Rather, the first language must not be abandoned before it is fully developed, whether the second language is introduced simultaneously or successively, early or late, in that process. This too accords with Lambert's notion of additive bilingualism and is reiterated by Hakuta, Ferdman, and Diaz (1987), who found that positive cognitive effects, including increased metalinguistic awareness and the use of language as a tool of thought, are found in additive bilingual situations (where the second language is acquired without loss of the mother tongue) that involve a somewhat systematic use of the two languages.

It is worth noting that a number of configurations exist as to the simultaneous or successive development of biliteracy and that these involve varying degrees of development of L1. A few examples will suffice to illustrate this point. There are cases where L2 literacy follows on varying levels of L1 literacy: Transitional bilingual education, as practiced in the United States, builds L2 literacy on minimal L1 literacy development; secondary schooling in a language of wider communication, such as English in many African nations, builds L2 literacy on moderate L1 literacy development; and foreign language studies at the college level build L2 literacy on highly developed L1 literacy.

Alternatively, there are cases where L1 literacy of varying levels of development follows on L2 literacy development: French immersion programs in Canada introduce English-speaking children to literacy through French, and later bring English literacy into the program, continuing to develop both throughout the years of schooling. On the other hand, immigrants who have been schooled in their second language may later apply their literacy skills to literacy in their first language, probably only for limited uses (Niyekawa, 1983:114). Finally, there are cases where L1 and L2 literacy are simultaneously acquired, for example, a U.S. Hispanic adult acquiring Spanish and English literacy in the same class (e.g., Lewis, 1988).

The Similar–Dissimilar Language Structures Continuum

Niyekawa (1983:98–99) suggested that learning to read in a second language that has no linguistic relation to the first language (e.g., Asian or Pacific language speakers learning European languages) will be "quite different" from learning a second language that is linguistically related to the first language (e.g., French and English). This would, in turn, be different than the case of two dialects of one language, or a pidgin and a language. Thus, not only multilingual settings, but also multidialectal settings (Collins, 1986; Collins & Michaels, 1986; Ferguson, 1985:140; Michaels, 1986; Simons & Murphy, 1986), and pidgin and creole settings (cf. Au et al., 1986:242; Durán, 1987:48), provide contexts for the study of biliteracy.

The Convergent–Divergent Scripts Continuum

Ferguson (1985:140) noted that cases around the world exemplify a range of possibilities as to writing systems: literacy in two languages with different writing systems (e.g., Bengali and English), in one language with two writing systems (e.g., Hindi and Urdu), or in two languages with one writing system (e.g., Marathi and Hindi). He invited research on consequences of this range of possibilities for literacy acquisition.

Thonis (1981:150), Barnitz (1982:565), Niyekawa (1983:97–102), and Feitelson (1987:180) suggested that the more characteristics two orthographic systems have in common, the greater or more immediate the potential for transfer of reading skills or strategies. On the other hand, Wong-Fillmore and Valadez (1986:662) reported that when students are learning to read in two languages at the same time, different writing systems (e.g., English and Chinese) appear to lead to less interference than do similar writing systems (e.g., English and French). Edelsky (1982:223, 225) found that although children in the bilingual program she studied generally used Spanish orthography when writing in English, they reserved the letter *k* for English and the tilde and accent for Spanish, thus reflecting knowledge of differences between the two writing systems from an early stage.

Fishman concluded from his study of four ethnolinguistic schools in New York City:

> With respect to mastering the various graphic systems employed in the ethnolinguistic schools we have studied [earlier he noted that the four graphic systems involved, Hebrew, Greek/Armenian, and French, may be said to be ordered on a continuum of decreasing divergence from English], it was our impression that divergence from or proximity to English made no noticeable difference in the rate or level of literacy acquisition by the time the second or third grade was reached. (Fishman, Gertner, Lowy & Milán, 1985:385)

In this case, whether because of transfer or not, convergence or divergence between the biliterates' two writing systems seemed to have little influence on the reading and writing of either.

CONCLUSION

Biliteracy is a complex phenomenon. In the course of this review, numerous biliteracy and, indeed, multiliteracy configurations have been cited. The motivation here was to contribute to theory, research, and practice with respect to biliteracy by attempting to elucidate that complexity. I have presented a framework for understanding biliteracy that uses the notion of continuum as its basis. It suggests that the nine continua provide a way to identify both relevant questions and incipient answers in research on biliteracy.

The important question as to the degree to which literacy knowledge and skills in one language aid or impede the learning of literacy knowledge and skills in the other has been answered partially through an understanding of the interrelated and nested nature of the continua. That is, the interrelatedness of the continua allows us to see why there is potential for positive transfer across languages and literacies, whereas the nested nature of the continua allows us to see that there are a myriad of contextual factors that may abet or impede such transfer.

Many unresolved issues remain for research with respect to the nature and development of biliteracy. Nevertheless, what is already known does have implications for the teaching of biliterate populations in our schools (see Hornberger, 1990, 1991, 1992, 1993, for more discussion on implications for teaching). Somewhat ironically, the framework outlined here suggests that the hope for understanding biliteracy, as well as literacy and bilingualism, seems to lie in the complexity of biliteracy. Once it is recognized that every instance of biliteracy shares in being situated on the same series of continua, it no longer seems to matter which particular configuration is under consideration. The important point becomes recognizing and understanding what the continua are and how they are related to each other. To return one final time to Sokhom, Maria, and Elizabeth, the implications of the model of biliteracy outlined here are that the more the contexts of their learning allow Sokhom, Maria, and Elizabeth to draw on *all* points of the continua, the greater are the chances for their full biliterate development.

NOTES

1. Names in the vignettes are pseudonyms.
2. Speech act is the minimal unit of the following set: speech act, speech event, speech situation, and speech community. Hymes (1974) gave an example: "a party (speech situation), a conversation during the party (speech event), a joke within the conversation (speech act)" (52). He also defined the speech community as a "community sharing knowledge of rules for the conduct and interpretation of speech" (Hymes, 1974:51).
3. A *domain*, as defined by Fishman (e.g., 1972, 1986) is a con-

struct based on congruences between patterns of language use and social situations, where social situations are made up by a particular conjunction of setting (place and time) and role relationships of the participants. The aggregates of situations in which place, time, role relationship, and patterns of language use correlate in the culturally appropriate way are termed *domains*.

4.   Ferguson (1959) originally introduced the term *diglossia* to refer to the speech community where "two varieties of a language exist side by side throughout the community, with each having a definite role to play" (325). The languages he selected to exemplify this concept were classical and colloquial Arabic in Arabic-speaking countries; katharevousa and demotiki in Greece; standard and Swiss German in Switzerland; and French and Haitian creole in Haiti. Fishman (1967:29) later extended the concepts of diglossia and of functional specialization to include not only varieties of one language but different languages.

5.   Code-switching refers to the switch from one code to another (i.e., one language to another) by a speaker within an "unchanged" speech event or situation (cf. Blom & Gumperz, 1986; Gumperz, 1972).

6.   Krashen (1987) claimed that comprehensible input is the "true and only causative variable in second language acquisition" (40; see also Krashen, 1985). His argument that the best form of input to the second-language learner is language that includes input that is a bit beyond the learner's current level ($i + 1$) but still comprehensible has influenced a number of language-teaching approaches (e.g., the natural approach) (McLaughlin, 1985:116; Krashen & Terrell, 1983).

7.   According to Swain (1985:252), learners must have the opportunity to produce comprehensible output in order to move from a purely semantic analysis to a syntactic analysis of the language (see also Pica, 1988; Pica et al., 1989).

8.   The beginnings of miscue analysis were in the 1960s, with a paper Goodman presented at the 1964 American Educational Research Association meetings, titled "A Linguistic Study of Cues and Miscues in Reading" (reprinted in Goodman, 1982). Working from the premise that a reader actively reconstructs a message from written language by using language cues, miscue analysis examines the "errors" readers make in oral reading as a clue to understanding the reading process. In that first paper, Goodman divided the cues into sets: those within words (e.g., letter-sound relationships), those in the flow of language (e.g., structural markers), those external to language and the reader (e.g., pictures), and those within the reader (e.g., conceptual background).

9.   Ellis (1986:47–48) explained that the term *interlanguage* refers to (a) "the structured system which the learner constructs at any given stage in his development" and (b) "the series of interlocking systems

which form . . . the interlanguage continuum." The L2 learner is seen as progressing along the interlanguage continuum by means of hypothesis testing. That is, L2 learners, like L1 learners, make errors in order to test out certain hypotheses about the nature of the language they are learning. The notion of L1 interference is not rejected entirely, but is seen as one of five principal processes operating in the interlanguage (others include overgeneralization of target language rules and transfer of training). L. Selinker's (1972) paper marked the first appearance of the term *interlanguage*.

10.   Cummins's (1979b) linguistic interdependence hypothesis posits that "the level of L2 competence which a bilingual child attains is partially a function of the type of competence the child has developed in L1 at the time when intensive exposure to L2 begins" (233). This hypothesis, along with the distinction between basic interpersonal communication skills (BICS) and cognitive/academic language proficiency (CALP) (Cummins, 1979a), later expanded into a four-quadrant model of language proficiency (Cummins, 1981), and the threshold hypothesis (which posits that there is a lower threshold of linguistic competence that a bilingual child must attain to avoid cognitive deficits and a higher threshold to gain positive cognitive effects), were offered as a way of explaining seemingly contradictory research results in bilingual education (Canadian immersion vs. U.S. transitional bilingual education) and bilingualism (positive vs. negative cognitive effects). (See also Cummins, 1985).

11.   For Lambert, an additive form of bilingualism is one in which a second, socially relevant language is added to one's repertory of skills without displacing or replacing the first or "home" language, whereas a subtractive form of bilingualism is the one "experienced by many ethnic minority groups who, because of national educational policies and social pressures of various sorts, are forced to put aside their ethnic language for a national language" (1985:119–120).

12.   The compound/coordinate distinction refers to whether or not the two languages of a bilingual are fused into one language system. The distinction originated with Uriel Weinreich's (1963:9–11) discussion of possible relationships between a sign and a sememe (unit of meaning) in bilingualism. In his discussion (a) a coordinative relationship meant that a word in either language had its own distinct referent, (b) a compound relationship was one where words from both languages shared one and the same referent, and (c) a subordinative relationship meant that access to the referent of a word in language A was made only *through* language B. Although Weinreich suggested that a person's or a group's bilingualism need not be entirely of one or another of these three types, the compound/coordinate distinction has been widely interpreted (beginning with Ervin & Osgood, 1954:141) to refer precisely to bilingual

types, an interpretation not without its problems (cf. Hakuta, 1986:95–101).

REFERENCES

Alderson, J.C. (1984). Reading in a foreign language: A reading problem or a language problem? In J.C. Alderson & A.H. Urquhart (Eds.), *Reading in a foreign language* (pp. 1–27). London: Longman.

Alderson, J.C. & Urquhart, A.H. (Eds.). (1984). *Reading in a foreign language*. London: Longman.

Au, K.H., Crowell, D., Jordan, C., Sloat, K., Speidel, G., Klein, T. & Tharp, R. (1986). Development and implementation of the KEEP reading program. In J. Orasanu (Ed.), *Reading comprehension: From research to practice* (pp. 235–252). Hillsdale, NJ: Lawrence Erlbaum.

Barnitz, J. (1982). Orthographies, bilingualism and learning to read English as a second language. *Reading Teacher, 35,* 560–567.

Basso, K. (1974). The ethnography of writing. In R. Bauman & J. Sherzer (Eds.), *Explorations in the ethnography of speaking* (pp. 425–432). New York: Cambridge University Press.

Baynham, M. (in press). Literate, biliterate, multiliterate? Some issues for literacy research. In B. Street & P. McCaffery (Eds.), *Literacy research in the U.K.*

Blom, J. & Gumperz, J. (1986). Social meaning in linguistic structure: Code-switching in Norway. In J. Gumperz & D. Hymes (Eds.), *Directions in sociolinguistics: The ethnography of communication* (pp. 407–434). New York: Basil Blackwell.

Bloome, D. (Ed.). (1987). *Literacy and schooling*. Norwood, NJ: Ablex.

Bloome, D. & Green, J. (1984). Directions in the sociolinguistic study of reading. In P.D. Pearson (Ed.), *Handbook of reading research* (pp. 395–421). New York: Longman.

Carlo, M.S., Sinatra, G.M. & Royer, J.M. (1989, March). *Using the sentence verification technique to measure transfer of comprehension skills from native to second language*. Paper presented at the annual meeting of the American Educational Research Association.

Carrell, P. (1987). Introduction. In J. Devine, P. Carrell & D.E. Eskey (Eds.), *Research in reading in English as a second language* (pp. 1–7). Washington, DC: TESOL.

Clarke, M.A. (1981). Reading in Spanish and English: Evidence from adult ESL students. In S. Hudelson (Ed.), *Learning to read in different languages* (pp. 69–92). Washington, DC: Center for Applied Linguistics.

Collins, J. (1986). Differential instruction in reading groups. In J. Cook-

Gumperz (Ed.), *The social construction of literacy* (pp. 117–137). New York: Cambridge University Press.

Collins, J. & Michaels, S. (1986). Speaking and writing: Discourse strategies and the acquisition of literacy. In J. Cook-Gumperz (Ed.), *The social construction of literacy* (pp. 207–222). New York: Cambridge University Press.

Cook-Gumperz, J. (Ed.). (1986). *The social construction of literacy.* New York: Cambridge University Press.

Cummins, J. (1979a). Cognitive/academic language proficiency, linguistic interdependence, the optimum age question, and some other matters. *Working Papers on Bilingualism, 19,* 197–205.

_____. (1979b). Linguistic interdependence and the educational development of bilingual children. *Review of Educational Research, 49,* 222–251.

_____. (1981). The role of primary language development in promoting educational success for language minority students. In California State Department of Education, *Schooling and language minority students: A theoretical framework* (pp. 3–49). Los Angeles: Evaluation, Dissemination and Assessment Center, California State University.

_____. (1985). The construct of language proficiency in bilingual education. In J. Alatis & J. Staczek (Eds.), *Perspectives on bilingualism and bilingual education* (pp. 209–231). Washington, DC: Georgetown University Press.

de Castell, S., Egan, K. & Luke, A. (Eds.). (1986). *Literacy, society, and schooling.* New York: Cambridge University Press.

Department of Education: Final research priorities; establishment (1988, June 20). Federal Register, pp. 23192–23195.

Dubin, F. (1989). Situating literacy within traditions of communicative competence. *Journal of Applied Linguistics, 10,* 171–181.

Durán, R. (1987). Factors affecting development of second language literacy. In S. Goldman & H. Trueba (Eds.), *Becoming literate in English as a second language* (pp. 33–55). Norwood, NJ: Ablex.

Duranti, A. & Ochs, E. (1986). Literacy instruction in a Samoan village. In B.B. Schieffelin & P. Gilmore (Eds.), *The acquisition of literacy: Ethnographic perspectives* (pp. 213–232). Norwood, NJ: Ablex.

Dutcher, N. (1982). *The use of first and second languages in primary education: Selected case studies* (World Bank Staff Working Paper No. 504). Washington, DC: World Bank.

Edelsky, C. (1982). Writing in a bilingual program: The relation of L1 and L2 texts. *TESOL Quarterly, 16,* 211–228.

_____. (1986). *Writing in a bilingual program: Había una vez.* Norwood, NJ: Ablex.

Ellis, R. (1986). *Understanding second language acquisition.* Oxford: Oxford University Press.

Engle, P. (1975). *The use of vernacular languages in education: Language medium in early school years for minority language groups.* Washington, DC: Center for Applied Linguistics.

Erickson, F. (1984). School literacy, reasoning, and civility: An anthropologist's perspective. *Review of Educational Research, 54,* 525–546.

――――. (1991). Advantages and disadvantages of qualitative research design on foreign language research. In B. Freed (Ed.), *Foreign language acquisition research and the classroom* (pp. 338–353). Lexington, MA: D.C. Heath.

Ervin, S. & Osgood, C. (1954). Second language learning and bilingualism. *Journal of Abnormal and Social Psychology, 49* (Suppl.), 139–146.

Faltis, C. (1986). Initial cross-lingual reading transfer in bilingual second grade classrooms. In E.E. Garcia & B. Flores (Eds.), *Language and literacy research in bilingual education* (pp. 145–157). Tempe: Arizona State University.

Feitelson, D. (1987). Reconsidering the effects of school and home for literacy in a multicultural cross-language context: The case of Israel. In D. Wagner (Ed.), *The future of literacy in a changing world* (pp. 174–185). Oxford: Pergamon Press.

Ferguson, C.A. (1959). Diglossia. *Word, 15,* 325–340.

――――. (1985). Patterns of literacy in multilingual situations. In J. Alatis & J. Staczek (Eds.), *Perspectives on bilingualism and bilingual education* (pp. 135–143). Washington, DC: Georgetown University Press.

Fishman, J.A. (1967). Bilingualism with and without diglossia; diglossia with and without bilingualism. *Journal of Social Issues, 23*(2), 29–38.

――――. (1972). The relationship between micro- and macrosociolinguistics in the study of who speaks what language to whom and when. In J.B. Pride & J. Holmes (Eds.), *Sociolinguistics* (pp. 15–32). New York: Penguin Books.

――――. (1986). Domains and the relationship between micro- and macrosociolinguistics. In J. Gumperz & D. Hymes (Eds.), *Directions in sociolinguistics: The ethnography of communication* (pp. 435–453). New York: Basil Blackwell.

――――. (Ed.). (1968). *Readings in the sociology of language.* The Hague: Mouton.

Fishman, J.A., Gertner, M.H., Lowy, E.G. & Milán, W.G. (1985). *The rise and fall of the ethnic revival: Perspectives on language and ethnicity.* Berlin: Mouton.

Gathercole, V.C. (1988). Some myths you may have heard about first language acquisition. *TESOL Quarterly, 22,* 407–435.

Gee, J.P. (1986). Orality and literacy: From *The Savage Mind* to *Ways with Words*. TESOL Quarterly, 20, 719–746.

Genesee, F. (1987). *Learning through two languages: Studies of immersion and bilingual education*. Cambridge, MA: Newbury House.

———. (1989). Early bilingual development: One language or two? *Journal of Child Language, 16*, 161–179.

Goodman, K. (1982). *Language and literacy: The selected writings of Kenneth S. Goodman* (Vols. I and II). Boston: Routledge & Kegan Paul.

Goodman, K. & Goodman, Y. (1983). Reading and writing relationships: Pragmatic functions. *Language Arts, 60*, 590–599.

Grosjean, F. (1982). *Life with two languages: An introduction to bilingualism*. Cambridge, MA: Harvard University Press.

Grosjean, F. (1985). The bilingual as a competent but specific speaker-hearer. *Journal of Multilingual and Multicultural Development, 6*, 467–477.

Grove, M.P. (1981). Psycholinguistic theories and ESL reading. In C.W. Twyford, W. Diehl & K. Feathers (Eds.), *Reading English as a second language: Moving from theory* (pp. 3–20). Bloomington: Indiana University.

Gumperz, J. (1969). How can we describe and measure the behavior of bilingual groups? In L.G. Kelly (Ed.), *Description and measurement of bilingualism: An international seminar*. Toronto: University of Toronto Press.

———. (1972). Verbal strategies in multilingual communication. In R. Abrahams & R. Troike (Eds.), *Language and cultural diversity in American education* (pp. 184–195). Englewood Cliffs, NJ: Prentice-Hall.

Hakuta, K. (1986). *Mirror of language: The debate on bilingualism*. New York: Basic Books.

———. (1987, December). *Properties of the bilingual mind*. Paper presented at the Harvard Institute on Bilingual Education: Research to Policy to Practice.

Hakuta, K. & Cancino, H. (1977). Trends in second language acquisition research. *Harvard Educational Review, 47*, 294–316.

Hakuta, K., Ferdman, B. & Diaz, R. (1987). Bilingualism and cognitive development: Three perspectives. In S. Rosenberg (Ed.), *Advances in applied psycholinguistics. Vol. 2: Reading, writing, and language learning* (pp. 284–319). New York: Cambridge University Press.

Heath, S.B. (1980). Functions and uses of literacy. *Journal of Communication, 30*, 123–133.

———. (1982). What no bedtime story means: Narrative skills at home and school. *Language in Society, 11*, 49–76.

———. (1983). *Ways with words*. New York: Cambridge University Press.

———. (1986). Sociocultural contexts of language development. In California State Department of Education, *Beyond language: Social and cultural factors in schooling language minority students* (pp. 143–186). Los Angeles: Evaluation, Dissemination and Assessment Center, California State University.

Hornberger, N.H. (1988). *Bilingual education and language maintenance: A southern Peruvian Quechua case.* Dordrecht: Foris.

———. (1990). Creating successful learning contexts for bilingual literacy. *Teachers College Record, 92,* 212–229.

———. (1991). Extending enrichment bilingual education: Revisiting typologies and redirecting policy. In Ofelia García (Ed.), *Bilingual education: Focusschrift in honor of Joshua A. Fishman on the occasion of his 65th birthday, Vol. 1* (pp. 215–234). Philadelphia: John Benjamins.

———. (1992). Biliteracy contexts, continua, and contrasts: Policy and curriculum for Cambodian and Puerto Rican students in Philadelphia. *Education and Urban Society, 24,* 196–211.

Hornberger, N.H. & Micheau, C. (1988, October). *Teaching reading bilingually.* Paper presented at the Ninth Conference on Spanish in the United States, Miami.

———. (1993). Getting far enough to like it: Biliteracy in the middle school. *Peabody Journal of Education* (to appear).

Hudelson, S. (1984). Kan yu ret an rayt en ingles: Children become literate in English as a second language. *TESOL Quarterly, 18,* 221–238.

Hymes, D.H. (1964). Introduction: Toward ethnographies of communication. *American Anthropologist, 66*(6, Pt. 2), 1–34.

———. (1974). *Foundations in sociolinguistics: An ethnographic approach.* Philadelphia: University of Pennsylvania Press.

———. (1986). Models of the interaction of language and social life. In J. Gumperz & D. Hymes (Eds.), *Directions in sociolinguistics: The ethnography of communication* (pp. 35–71). New York: Basil Blackwell.

Indrasuta, C. (1988). Narrative styles in the writing of Thai and American students. In A.C. Purves (Ed.), *Writing across languages and cultures: Issues in contrastive rhetoric* (pp. 206–226). Newbury Park, CA: Sage.

Kaplan, R.B. (1988). Contrastive rhetoric and second language learning: Notes toward a theory of contrastive rhetoric. In A.C. Purves (Ed.), *Writing across languages and cultures: Issues in contrastive rhetoric* (pp. 275–304). Newbury Park, CA: Sage.

Kelly, L.G. (Ed.). (1969). *The description and measurement of bilingualism: An international seminar.* Toronto: University of Toronto Press.

Krashen, S. (1985). *The input hypothesis: Issues and implications.* London: Longman.

————. (1987). Applications of psycholinguistic research to the classroom. In M. Long & J. Richards (Eds.), *Methodology in TESOL: A book of readings* (pp. 33–44). New York: Newbury House.

Krashen, S. & Terrell, T. (1983). *The natural approach.* Hayward, CA: Alemany Press.

Lambert, W.E. (1985). Some cognitive and sociocultural consequences of being bilingual. In J. Alatis & J. Staczek (Eds.), *Perspectives on bilingualism and bilingual education* (pp. 116–131). Washington, DC: Georgetown University Press.

Lambert, W.E. & Tucker, G.R. (1972). *The bilingual education of children: The St. Lambert experiment.* Rowley, MA: Newbury House.

Langer, J. (1988). The state of research on literacy. *Educational Researcher, 17*(3), 42–46.

Leap, W.L. (1987, November). *Pathways and barriers to literacy-building on the Northern Ute Reservation.* Paper presented at the annual meeting of the American Anthropological Association.

Lewis, M. (1988, September). *Adult literacy students: Perceptions of reading held by English and Spanish speakers.* Paper presented at the Modern Language Association Right to Literacy Conference, Columbus, Ohio.

Lytle, S. & Botel, M. (1988). *The Pennsylvania Comprehensive Reading and Communication Arts Plan II (PCRP II). Reading, writing, and talking across the curriculum.* Harrisburg: Pennsylvania Department of Education.

Mangubhai, F. (1987). Literacy in the South Pacific: Some multilingual and multiethnic issues. In D. Wagner (Ed.), *The future of literacy in a changing world* (pp. 186–206). Oxford: Pergamon Press.

McLaughlin, B. (1985). *Second language acquisition in childhood: Volume 2. School-age children.* Hillsdale, NJ: Erlbaum.

Michaels, S. (1986). Narrative presentations: An oral preparation for literacy with first graders. In J. Cook-Gumperz (Ed.), *The Social construction of literacy* (pp. 94–116). New York: Cambridge University Press.

Modiano, N. (1973). *Indian education in the Chiapas highlands.* New York: Holt, Rinehart and Winston.

Moll, L. & Díaz, S. (1985). Ethnographic pedagogy: Promoting effective bilingual instruction. In E.E. Garcia & R.V. Padilla (Eds.), *Advances in bilingual education research* (pp. 127–149). Tucson: University of Arizona Press.

Murray, D.E. (1988). The context of oral and written language: A framework for mode and medium switching. *Language in Society, 17,* 351–373.

Niyekawa, A.M. (1983). Biliteracy acquisition and its sociocultural effects. In M. Chu-Chang (Ed.), *Asian- and Pacific-American perspectives in bilingual education* (pp. 97–119). New York: Teachers College Press.

Olson, D., Torrance, N. & Hildyard, A. (Eds.). (1985). *Literacy, language, and learning: The nature and consequences of reading and writing.* London: Cambridge University Press.

Ong, W. (1982). *Literacy and orality: The technologizing of the word.* New York and London: Methuen.

Parry, K.J. (1987). Reading in a second culture. In J. Devine, P. Carrell & D.E. Eskey (Eds.), *Research in reading in English as a second language* (pp. 59–70). Washington, DC: TESOL.

Pica, T. (1988). Interlanguage adjustments as an outcome of NS-NNS negotiated interaction. *Language Learning, 38,* 45–73.

Pica, T., Holliday, L., Lewis, N. & Morgenthaler, L. (1989). Comprehensible output as an outcome of linguistic demands on the learner. *Studies in Second Language Acquisition, 11,* 63–90.

Pride, J.B. & Holmes, J. (1972). *Sociolinguistics: Selected readings.* New York: Penguin Books.

Reyes, M. (1987). Comprehension of content area passages: A study of Spanish/English readers in third and fourth grade. In S.R. Goldman & H.T. Trueba (Eds.), *Becoming literate in English as a second language* (pp. 107–126). Norwood, NJ: Ablex.

Roller, C.M. (1988). Transfer of cognitive academic competence and L2 reading in a rural Zimbabwean primary school. *TESOL Quarterly, 22,* 303–318.

Rosier, P. & Holm, W. (1980). *The Rock Point experience: A longitudinal study of a Navajo school program* (Bilingual Education Series 8). Washington, DC: Center for Applied Linguistics.

Scribner, S. (1984, November). Literacy in three metaphors. *American Journal of Education, 93*(1), pp. 6–21.

———. (1987). Introduction. In D. Wagner (Ed.), *The future of literacy in a changing world* (pp. 19–24). Oxford: Pergamon Press.

Scribner, S. & Cole, M. (1981). *The psychology of literacy.* Cambridge: Harvard University Press.

Selinker, L. (1972). Interlanguage. *International Review of Applied Linguistics, 10,* 209–230.

Simons, H.D. & Murphy, S. (1986). Spoken language strategies and reading acquisition. In J. Cook-Gumperz (Ed.), *The social construction of literacy* (pp. 185–206). New York: Cambridge University Press.

Smith, J. (1967). *Creative teaching of the language arts in the elementary school.* Boston: Allyn and Bacon.

Söter, A.O. (1988). The second language learner and cultural transfer in narration. In A.C. Purves (Ed.), *Writing across languages and cultures: Issues in contrastive rhetoric* (pp. 177–205). Newbury Park, CA: Sage.

Street, B. (1984). *Literacy in theory and practice.* New York: Cambridge University Press.

———. (1988a). A critical look at Walter Ong and the "Great Divide." *Literacy Research Center,* 4(1), 1, 3, 5.

———. (1988b). Literacy practices and literacy myths. In R. Saljo (Ed.), *The written world* (pp. 59–72). New York: Springer Press.

———. (in press). Literacy, pedagogy, and nationalism. In *Occasional Papers.* New York: Columbia University Teachers College.

Swain, M. (1985). Communicative competence: Some roles of comprehensible input and comprehensible output in its development. In S. Gass & C. Madden (Eds.), *Input in second language acquisition* (pp. 235–253). Rowley, MA: Newbury House.

Szwed, J.F. (1981). The ethnography of literacy. In M.F. Whiteman (Ed.), *Writing: The nature, development, and teaching of written communication. Volume 1:* Variation in writing: Functional and linguistic-cultural differences (pp. 13–23). Hillsdale, NJ: Erlbaum.

Tannen, D. (1985). Relative focus on involvement in oral and written discourse. In D. Olson, N. Torrance & A. Hildyard (Eds.), *Literacy, language, and learning: The nature and consequences of reading and writing* (pp. 124–147). London: Cambridge University Press.

Thonis, E. (1981). Reading instruction for language minority students. In California State Department of Education, *Schooling and language minority students: A theoretical framework* (pp. 147–181). Los Angeles: Evaluation, Dissemination and Assessment Center, California State University.

Tucker, G.R. (1986). Implications of Canadian research for promoting a language-competent American society. In J.A. Fishman (Ed.), *The Fergusonian impact* (Vol. 2, pp. 361–369). Berlin: Mouton.

UNESCO. (1953). *The use of vernacular languages in education* (Monographs of Fundamental Education No. 8). Paris: Author.

Wagner, D., Messick, B.M. & Spratt, J. (1986). Studying literacy in Morocco. In B.B. Schieffelin & P. Gilmore (Eds.), *The acquisition of literacy: Ethnographic perspectives* (pp. 233–260). Norwood, NJ: Ablex.

Wagner, D., Spratt, J.E. & Ezzaki, A. (1989). Does learning to read in a second language always put the child at a disadvantage? Some counterevidence from Morocco. *Applied Psycholinguistics, 10,* 31–48.

Wald, B. (1987). The development of writing skills among Hispanic high school students. In S. Goldman & H. Trueba (Eds.), *Becoming literate in English as a second language* (pp. 155–185). Norwood, NJ: Ablex.

Weinreich, U. (1963). *Languages in contact: Findings and problems.* The Hague: Mouton.

Wilde, S. (1988, September). *Teaching skills or learning language? Spelling in the whole language classroom.* Paper presented at the Modern Language Association Right to Literacy Conference.

Williams, J. (1987). *Singaporean non-native institutionalized English, production principles, and language acquisition.* Unpublished doctoral dissertation, University of Pennsylvania.

Wong-Fillmore, L. & Valadez, C. (1986). Teaching bilingual learners. In M.C. Wittrock (Ed.), *Handbook of research on teaching* (pp. 648–685). New York: Macmillan.

Zentella, A.C. (1981). *"Hablamos los dos. We speak both.": Growing up bilingual in El Barrio.* Unpublished doctoral dissertation, University of Pennsylvania.

Zutell, J. & Allen, V. (1988). The English spelling strategies of Spanish-speaking bilingual children. *TESOL Quarterly, 22* 333–340.

PART 3

Social and Cultural Perspectives

CHAPTER 5

Sociocultural Change Through Literacy: Toward the Empowerment of Families

Concha Delgado-Gaitan

In arguing for a theory of literacy as a social practice, Street (1984) challenges the concept of an autonomous model that represents literacy as neutral technology, acquired through formal schooling and detached from other specific social contexts. The autonomous model isolates literacy as an independent variable, a collection of discrete cognitive skills. In contrast, Street takes the position that literacy practices are always accompanied by specific forms of social organization. Literacy, then, becomes the concrete social form and the institution that gives meaning to the discrete practices of reading and writing (95–125).

This perspective provides a context in which literacy practices take different forms depending on the organizational nature of the family. It takes into account the ecocultural niche that explains the family's socioeconomic level, social and political relations, religious beliefs, regional ecological location, as well as the family's relationship to other institutions including neighborhood, media, health institutions and schools (Delgado-Gaitan, 1990; Moll & Diaz, 1987; Trueba, 1984). These activities are culturally variable

I am grateful for the research assistance of Martha Allexsaht-Snider and Hector Mendez. Funding for parts of this study were provided by Johns Hopkins Center for the Study of Disadvantaged Students and the University of California, Santa Barbara, Center for Chicano Studies.

in that there is wide diversity among families as they interact in different settings. Literacy in particular enters as a socioculturally constructed activity (Leichter, 1984; Schieffelin & Cochran-Smith, 1984). At the same time, families' linguistic interaction, especially through questioning, plays a significant part. Research on questioning in family and school settings (Green, Wade & Graham, 1988; Heath, 1982) affirms that asking questions is a sociocultural activity and that there is diversity in formulating and responding to questions, especially among those children who are not reared in middle class White families. Further, it is clear from my work that as families interact in new settings and acquire new literacy skills, they become empowered through the process of social interaction and community organization (Delgado-Gaitan, 1990).

Empowerment principles state that people who have been historically underrepresented can organize and through a process of critical reflection recognize their potential and state their goals for access to resources, thus power. Empowerment process principles have been advanced by Freire (1970), Freire and Macedo (1987), Delgado-Gaitan (1990), Delgado-Gaitan and Trueba (1991), and the Cornell Empowerment Group (Allen, Barr, Cochran, Dean & Green, 1989). Theoretically, in order to understand families as contexts for human development, we need to consider not only how family members interact with each other in their daily activities but also the social and structural systems that surround the family, including institutional systems such as workplaces and schools. For example, how families exercise their power relative to schools speaks to the level of involvement parents have with the schools and their knowledge about their role as educators in the home.

The Family Matters Program designed by Bronfenbrenner and Cochran in 1976 has successfully exemplified how empowerment occurs on a continuum that varies for everyone involved. Cochran (1988) suggests that empowerment occurs in varying stages for families in the study because families start at different points in the process. Five stages are outlined, depicting sociocultural change leading to empowerment in the community:

1. Positive changes in self-perception
2. Alteration of relations with members of the household or immediate family

3. Establishment and maintenance of new relations with more distant relatives and friends

4. Information-gathering related to broader community involvement

5. Change-oriented community action

The interrelationships among individuals, the social context, and acquisition of social knowledge establish the conditions for social change—the fifth stage—to occur as noted. This framework for empowerment has significant implications for the family literacy study reported here.

The families' perception of social reality and need to enhance communication within their family gave rise to the study reported here. In this case, the research team departed from the current trend of defining family literacy as benefiting children's academic achievement in school, as others have done (Clark, 1984; Goldenberg, 1987; Seppanen, 1988). Beyond the need to improve children's academic performance is the parents' desire to understand how they, together with their children, read to learn, a concept raised as a theoretical construct for literacy in practice by Auerbach (1989). Reading to learn focuses on literacy as a means for deriving meaning from text in relation to the reader's sociocultural experience as it occurs in the natural setting (Auerbach, 1989; Cook-Gumperz, 1986; Taylor, 1983). In this theoretical framework, the emphasis is on the readers' literacy practices for the purpose of enhancing their self and group identity and/or for instrumental means to accomplish a specific goal. It underscores the five stages of change outlined in Cochran's empowerment process.

This chapter presents the results of the Carpinteria family-literacy study (Delgado-Gaitan, 1990) pursued from a sociocultural perspective with regards to empowerment for Spanish-speaking children and their families. In particular, the Carpinteria community case is used to illustrate the potential of collective work in parents' learning to read with their children for the purpose of understanding texts in relation to their experience.

Family literacy has power as its basis because it creates access to participation and breaks patterns of social isolation. When change occurs by choice, as a result of self-reflection, it is accepted and internalized by those affected. This allows the person or group to determine its own direction and change. Implicit here is knowledge and responsibility for one's behavior and willingness to take action to help shape it as desired.

Outcomes of the empowerment process manifest themselves through access to resources. Power is the capacity to influence foreseen and unforeseen effects for oneself and others, and the increased ability to create desired change as the individual, parents, family, teacher, and school deem appropriate. At an individual level, empowerment takes place by building self-esteem and self-confidence. At the family level empowerment occurs when barriers are removed or incentives provided in local settings.

Research has found that parents teach more than the mechanics and strategies of reading during this activity with children; they impart sociocultural knowledge based on their own experience (Heath, 1983; Leichter, 1984; Wells, 1986). They convey values, a world view about their position in society, and they imbue their children with a sense of confidence that they are important enough to receive their parents' attention.

Ada (1988) attempted to examine the intersection between children's literature, parent-child interaction with each other and the text, questioning strategies for reading comprehension, and the notion of self-concept through Freire's notion of liberation. Following Freire's (1970) concept of liberation and his work on literacy with Brazilian peasants, Ada attempted to have parents learn how to motivate their children to read by utilizing four questioning strategies. These strategies were intended to teach the children to reflect on their own experiences and liberation. She reasoned that if parents were to apply knowledge of their status and experience in society by teaching their children to do the same thing, they would require primary experience in examining text for their own purposes. They would become better teachers if they read texts that interested them and that were relevant to their own experiences. Parents who reflected on their own experience relative to the material they read would be better able to teach their own children how to relate storybooks to the children's experience.

Ada proposed four categories of questions that framed the interaction between adults and children: descriptive, personal interpretive, critical, and creative. Descriptive questions solicited factual recall; for example, "What did the female elephants wear?" Personal interpretive questions asked readers to think about their personal experience in relation to what they read; for example, "Have you ever felt that you were prevented from doing things that others had permission to do? How did you feel?" Critical questions revealed the child's ability to analyze the text in terms of sociopolitical perspective; for example, "Could the male and female monkeys have divided the work and responsibilities better?" Creative questions made readers think about ways they would resolve similar questions to those in the story; for example, "If you had been one of the female monkeys, what could you have done to improve the situation?"

Essentially, Ada found that Spanish-speaking children and their parents become empowered when they learn to interpret literature in relation to their own experience and reality. She showed that parents of Spanish-speaking children learned to read to their children by reading selected children's literature books and using a hierarchy of questions designed to generate discussion between children and parents.

THE INTERVENTION STUDY

Studying Family Literacy

Four years prior to the beginning of the study reported here, I conducted an ethnographic study on home and school literacy and parent involvement in Carpinteria, California (Delgado-Gaitan, 1990). The results indicated that by the time Spanish-speaking children reached the third or fourth grade, parents were intimidated by the language barrier presented in homework, which was almost totally in English. This intimidation was a distancing factor in the parent-child relationship that was crucial to maintaining a supportive system for children.

Another issue emerged in that study: because homework consumed most of the children's time at home, parents found little time to do leisure reading with their children. The findings of this study were shared with a parent group, COPLA (Comité de Padres Latinos), which had been organized to deal with issues pertaining to their children's education. As parents became aware of their literacy practices in the home they expressed an interest in increasing their reading at home with their children; parents who had children who did not excel in reading were especially interested.

When I was funded to conduct an intervention study, the focus of the research was decided jointly by the researchers, their assistants, the COPLA committee, and school administrators. Family literacy received strong support as a potential project for children. Students in the third and fourth grades who needed support in their reading skills seemed likely participants, according to earlier findings by Delgado-Gaitan (1990). The students were evaluated by their teachers as Spanish-speaking readers who could benefit from additional support in their reading. Three major research questions guided this study:

1. How does parental use of literature with their children influence the parents' perception of self efficacy regarding literacy tasks?
2. How are household relations affected as a result of parent-child literacy activity?
3. How did the literacy project create new social networks for parents?

Over a five-year period, ethnographic data were collected in Carpinteria, California, on home-school communication in second, third and fourth grades, especially pertaining to literacy activities in home and school. In addition, ethnographic data on parents' involvement with the school district, from preschool to high school, were collected. Data from the latter included policies and practices. Data on the community parent organization showed the development of the power base for Spanish-speaking parents.

Using the background data on children's literacy performance in school, families, and the home-school relationships, the research team consulted with the parents and Morgan Elementary School for their input on a literacy project that would best suit their needs and goals. We created a family literacy program where parents could engage in reading with their children at home.

The eight books for the project were screened intentionally for topics that would generate discussion in families in this community. Nonsexist, nonracist, and nonclassist stories received major consideration. We departed somewhat from the recommendation of Ada (1988) in her curriculum simply because we considered some of the books used in the Pajaro Valley project inappropriate, potentially offensive, or uninteresting. We did overlap with Ada's recommended list when our criteria fit. The books selected were: *Rosa Caramelo, ¿A Dónde Vas Osito Polar?, Historia de los Bonobos con Gafas, El Primer Pájaro de Piko-Niko, Tío Elefante, El Perro del Cerro y la Rana de la Sábana, Monty,* and *Mira Como Salen las Estrellas.* The project began with the shorter books and progressed to the longer ones.

The parents of the selected children learned how to discuss book content with their children. At eight monthly sessions, held in the school setting, parents were given a children's literature book and taught the four types of questioning strategies that would improve their child's involvement in reading. Parent-participants were then observed reading to their children in the natural home setting on five different occasions. A recording was made during each of these periods. These occasions provided the researchers with observation and interview data on parent-child interaction regarding literature content.

At each monthly meeting parents discussed the new books. Working in small groups, they asked each other questions to model possible ways of interacting with their children. Mrs. Reyes, a parent from the community who had a great deal of experience in reading with children and in working with the COPLA parent group, assisted in the literacy classes, and another parent, Mrs. Mata, organized childcare during the parent meetings. By involving active parents in the project in a variety of capacities, the family literacy project was strengthened because parent leaders served as role models to those learning new practices regarding their children's schooling.

Three major areas in family literacy are delineated in the sections that follow, including background of families, parent-child interaction around literature texts, and parent-parent interaction.

FINDINGS: FAMILY LITERACY

Parents' Backgrounds

Families shared a number of characteristics. They were immigrants from Mexico, working class, and predominantly Spanish-speaking. Reading skills of the parents varied along two continua. One was that of Spanish reading and writing: only two parents who had attended school in Mexico had gone beyond the sixth

BACKGROUND DATA ON FAMILY

| Family Name | Number of Siblings in Household | Parents' Schooling | | Parents' Employment | |
		Mother	Father	Mother	Father
Romo	2	12th	12th	housekeeping	clerk
Alvarez	3	6th	6th (Mexico) 2 yrs. HS (US)	factory	gardener
Samora	3	1st	2nd	factory	unemployed
Gomez	3	5th	2nd	factory	gardener
Lara	4	6th	4th	housekeeping	tree cutter gardener
Mendez	2	1st/US	5th/City College	housewife	gardener
Quinta	2	6th	6th	housewife	gardener
Rios	7	none	none	housewife	gardener
Macias	2	7th/US	10th/US	Self-employed Caterer	divorced
Soto	3	did not finish primary	attended secondary school	Supv. of maids hotel	driver, delivery

grade. Table 5.1 describes the families who participated in the intervention project.

All parents valued literacy skills for their children and had definite opinions about what a good or poor reader was. Most of the parents provided a detailed profile of their child as a reader and of their reading competencies. In giving a definition of what makes a good or poor reader, the parents usually described a good reader as a person who read all types of materials, read avidly, and read well, in contrast to a poor reader as a person who did not like to read and had difficulty reading text. Most of the parents read with their children at home prior to the intervention, although many said that they did not read regularly due to time constraints. Once children moved into higher grades in school, parents waited for their children to initiate a reading activity that usually involved school texts.

Parent-Child Interaction

Ada (1988) stated that the four questioning strategy categories (descriptive, personal, critical, and creative) comprise a hierarchy from simple to more complex, which suggests that the more complex questions, in the creative mode, are more likely to evoke the kind of reflection that enables the child to be analytical about sociocultural conditions. Ada's (1988) literature curriculum designated types of questions for teachers to use with the students. Her initial intent was to train teachers to use her literature books and then rely on the children's enthusiasm to motivate the parents to come to the school to learn about the books. She intended that parents, in her study, use similar questioning strategies as those of the teacher.

In the Carpinteria family-literacy study, a principal criterion of analysis was the question-response interaction in the literacy activity in the home. Our project in Carpinteria varied somewhat from Ada's project in that we began training the parents rather than the teachers. However, we maintained the concept of the questioning strategy as way of organizing the presentation of children's storybooks to the parents. The different themes of each book lent themselves to discussion. Another variation in our project was to have the parents design their own questions for each book. We as the researchers had a preconceived notion based on the concept of empowerment; given the opportunity to create their own questions about the storybooks, parents could build on their personal experience and knowledge. In the parent-training meetings, adults were allowed to spontaneously create the questions they would ask their children when reading the project's books. In order to ascertain how parents actually used these questions with their children in a reading activity, the intervention included an opportunity to discuss the content of the books with them. They practiced constructing questions with each other. By devising these questions, they learned how to think about the story and its relationship to their experience, making it possible to pose appropriate questions for their children.

The five phases of videotaped observations yielded rich data about the way that parents posed questions to children about the text. The first videotaped session was collected prior to the intervention. Four subsequent sessions were scheduled on alternate months during the project.

Although parents read to their children in most of the families, the first preintervention video revealed that all but one set of parents listened to their children read without verbal interaction. The one exception was the Alvarez parents, who asked several questions as they read the book to their child. Table 5.2 shows a general pattern of parent-child interaction regarding text through descriptive and experiential (personal, opinion, creative) questions. The numbers in and of themselves are not meaningful unless the development of the interaction among the families can be seen along a time continuum. Each family has its own particular story about its experience with literacy before and during the project. For the purpose of this chapter, however, I will discuss briefly three individual family cases to illustrate empowerment within the family as well as with the community.

Rios Family

The Rios family was particularly significant to the project with respect to the development of their effort to participate in their daughter Rosa's reading. Nahuatl is the family's first language, Spanish is the second, and English is the third for the children. The ten family members live in a small dirt-floor shack high up on the mountainside in the outskirts of town. They tend the ranch on the land where they live. In the first project session, both parents attended and brought one of their oldest sons with them; all their other children went to the childcare room. When the parents introduced themselves to the group they revealed that they had to bring all of the younger children because the owner of the ranch did not allow the children to stay in the shack unsupervised, and that they were interested in supporting their children's literacy because they had not had the opportunity to study in either Nahuatl or Spanish in Mexico.

Neither Mr. or Mrs. Rios could read Spanish. Their son, Rogelio, sat next to them and read aloud. During the first class all their children joined the parents in the classroom to listen to a story. I asked the children questions about the text. Rosa, a fourth grader, was the only child who raised her hand and responded to the questions enthusiastically. It was apparent to the research team that this family's literacy development held great promise and they deserved close observation over the course of the project. In point of fact, we found ourselves involved with the Rios family sooner and more deeply than we had anticipated. The family had transportation problems that prevented them from continuing the literacy classes. Round-trip transportation was arranged, thanks to other families in the project, and the Rios family was able to continue participating.

A new challenge was raised, however, when the older son called, a short time later in the project, to state that Mr. Rios had to work late every Friday night (when class was scheduled) and that Mrs. Rios was getting along in her pregnancy to the point where the trip to class was too tiring. He concluded his telephone call with the reluctant conclusion that they would have to "drop out" of the project. But the research staff would not permit this; they had quickly become enamored of the family for personal as well as scholarly reasons, and arranged to have Rogelio assume the responsibility of working with his enthusiastic little sister, Rosa. Following the first class, we learned that generally the parents did not listen to the children read, rather that the older brothers helped the younger ones with their schoolwork. Therefore, Rogelio's participation was appropriate.

Before starting the literacy classes in this project, Mr. Rios listened to Rosa read but did not interact with her verbally in any way. He did express an interest in her reading to him.

TABLE 5.2
BOOKS THEMES AND QUESTIONING CATEGORIES

	Pre-intervention		Rosa Caramelo — Theme: Gender Socialization		A Dónde Vas Osito Polar — Theme: Separating and Re-Uniting		Historia De Los Bonobos Con Gafas — Theme: Gender Equality and Status		El Primer Pájaro De Piko-Niko — Theme: Self-Discovery and Identity		Tío Elefante — Theme: Separation and Familial Support		El Perro Del Cerro Y La Rana De La Sábana — Theme: Rhyming		Monty — Theme: Problem Solving		Mira Como Salen Las Estrellas — Theme: Immigration	
	D	E	D	E	D	E	D	E	D	E	D	E	D	E	D	E	D	E
Romo (David)	0	0							15	6							0	2
Romo (Mona)	0	0							8	4							0	2
Alvarez	10	0					45	19	11	8							19	6

Name														
Samora	1	2			10	0	19	1					9	3
Gomez	3	0			10	12	7	2						
Lara	0	0			45	14							29	10
Mendez			10	2	17	1	52	6					15	0
Quinta	0	1							4	12	12	4	5	30
Rios	0	0					5	0	18	0			26	0
Macias	1	2	13	9									4	9
Soto	0	0			1	4	7	0					7	5

D: descriptive
E: experiential

The second video session showed Rogelio and Rosa in their home reading the book *El Primer Pájaro de Piko-Niko*. This book is about a bird who was born in a part of the forest that did not have other birds and who therefore did not know how to fly. He sought his identity with other animals but they could not help him. Just as he was falling from a cliff he passed a group of birds who called out to him "¡Vuela, Pájaro, en el viento!" (Fly, bird, in the air!) The bird did so and discovered his identity as a bird.

This session showed Rogelio asking a few questions referring to particular facts of the story. The questions were of a descriptive nature: for example: "¿A dónde fue?" (Where did the bird go?), to which Rosa answered, "A una cueva" (To a cave).

The third reading was *Tío Elefante*. This story was considerably longer than the previous one, with five short chapters of a few pages each. The story concerned a baby elephant that had been separated from its parents. An uncle tried very hard to help the baby elephant to deal with his sorrow and the pain of not knowing his parents' whereabouts. He took him on a train trip to his own house and helped him to pass the time by playing a variety of games such as counting houses, telephone poles, and peanut shells.

During this third video interaction, Rogelio posed numerous questions to Rosa. Although the questions to Rosa appeared to be mostly of a descriptive nature, they differed qualitatively in their complexity. Earlier questions required brief direct responses, while Rogelio's questions in this third video showed growth, as responses required Rosa to consider purpose on the part of the character as opposed to simpler name or location. For example, this set of questions called for Rosa to complete the question with actual text. Pointing to the text, Rogelio asked, "¿Qué intentó?" (What did he intend?); Rosa answered, "Intentó contar las casas" (He intended to count the houses). Recalling the character's intentions meant that Rosa had to understand his role.

Immigration was the theme in the eighth book read by the families in the project. *Mira Como Salen Las Estrellas* was the title and it was read on the fourth videotaping of the family in the home. The story was about a young boy and girl who took a long trip to America on a ship with their aunt to join their father and mother. The story was told from the children's point of view, relating their experiences on a ship with other people who were immigrating to America. Various trials and tribulations, such as watching others become sick and die, were reported by the children. Their arrival and reunion with their parents made it all worthwhile.

Rogelio and Rosa's interaction concerning this book was somewhat different from the three previous ones. He asked Rosa over twenty predominantly descriptive questions involving causal links, such as, "¿Por qué se iban temprano a la cama?" (Why did they go to bed early?), to which she answered, "Para ver como salían las estrellas" (To see the stars come out). Development was evident in this video as Rogelio posed so many questions that they engaged Rosa into formulating a sequence of events almost at a level of summarizing the story with precise detail. Increased interaction between Rosa and Rogelio during their reading sessions over the course of the project reflected Rogelio's growth in checking on Rosa's comprehension for sequencing events and in developing a format that allowed her to demonstrate her recall on the "what, why, where, when, and how" questions. Rosa became more focused on the text, which built a strong foundation for other types of questions involving her opinion or relating the text to her experience. Revealed in the videotapes also was Rosa's marked enthusiasm for answering the questions, which indicated the importance of being challenged as Rogelio's questions encouraged her to think about what she had read.

Quinta Family

Luis Quinta, a third grader, was having a particular problem with reading, as well as in his overall social adjustment in school, in spite of the fact that his parents read at home. His parents believed that Luis was discouraged because the teacher scolded him when he made mistakes. Luis's overall attitude toward reading and school suffered as a result and the parents were concerned. They had met with the teacher and tried to find out how to help him at home. Although the parents encouraged him to do his homework and rewarded him by taking him for a ride, he defied them and the problems persisted. On some nights, Luis's parents read to him from the Bible, but usually they read only the school texts, since his academic work was in jeopardy.

The first session we videotaped with the Quinta family showed the father reading Luis's favorite story about a pirate and a treasure at sea. About midway through the book Mr. Quinta stopped reading and asked Luis if he wanted to read part of the book. Luis declined by not responding to the invitation.

The second video, however, showed over twenty question and answer responses between Luis and his father as they read the book *Tío Elefante* (Uncle Elephant). The father, for example, asked "¿Por qué lo invitó el tío elefante?" (Why did his uncle elephant invite him?), to which Luis responded, "Porque el niño estaba solo" (Because the little boy was alone). Mrs. Quinta also posed questions to Luis as she listened to him read. She asked a variety of questions that required Luis to call on his experience. "¿Alguna vez te has sentido solo, triste?" (Have you ever felt alone, sad?) "No." "¿Alguna vez te pasó algo parecido?" (Have you ever had something like this happen to you?) Luis was reluctant to answer his parents' questions, but they were quick to elicit the information with a variety of questions.

In the third session, a number of question-answer interactions were recorded as the parents and Luis read the book *El Perro del Cerro y la Rana de la Sábana*. This was a very small book of a nonsensical nature written in rhyme verse, and it provided material for some comparison questions that the parents asked Luis. "¿Quién crees tú que sea el más valiente, el perro o la rana?" (Who do you think is braver, the dog or the toad?) "El perro" (The dog). "¿Por qué?" (Why?) "Porque el perro es más grande" (Because the dog is bigger). Even though the book was brief and of a ludic nature, the parent-child interaction advanced in the question-answer formulation.

Parents continued to elaborate on their interaction with their son and the storybooks. Both Mr. and Mrs. Quinta joined Luis in reading the book in the fourth recorded session, *Mira Como Salen Las Estrellas*. An increased number of interactions showed a focus on Luis's opinions and personal experience. For example: "¿Tú qué piensas, por qué estaban contentos?" (What do you think, why were they happy?) "Porque miraban la Estatua de la Libertad" (Because they saw the Statute of Liberty). "¿Y eso qué quería decir?" (And what did that mean?) "Que estaban en América" (That they were in America). "¿Si a tí te hubiera pasado una cosa así, tu qué hubieras sentido?" (If something like that had happened to you, what would you have felt?) "Alegría." (Happiness). Luis was also asked to imagine what the children in the book might have liked to read: "¿Cuáles historias crees que le gustan?" (What stories do you think he likes?) "De cuando estaba chiquito" (Stories from when he was little). "¿Por qué te gusta que te cuenten historias?" (Why do you like stories told to you?) "Porque hacen que me duerma" (Because they help me go to sleep).

Both parents read together with Luis during the sessions dealing with the project, although they indicated that at other times it was either the father or mother who read with him. Each asked different questions within the same categories to get Luis to think about his reading and simultaneously create meaning with him.

Alvarez Family

The Alvarez family read a great deal at home. Mr. Alvarez had learned to read in Spanish in Mexico and spent two years in a high school in the United States, where he learned to read in English. Both parents in the Alvarez family had a history of reading with Mona, but Mrs. Alvarez admitted that she read less with the children than her husband. Mr. Alvarez had been very involved in the parent group, COPLA. He attended meetings regularly and was very vocal about parents assuming responsibility for their children's success in schooling. The reading sessions reflect the systematic work that the Alvarezes did with their children.

In the first reading session prior to the intervention, Mr. Alvarez did not pose any questions to Mona when she read, except to ask if she liked what she read. She answered, "Sí". When Mrs. Alvarez read with Mona, a few parent-child interactions were noted; most of them were descriptive questions to which Mona gave factual answers about the story. A couple of times Mrs. Alvarez told Mona to talk to her about what she had read and Mona recounted the story.

Mrs. Alvarez read to Mona and asked her a few questions; then Mona read to her mother and asked her questions. The book they read was *El Primer Pájaro de Piko Niko*. As her mother read, Mona asked questions such as, "¿Qué es floresta?" (What is a grove?), to which her mother replied, "Como un tipo de selva florestal" (Like a type of dense jungle). "¿Qué apareció en el cielo?" (What appeared in the sky?) "Un pajarito" (A bird).

The two reversed roles and Mona read the book while her mother asked questions, "¿Por qué no le salía la voz, mi hija?"

(Why didn't he have a voice, dear?) "Porque estaba muy espantado" (Because he was very shocked). "¿Como tú por ejemplo, si te encontraras en un lugar oscuro te iba a salir la voz, si te dijeran, entra ahí?" (Like you for example, if you found yourself in a dark place wouldn't you lose your voice, if someone told you, enter there?)

In the third session, Mr. Alvarez allowed Mona to read the entire book, *Historia de los Bonobos,* and he posed the questions after she finished reading the story. He asked a variety of questions within the framework of questions we suggested—some descriptive, others more personal.

"¿Y los bonobos, qué era lo que hacían?" "Ellos nomás comían y parloteaban." "¿Si alguien te hiciera mucho ruido en tu casa donde tú vivieras te enfadarías también?" "Sí." (And what did the monkeys do?) (They just ate and talked without stopping.) (If someone made too much noise in your home where you lived would you become fed-up too?) (Yes.)

Mr. Alvarez tried to engage Mona to talk about her feelings about someone invading her territory. Framed as a yes-no question, Mona found it easy to respond with one word. Mrs. Alvarez succeeded in inviting more reflection in subsequent questions, as in the illustration that follows. Mona read the book *Mira Como Salen las Estrellas* to her mother, and Mrs. Alvarez interacted with her daughter to induce her to recall her personal experience.

"Como cuando nosotros fuimos a Mexico. ¿Te acuerdas cuando tú estabas más chiquita, que fuimos para allá y tu papá no fué? Estabas feliz con tus tías y tus primos, ¿verdad? ¿Pero lo extrañabas a él?" "Sí." "¿Y cuando volvimos qué sentiste?" "Contenta." "¿Y le diste un abrazo?" "Ya no me acuerdo." (Like when we went to Mexico, do you remember? When you were younger, we went over there and your father didn't go? You were happy with your aunts and cousins, right? But, you missed him?) (Yes.) (And how did you feel?) (Happy.) (And did you give him a hug?) (I don't remember.)

The Alvarezes exemplified a family who read regularly together and demonstrated the importance of relating text to personal opinions and experiences in their lives. The mother encouraged Mona to think about her feelings about her father's absence, prompting her experience of being distant from her father.

The three families discussed here varied in their development in the sense that they entered the project at various points on the continuum of empowerment from changes in self-perception to community action. Regarding the questioning strategies, for example, the families generally stayed within the descriptive phase of questioning when reading, but they gradually ventured into framing a more elaborate discussion about the text. As parents read more with their children and became more experienced, they developed a more expanded repertoire of questions. Further, we observed a strong bond developing within the families as they shared a special time and space. Parents also increased their confidence in dealing with the schools because they had become more experienced in academic tasks, as was revealed in the follow-up interview with the families a year after the family literacy classes ended. They also developed networks with other parents in the family literacy classes and were encouraged to become more involved in the COPLA organization to continue their learning about their children's schoolwork. Parents who were active in COPLA made it a point to contact families who were enrolled in literacy classes.

Parent Classes

The format of the literacy classes was designed purposely not only to encourage parents to practice cognitive skills but also to provide them with a setting that invited discussion about their perceptions, emotions, fears, and concerns, and with a place where they could link with others who shared their experience in learning literacy in a new culture. The literacy classes began with an introduction about the beauty of stories. The trainer/researchers and the community member/trainer talked to the families about the importance of reading in the home and the parents' role in that activity. Conditions for participation in Family Literacy Project were discussed with particular emphasis on the following:

1. The parents should meet regularly with researchers and other parents, including a community leader, to share and discuss storybooks they would read to their children at home

2. Both parents (where possible) should attend the monthly classes and read to their children nightly

3. A quiet time should be allotted daily to read with the child and discuss the story by asking the child appropriate questions

4. Television time should be minimized and substituted with reading activity

5. Monthly reports should be submitted by the families on the books read by the children during the month

6. Families should be available for an interview and videorecording on alternate months during the course of the project

Agreements between the parents and researchers were necessary to establish continuity for the Family Literacy Project. In addition to the parents' role, the researchers were required to provide specific things to the families during the course of the project:

1. Each family would receive one storybook per month

2. Childcare would be provided at every class meeting

3. Home visits would be made on alternate months of the scheduled project at the parents' convenience

4. A nominal monetary compensation would be allocated to each family for their participation in the project

Structure and content were particularly significant in the literacy classes. The format was designed to involve parents. It was intended to facilitate the presentation of text content, which, for the most part, was in the form of a discussion using a variety of questioning strategies.

Parents welcomed the opportunity to participate in the literacy classes although some were rather reticent at first because of their own limited literacy skills. The class format accommodated the variation of literacy skills among the adults. Those parents who opted not to read because they felt embarrassed or because they lacked the skills were allowed to refrain from reading in the small groups. As the classes progressed, however, those parents who initially would not read at all were encouraged to read along with other parents in choral reading. In one case, the couple's older son sat in the classes and read the book to the parents so that they were able to follow along with the group. By the last class, parents who initially did not want to read aloud in the small group sessions were observed reading aloud, even though some read very slowly. They also were encouraged to participate more in the group discussions about the themes of the stories and to share their personal experiences to illustrate. Parents left their children at childcare in a nearby room while they attended class in the library.

At the beginning of the class, I welcomed the parents and we talked informally about general issues of urgency to them such as the possible difficulty in dealing with their children's schoolwork or meeting with the teacher. This was usually an opportunity for the parents who were active in the COPLA parent organization to invite others to participate and to learn about getting involved in the schools and helping their children that in this manner.

Following the opening discussion, Mrs. Reyes, the experienced parent, read the new story to the group as they listened and responded to her questions. When Mrs. Reyes completed the story the parents separated into three small groups led by herself and two researchers.

In the groups, parents took turns reading the story that had been read to them and asked questions of each other. At least four of the parents had approached this entire task rather reluctantly because they considered themselves nonreaders. During earlier classes they were allowed to skip their turn to read, but gradually they were encouraged to read aloud with the entire group. In this way they could follow the text as they read aloud with the group. These parents were also encouraged to listen to others read and pose questions about the content; this led to group discussions about the theme of the book. Thus, by the third meeting at least two of the parents who initially claimed to be nonreaders were actually participating in the discussion with the other parents.

As presented to the parents, the questioning strategies— descriptive, personal, critical, and creative—lent a framework to generate discussion. Initially, the questioning strategies were described to the parents as four types of questions to ask children during a reading activity. We soon realized the mistake of describing the strategies as labelled categories. Parents were quite capable of generating questions about the story on their own, and in fact, their questions fit well into the four categories we presented. Yet, when they saw the white sheets of paper with the four types, upon which they were to write their own questions, they became confused as to this competence. The error was in imposing an artificial structure on the process of organizing their thoughts about the texts so that they lost confidence and spontaneity in the discussion.

For the duration of the project, the seven months that followed, some time in class was spent undoing that mistake. When parents asked questions in their small groups, they usually prefaced it by commenting, for instance, "No sé que tipo de pregunta es ésta, pero, ¿Qué hacían los bonobos en los árboles?" (I don't know what type of question this is but, what did the monkeys do in the trees?) Eventually, the confusion of what the abstract categories meant dissipated, or so we thought. On the last interview with families in their homes, two parents, one of them Mrs. Alvarez, mentioned to me that they were so grateful for what they had learned in their classes, but one thing concerned her: "Yo nunca pude aprender los cuatro tipos de preguntas. Eso siempre me confundía." (I never could learn the four types of questions. That always confused me.) Of course, I assured them that the labels were not important since they had actually accomplished a great deal in the way they interacted with their children about the stories.

How did parents learn ways to discuss the book with their children? Parents learned through modeling, group discussion, and actual practice, which allowed them to define what ideas they had about the story and through open discussion. Parents approached each book from their experience, which shaped the discussion. At the beginning of each class, Mrs. Reyes modeled the reading activity and she posed questions to them as a group, just as they would read with their children at home. The research team reinforced the practice in the small-group sessions.

By the sixth session, the parents who had become integrated into the reading process had begun to read text in the small groups. Mr. Samora claimed not to be able to read and when we visited their home, he always let Mrs. Samora read with their son. In class, he learned to quietly ask a question or two during group discussion. By the sixth class, Mr. Samora actually read a page from the text with his wife's assistance, as she read along with him. In the small-group sessions of the last class, Mr. Samora read a page by himself without his wife's assistance, and in the last video session recorded in their home, he read with his son and asked him questions. His wife, overburdened by her solitary role as Augusto's tutor, was grateful for Mr. Samora's assistance. In the project, she learned that her husband, too, had developed new skills. Before the project, Mr. Samora expressed discomfort about reading because he had only completed the first grade in Mexico. In the process of learning cognitive skills in reading, parents also learned to express feelings about their relationship to literacy and to redefine it.

Parent-Community Interaction

Mrs. Reyes played a key role not only as a project trainer but also as a cultural broker between the COPLA parent group and this group of parents who had been less involved in the schools. After the first phase of the classes terminated, the School District Migrant Programs sponsored a one-day conference for Spanish-speaking families. The organizers asked the COPLA organization to participate, and Mrs. Reyes volunteered to work with Mrs. Mata, the childcare provider for the Family Literacy Project, to present a workshop on literacy for other Spanish-speaking parents in the larger community. The conference sessions were videotaped and the two parents used them to evaluate their performance. The teacher, Mrs. Reyes, and Mrs. Mata held two two-hour workshops. They had about twenty participants (both men and women) in each session and they used the same format of reading and discussing as was done in the Family Literacy Project. Mrs. Reyes read the story of *Rosa Caramelo:*

> A herd of elephants discriminated against the female elephants by making them dress in pink frilly collars and pink booties. The only different one in the bunch was a grey elephant that was quite unhappy because she could not do a lot of the things that the male elephants did until one day she broke out of the fenced area where the female elephants were restricted. The other female elephants liked what they saw and joined the grey elephant. (Translated from Spanish).

This gender theme was of particular interest to the parents. Mrs. Reyes read the story and posed questions to the group in the familiar way she had done in the literacy class. The parents separated into two smaller groups, where they engaged in a discussion about the unfair treatment of the female elephants. In one group, for example, this position was countered with arguments that girls should be protected and if given too much freedom they might get into trouble. This seemed to sway the conversation to the need to protect all children because of drugs and other evils "allá en el mundo" (out there in the world). Following their half-hour discussion, parents returned to the large group and Mrs. Mata and Mrs.

Reyes guided the discussion, inviting both groups of parents to share ideas that emerged about the book.

Another level of extended community awareness that resulted from the Family Literacy Project was the increased networking of parents with the COPLA organization. When the literacy classes began, only Mr. Alvarez, Mrs. Mata, and Mrs. Reyes were active. The classes became a focal area for recruitment for COPLA because the parents saw the importance of linking what they were learning with the rest of the Spanish-speaking community. They believed that by working together to transmit this type of knowledge to others, they could all better assist their children, and COPLA was the vehicle by which they could unite and share this knowledge. Mr. Alvarez usually announced forthcoming activities for the local COPLA meetings. The increase in participation in monthly meetings became evident about five months after the literacy project began. The attendance was more consistent than it had ever been once parents from the literacy class began attending. This meant the end of organizational difficulties in the school, but it also indicated the need for the school to reach out to parents in a way that is meaningful to them. Furthermore, it showed the influence of forming parent networks for the purpose of sharing knowledge and skills to find ways to help their children both at home and at school.

A year after the literacy classes ended, one of the parents gave testimony to the importance of using parental classes as linkages to other parent organizations. Mr. Quinta attended a district-wide meeting of the COPLA organization where he spoke to the issue:

> Yo he visto que es muy necesario que uno como padre de familia tome interés en la escuela de sus hijos. Nosotros (yo y mi esposa) participamos en el proyecto de lectura para la familia y hemos visto que nuestro hijo se ha desarrollado mucho y yo creo que es porque nosotros tenemos más interés en su lectura y él sabe que nos importa. También hemos aprendido mucho en las juntas de COPLA sobre los derechos que tienen los padres en las escuelas. Y, pues, yo estoy muy agradecido del apoyo que nos han dado todos.

> (I have learned that it is very necessary that parents take an interest in their children's schooling. We (me and my wife) participated in the Main School Family School Project and we have seen our son develop so much and it's because we have taken

more of an interest in his reading and he knows that it is important to us. We have also learned a great deal from the COPLA
meetings about the rights that parents have in the schools. I, for
one, am very appreciative of everyone's support).

Much was learned about empowerment in this study by observing how parents and children drew meanings from reading
together and how they shared and related their experiences to the
texts. As we learned more about empowerment by the families vis-
à-vis the schools and the community, the families in the study
increased awareness of their identity as community members who
shared a common cultural base. Sharing this cultural heritage, as
they read the books with their children, provided parents with
support and confidence. On another level, the empowerment families obtained in this process encouraged them to teach other parents. In a real sense, then, the project had a networking effect and
strengthened the empowerment of the group as well as individuals.

Conclusion

Literacy in the Carpinteria project was much more than interpreting text from a book and relating it to the individual's experience.
Embedded in a social process, literacy transforms people's organization in the home as a result of the new ideas and practices
acquired. Parents and children may have been engaged in a direct
question-and-answer interaction about the storybook text, but
what they shared was more; they shared values and opinions about
the importance of the family, identity with a group, emotional
support, and freedom. This sociocultural knowledge was transmitted and reconstructed in their literacy classes.

Increased awareness among parents was evidenced by a positive change in their self-perception and efficacy in being able to
participate directly in their children's literacy learning. In the cases
where reading with their children was not a common activity, parents accepted changes in their family organization to accommo-
date the new behavior. Through classes they established new relationships with other members of their cultural group and shared
common concerns, fears, and successes as they learned from one
another. Part of the families' overall development was evident as
they reached out to other members of the community by teaching
what they learned in the literacy project and by becoming involved

in COPLA activities. Although the project was designed to deal only with family literacy within the home, the ramifications extended beyond the household. Families became empowered on numerous levels beyond the home reading activity as parents became knowledgeable about the importance of encouraging literacy in the home, learning collectively with other community members, and becoming more involved in their children's education through an established parent group.

REFERENCES

Ada, A.F. (1988). The Pajaro Valley experience: Working with Spanish-speaking parents to develop children's reading and writing skills in the home through the use of children's literature. In T. Skutnabb-Kangas & J. Cummins (Eds.), *Minority education: From shame to struggle* (pp. 224–238). Philadelphia: Multilingual Matters.

Allen, J., Barr, D., Cochran, M., Dean, C. & Green, J. (1989). Empowerment process. Empowerment Project, College of Human Ecology, Cornell University. Unpublished manuscript.

Auerbach, E. (1989). Toward a social-contextual approach to family literacy. *Harvard Educational Review, 59,* 165–181.

Clark, M. (1984). Literacy at home and at school: Insights from a study of young fluent readers. In H. Goelman, A. Oberg & F. Smith (Eds.), *Awakening to literacy* (pp. 38–50). Portsmouth, NH: Heinemann.

Cochran, M. (1988). Between cause and effect: The ecology of program impacts. In A.R. Pence (Ed.), *Ecological research with children and families* (pp. 143–169). New York: Teachers College Press.

Cook-Gumperz, J. (Ed.). (1986). *The social construction of literacy.* Cambridge: Cambridge University Press.

Delgado-Gaitan, C. (1990). *Literacy for empowerment: The role of parents in children's education.* London: Falmer Press.

Delgado-Gaitan, C. & Trueba, H. (1991). *Crossing cultural borders: Education for immigrant families in America.* London: Falmer Press.

Freire, P. (1970). *Pedagogy of the oppressed.* New York: Seabury Press.

Freire, P. & Macedo, D. (1987). *Literacy: Reading the word and the world.* South Hadley, MA: Bergin and Garvey.

Goldenberg, C.N. (1987). Low-income Hispanic parents' contributions to their first-grade children's word recognition skills. *Anthropology and Education Quarterly, 18,* 149–79.

Green, J.L., Wade, R. & Graham, K. (1988). Lesson construction and student participation: A sociolinguistic analysis. In J.L. Green & J.O.

Harker (Eds.), *Multiple perspective analyses of classroom discourse* (pp. 11–48). Norwood, NJ: Ablex.

Heath, S.B. (1982). Questioning at home and at school: A comparative study. In G. Spindler (Ed.), *Doing the ethnography of schooling: Educational anthropology in action* (pp. 102–131). New York: Holt, Rinehart & Winston.

————. (1983). *Ways with words*. New York: Cambridge University Press.

Leichter, H.J. (1984). Families as environments for literacy. In H. Goelman, A. Oberg & F. Smith (Eds.), *Awakening to literacy* (pp. 38–50). Portsmouth, NH: Heinemann.

Moll, L. & Diaz, S. (1987). Change as the goal of educational research. *Anthropology and Education Quarterly, 18,* 300–311.

Schieffelin, B. & Cochran-Smith, M. (1984). Learning to read culturally: Literacy before schooling. In H. Goelman, A. Oberg, & F. Smith (Eds.), *Awakening to literacy* (pp. 3–23). Portsmouth, NH: Heinemann.

Seppanen, P.S. (1988). Community education as a home for family support and education programs. Research Report, Harvard Family Research Project. Harvard University.

Street, B. (1984). *Literacy in theory and practice*. Cambridge: Cambridge University Press.

Taylor, D. (1983). *Family literacy: Young children learning to read and write*. Exeter, NH: Heinemann.

Trueba, H.T. (1984). The forms, functions and values of literacy: Reading for survival in a barrio as a student. *NABE Journal, 9,* 21–40.

Wells, G. (1986). The language experience of five-year-old children at home and at school. In J. Cook-Gumperz (Ed.), *The social construction of literacy* (pp. 69–93). New York: Cambridge University Press.

CHAPTER 6

"Not Joined In": The Social Context of English Literacy Development for Hispanic Youth

Virginia Vogel Zanger

Although learning to read and write in another language is an individual accomplishment, it takes place within a social and political context. Furthermore, the act of acquiring literacy has social and political consequences that go beyond the individual. In recent years, scholars have argued persuasively that literacy cannot be divorced from specific sociopolitical contexts, in the same way that that pedagogy cannot be separated from ideology (Bennett, 1983; Ferdman, 1990; Freire, 1968; Giroux, 1983; Macedo, 1983; Roth, 1984; Trueba, 1987).

Data from international studies (Cummins, 1989) show a clear link between the economic and social status of minority groups and the academic achievement of students from those groups. The question of just how schools manage to reproduce the social stratification of groups within the larger society is one with important implications for educational practice. Efforts to promote English literacy development, for example, must be based on a clear under-

Portions of the data and analysis presented here are discussed in the author's chapter "Academic Costs of Social Marginalization: An Analysis of Latino Students' Perceptions at a Boston High School," which appears in R. Rivera & S. Nieto (Eds.), *The Education of Latino Students in Massachusetts: Issues, Research and Policy Implications,* Amherst: UMass Press, 1993. Videotapes from which the data for this study were transcribed were subsequently edited into a commercially distributed video *'How We Feel': Hispanic Students Speak Out* (1990), available from Landmark Films, Falls Church, VA.

standing of the ways in which social conditions in which learning takes place either promote or hinder that development for linguistic-minority students.

In this chapter, I will present and discuss qualitative data from a study that explored the social context of English literacy development for a group of Hispanic high-school students.[1] Focusing on the perspectives of the students themselves, three themes that emerged from the data are analysed and discussed: marginalization, cultural respect, and student–teacher trust. The final section highlights implications of the analysis for school restructuring efforts.

THEORETICAL FRAMEWORK:
A SOCIAL VIEW OF LEARNING

Moll and Diaz (1987) propose that to understand literacy development within linguistic-minority communities it is necessary to grasp the dynamics of the social organization of schooling at the level of the school. Trueba (1989) also recommends "context-specific" investigations at the micro level for gaining a more precise understanding of the dynamics of academic success for linguistic-minority students. Within this context-specific approach, he recommends using a neo-Vygotskian framework that conceptualizes learning as a socially constructed phenomenon. Vygotsky (1978) proposed that central to cognitive development is the cooperation between children and their teachers—or peers who function as teachers. From this perspective, student failure may be seen as a failure of the social system to provide linguistic-minority students with the appropriate social interactions necessary for literacy development. The neo-Vygotskian framework, by focusing on the interpersonal elements of learning, allows us to see the link between individual cognitive processes and the broader sociopolitical structure.

Vygotsky theorized that, contrary to the tenets of behavioral psychology that have shaped much of American educational research, animals and humans learn in profoundly different ways because of the social nature of human beings. Human learning is a profoundly interactive phenomenon according to Vygotsky. Internal cognitive development, he argued, is triggered "when the child is interacting with people in his environment and in cooperation with his peers" (1978:90). Intellectual guidance provided by a teacher or peers and an environment conducive to mental risk-taking are necessary conditions for learning within a Vygotskian framework. The framework has been used to help explain how the sociopolitical context of an educational environment produces academic success (Abi-Nader, 1990) and failure (Trueba, 1989) for language-minority students. It will be used to help interpret the data.

In the following section I present data on the perceptions of Hispanic high-school students about aspects of the social organization of their school, specifically the relationships between Hispanic students and their non-Hispanic peers and teachers. While the data do not focus directly on literacy, they illuminate some of the social, cultural, and psychological conditions that may profoundly shape English literacy development for these linguistic-minority students.

THE STUDY: AN EXERCISE IN ACTION RESEARCH

The data were collected as part of a larger action research project in which Hispanic students were asked to help non-Hispanic teachers in their school gain a better understanding of their needs (Zanger, 1989). The objective of the larger project was to enhance the effectiveness of monolingual program teachers. A class of Spanish-speaking students was selected to prepare a panel presentation for the teachers on their educational experiences and needs as Hispanics. Their teacher was an Anglo whose exceptional ability to motivate his Hispanic students was profiled in an ethnographic study by Abi-Nader (1990). He saw the panel presentation as an opportunity to develop critical thinking skills among his students through discussion, reflection, and writing. The panel presentation, as well as the preparatory class discussions, were videotaped and subjected to thematic analysis following procedures described in Bogdan and Taylor (1975) and Spradley (1979).

After transcription, the data were analyzed according to the themes mentioned by the students. The following broad categories were identified, based on the themes that emerged: language issues, teacher expectations, support, stigmatization, intercultural understanding, peer relations, curriculum, and mutual exchange. After the data were sorted into these categories, a broader lens was used to refocus them into the three final categories: marginalization, cultural respect, and breakdown in student–teacher trust emerged as key themes. Students' language was then analysed for imagery relating to their marginalized position within the school. This discourse analysis yielded three further themes: exclusion, subjugation, and invisibility. These will be presented and explored in the next section.

The students who participated in the study were eleventh and twelfth graders attending a neighborhood high school in Boston. The student body at the school was 40 percent Hispanic, 40 percent African-American, and 20 percent White. The headmaster and assistant headmaster at the school were African-American; the majority of the teachers were White. A large bilingual program was staffed by Hispanic and White teachers, but there were no Hispanic teachers in the monolingual program.

One-third of the students who participated in the videotaped discussions and panel presentations were Puerto Rican, one-third were Dominican, and the rest were Central and South American. Many were enrolled in the school's transitional bilingual education program. Of those who were not, some had been bilingual program students in previous years, while others had been educated exclusively in the monolingual program. While some students had been born in the United States to Puerto Rican or Dominican parents, others had immigrated from Latin America as recently as three years prior to the time that this study took place. While all the students were fluent in English and in Spanish, some were clearly Spanish dominant while others were English dominant. Students fell into both categories of linguistic-minority literacy students identified by Weber (1991): those who had become literate in their native language as children and acquired English literacy later on, and those who first learned to read in English, along with their English-speaking peers. It is not known how many of the English-dominant students were literate in Spanish. One of the most articulate and outspoken students, Elsa, had been raised in the United States, but had gone to study in her parents' native Dominican Republic for a time because, she said, she wanted the experience of feeling like one of the majority, rather than being a minority. All the discussions that were transcribed took place in English because their audience of teachers were monolingual English-speakers. Despite these variations in the students' linguistic, national, and educational backgrounds, all shared a commitment to finishing high school and going on to college. Their academic success and motivation had been a prerequisite for admission to the college skills class for bilingual students in which the videotaping took place.

To generate students' insights into the social dynamics of their schooling experience, they were asked to reflect upon and respond in writing to a series of questions about their experience as Hispanics in schools. The next day, in class, these reflections served as the basis of a discussion in which students were asked to address the reasons for the high drop-out rate of Spanish-speaking students at the school and to recommend ways to make the school better for students from Spanish-speaking backgrounds. The students understood that their reflections and discussions would have an actual impact on the attitudes and practices of teachers in their school as a result of the panel presentation to teachers.

HISPANIC STUDENTS' PERSPECTIVES: ANALYSIS AND DISCUSSION

In this section, data will be presented that describe the perspectives of this group of Hispanic students on the sociocultural context of their schooling experiences. The three themes which emerge from the data are marginalization, cultural respect, and breakdown in student–teacher trust. As each theme is elaborated, its implication for literacy development is discussed in the context of relevant educational research.

Marginalization

In their accounts of their experiences as Hispanics in North American schools, these students describe what it feels like to exist on the social and academic periphery of the school. This is stated most succinctly by a Central American girl who says, "Just because we're Hispanics, we're left out." This impression is echoed in the imagery chosen by her classmates to describe their experiences. One set of images revolves around students' exclusion from the group by teachers and by their non-Hispanic peers. A second set of images describes their perceptions of being relegated to an inferior status in the school's social hierarchy. And a third group of images projects their sense of being ignored, of feeling almost invisible.

Students convey their isolation and sense of exclusion with phrases like "not joined in" and "pushed out," an image that occurs four separate times. Sandra, a Dominican girl, describes the pressure from African American peers to assimilate or face rejection:

> They won't accept you if you're not like them. They want to monoculture [you]. If you don't do that, they just take you out of the group. Put you out.

Teachers, too, are perceived as contributing to the students' sense of being excluded, for they are described as "pushing" students "right to the side," "right from outta the class," and "out to the edge."

Another distinct group of images depicts the position of low status to which students feel themselves relegated. Here is Sandra's analysis of the hierarchical relations at the school:

> They [the other students] think that we're much, much under them. They want to step on us. And it shouldn't be like that. That's why some of students drop out of school, because they feel under them.

Prepositions that students select to describe their position in the school are "below," "under," "low," and "down." According to the Hispanic students, both "Black" and "American" [presumably Americans of European ancestry] students rank higher in the school's hierarchy.

Students' accounts of their low status in the school also reveal a sense of stigmatization for their Hispanic backgrounds and Spanish language, for their English skills, even for their accents. One Guatemalan boy describes his experiences as a new student this way:

> They [monolingual peers] use you as a joke. When you come in, and they hear you're Hispanic, the Black kids and Americans they start making fun of you. They don't like the way you dress, cause if you're not wearing Adidas, you're not joined in, that's what they say. And some people can't take it. Some of them can't take that people laughing at them, but some of us have the guts to keep going.

A Guatemalan girl tells of a recent "terrible experience" that made her furious, when a classmate told her, "You talk so funny, you have a funny accent."

Some students also recount interactions with teachers who seem to be just as contemptuous of them as the most racist of their peers are. It is the Puerto Rican students who seem to have encountered the worst instances of racism on the part of teachers. One accuses her teachers of "treat[ing] us just like cats and dogs." A Puerto Rican boy describes his shock when a teacher called him a "spic" in class (he adds that the teacher was later suspended). And Alicia, an outspoken Puerto Rican girl, tells of her teacher's penchant for asking only White students to watch her purse for her, rejecting Alicia's offers to help. Alicia concludes: "They [teachers] think that just because you don't have blond hair and blue eyes you're not honest."

A third set of images reflects the ways in which students feel ignored, which further reinforces their position on the periphery. These images highlight the social distance which seems to separate them from non-Hispanic classmates and teachers. In the minds of these Hispanic students, this social distance is linked to the refusal of teachers and peers to acknowledge their cultural identity in a positive way. These students interpret the larger school community's failure to validate their Hispanic culture as a signal that they are not wanted in the school. Marla, a Bolivian girl, describes teachers as "looking away from us, they're saying 'Oh, they're Hispanics, they can't do as much as the other kids can do.' They're saying that we're not good enough." Ana, a Puerto Rican, echoes this feeling of abandonment by American teachers: "They don't try for us to learn anything . . . they just leave us." Another classmate accuses teachers of failing to challenge Hispanic students for fear of pushing them "over the edge."

Students' belief that teachers fail to "push" them, a perceived lack of support that is voiced over and over, is experienced emotionally by the students as neglect. And the consequences of neglect are spelled out by one student's description of what happens to many of her Spanish-speaking peers: "They just feel left out, they feel like if no one loves them, no one cares, so why should they care? No one wants to hear what they have to say, so they don't say anything."

According to the students, then, the social dynamics of the school result in the alienation, the silencing, and the decline in motivation found among many of their peers. Dropping out is yet another consequence, according to Ana:

> The reason why most Hispanics drop out of school is because
> we're very sentimental, we like people to think of us as human
> beings. . . . People say, "Well most Hispanics have attitude prob-
> lems." Some of us do—why? Because we've been kicked around
> too many times, and we feel that we need to speak out.

Unfortunately, these perceptions are not isolated instances of
the stigmatization that Hispanic students have been known to experience. Similar perceptions of stigmatization reported by
linguistic-minority adolescents in public high schools in the United
States appear in studies by Gibson (1987), Zanger (1987, 1989),
Hoffman (1988), the Massachusetts Advocacy Center (1990), and
The National Coalition of Advocates for Students (1988). The
latter study, which was the result of a national two-year research
project in United States public schools, reported "immigrant students in every part of the country facing harassment and intergroup tensions as part of their daily school experience" (60).

How does a climate of perceived racism, of being treated "like
cats and dogs" as one informant put it, influence the learning
process? One consequence, most clearly articulated by the students
in this study, is that many students simply leave school. One boy
quoted above explains the high dropout rate among Hispanics as
the result of not being able to "take" the ridicule to which they are
all subjected. Some of his classmates attribute feelings of being left
out as the reason that many Hispanics do not remain in school.
Language-minority students who leave school—more than 50 percent of the Hispanic students in the school system in which this
study was done—have few other opportunities to develop their
English literacy.

For those who do stay, what impact does the racist atmosphere
perceived by these students have on their learning? An intriguing
experimental study by Gougis (1986) suggests that a climate of
racism functions as an "environmental stressor," which reduces
motivation and interferes with cognitive processes. In an experiment with African-American subjects, those who were asked to
perform a task of memorization in a situation where they were
exposed to racial prejudice experienced more emotional stress,
spent less time studying, and were less successful in recalling the
assigned material than were a control group who were not exposed
to racial prejudice. Another study, which analyzed case studies of
Puerto Rican and Vietnamese adolescents' acculturation experi-

ences, also pointed to the adverse effects that a climate of racial hostility can have on learning (Zanger, 1987). Puerto Rican students in the study, who had spent more time in U.S. schools than the Vietnamese students, had internalized the negative messages of the school environment to some extent, and although they had achieved quite a high degree of English proficiency, their lowered expectations for themselves and decreased motivation had resulted in significant academic underachievement. The Vietnamese students reacted in a different way to the racial hostility, which they also experienced: they withdrew from contact with native English-speakers, which severely impaired their English language development; nonetheless, their academic motivation remained so high that they were able to compensate for their low English literacy skills enough to continue on a college-bound academic track.

This link between second-language learning and intergroup relations is the subject of a body of literature that has sought to develop a psychosocial model of second-language acquisition (Beebe & Zuengler, 1983; Gardner & Lambert, 1972; Giles & Coupland, 1991; Schumann, 1978). How well and how fast students learn a second language may depend significantly upon social factors such as intergroup relations (Schumann, 1978), ethnocentrism (Gardner & Lambert, 1972), and ethnic identity (Giles & Coupland, 1991). These studies clearly have important implications for linguistic-minority English literacy development; as Trueba (1989) argues: "The isolation of linguistic minorities has been highly instrumental in retaining low levels of literacy" (120). Our data indicate that isolation within the context of an exclusionary school setting is a factor that should not be overlooked.

Cultural Respect

Cultural pride is a strong current running throughout much of the data, and it is a desire to be accepted *for who and what they are* about which students are most adamant. Elsa's demand for respect from teachers and other students is predicated on their recognition of her cultural identity as a Dominican American: "You can't succeed in a place where no one respects you for what you are," she says.

One of the students' major grievances against their school is its failure to grant them cultural respect by incorporating Hispanic culture and history into the curriculum, despite the fact that four out of ten students at the school are of Hispanic origin. According to Marla,

> I would put some of the blame on the school system. Because they say they have programs for ethnic backgrounds, for multi-cultural communities, but that isn't really true, all the way. It's true to some extent, [but] they only focus on certain ethnics, besides Whites, but they don't really focus on ours. They ignore ours. They don't give us the respect that we deserve. They ignore our culture, our Hispanic culture.

Furthermore, several students assert that if teachers incorporated their cultures into the curriculum, it would help dispel some of the racist misconceptions of their classmates, and raise their status by legitimizing their ethnicity. Elsa calls for "put[ting] our culture into the curriculum, let it be enforced who we are, what we feel." Similarly, Alicia, a Puerto Rican student, says,

> I'd like to know more about my history, and stuff like that. Cause they teach us all about Benjamin Franklin, Jesse Jackson . . . Martin Luther King, and those things are interesting, but I'd like to know more about things that happened when I wasn't around, you know back where I come from. Cause there's not much that I know, cause ever since I came here . . . my ethnic background was like pushed away, and they don't want me to know, they just want me to be as American as apple pie.

The exclusion of her cultural background from the curriculum upsets Alicia, and she clearly wishes that the curriculum were more reflective of her culture. How does this theme of cultural respect/cultural exclusion affect her opportunities to develop English literacy, and those of her Hispanic peers? According to research studies cited by Cummins (1989), cultural and linguistic incorporation in the school curriculum is a significant predictor of academic success, measured most often by standardized tests of reading. Further discussion of this question may benefit from exploring it in the context of three theoretical constructs from the research literature: additive/subtractive orientations, resistance theory, and cultural capital.

Within a theoretical framework developed by Cummins (1989), schools' treatment of students' language and culture is one of four key areas that determine whether students from minority backgrounds emerge from schools academically empowered or academically disabled. Defining different approaches, or treatments, Cummins makes a useful distinction between linguistically and culturally "additive" versus "subtractive" orientations toward students who bring to school languages and cultures that differ from that of the dominant majority. The concepts are adapted from Lambert's (1975) observations about differences in learning a second language in a context of additive bilingualism, in which the expectation is that students will retain their mother tongue, and a subtractive bilingual context, in which students are pressured to give up their native language for their new language. The incorporation of minority students' language and culture into the school curriculum supports students by providing a culturally additive environment, rather than asking that they choose between their home culture and the school culture.

The data in this study suggest that the school is communicating to this group of students a strongly subtractive context, which they resent. One student coins a new phrase in condemning the school's attempts to "monoculture" her and her Hispanic peers. Students sense that their culture is under attack, that it will be lost if they do not "defend" it. Marla speaks passionately when she says, "See, they're [the schools are] taking away our heritage. They're saying if you're not what we are, then you're not *it*."

Students' outspoken defense of their culture does not mean that they do not want to learn English or adapt to the dominant American culture. Rather, they are adamant that this be done in an educational context that is additive rather than subtractive in nature, one that does not seek to supplant their language and culture with another. Elsa articulates this sophisticated and inspiring vision of additive bilingualism and biculturalism:

> I think we should try to learn English, but not lose our Spanish. They want us to learn English and lose our cultural backgrounds. And I think there's a way they can work up on our already [*sic*] culture. And build it to be strong and better than what they are and we are. Two things combined can be very good. I mean we take the Spanish culture and a little bit of the English culture, we can be great students, we can be great people, we can be great leaders of this country.

In this exhortation, Elsa not only outlines a framework for reorienting schools' approach to educating Hispanic students. She also challenges schools to view them as potential leaders. In challenging the deficit model, which ascribes to linguistic minorities the role of academically needy student, Elsa also reminds us what they have to offer. She tells teachers: "You can learn a lot from us and we can learn a lot from you. Try to learn from us, 'cause we can teach you a lot."

Other accounts of the schooling experiences of linguistic minorities have described the alienation that occurs in a culturally subtractive environment, where school is seen as presenting a choice between the culture and language of the dominant culture or of their own. Richard Rodriguez (1975), reflecting on his own experience as a Chicano student, concludes that his education meant not only a gradual dissolving of familial and class ties but also a change of racial identity. Trueba (1989) asserts that second-language development is contingent on some degree of acculturation into the second culture. And when acculturation is perceived to be such an either/or proposition, some students' reluctance to trade in their cultural identity will translate into negative attitudes toward English literacy. If English literacy is framed in such subtractive terms, it is obvious that many will see the price of academic success as simply too high to pay. Nearly half of the Hispanic classmates of the students we heard from above chose to drop out of the school, and according to some of those who have decided to stay, dropping out is a direct response to the school's assimilationist pressures.

While some linguistic-minority students may react to these pressures by leaving school, others may respond by mentally withdrawing. Recent research among younger linguistic-minority students who have been labelled learning disabled identifies withdrawal as the response by some students to the stress engendered by the cultural demands of the American school (Trueba, 1989; Jacobs, 1990). Some students try to cover up their withdrawal with behaviors that often allow them to "pass for" competent students, while others simply give up "when the rewards of trying [do] not compensate for the pain" (Trueba, 1989).

If withdrawal is one possible response to the failure of the school to incorporate students' language and culture, resistance is another. There is a growing body of literature linking Giroux's

(1983) theories of resistance to schooling to the experiences of linguistic and racial minorities in United States schools (Erickson, 1987). This framework suggests that "consistent patterns of refusal to learn can be seen as a form of resistance to a stigmatized ethnic or social class identity that is being assigned by the school" (Erickson:350). Matute-Bianchi (1986) identified the ways in which some Chicano students resist adopting cultural behaviors dictated by the school because to do so is seen as undermining their cultural identity: "They must choose between doing well in school or being a Chicano" (254). Ogbu and Matute-Bianchi (1986) postulate the development of a collective oppositional identity among castelike minorities, a way for minorities to protect themselves emotionally from the inequities of institutionalized racism. White working-class youth may also refuse to "enter the race" because they perceive that the achievement ideology of the dominant culture is a hoax (MacLeod, 1987). Walsh (1987, 1991) describes the struggles of Puerto Rican students to maintain their own voice in the face of the assimilationist demands of the school, a resistance manifested in their behavior and maintenance of Puerto Rican linguistic style and discourse forms. Student resistance is suggested in the data presented above in Alicia's discussion of Hispanic students' "attitude problems." In her remarks, she acknowledges the existence of her peers' negative attitudes toward school, the perception of those attitudes by the school authorities, and the justification of students' resistance as a legitimate response to being "kicked around too many times."

Student resistance is one dynamic in a complex process, which may be set into motion when schools impose cultural hegemony on minority students, insisting on cultural assimilation and submissive attitudes as a precondition for literacy development (Erickson, 1987). According to Gilmore's (1985) ethnographic work, access to literacy was denied to students whom the school perceived as having, in Alicia's words, "attitude problems." Gilmore details the ways in which fourth-, fifth-, and sixth-grade African-American students demonstrate resistance to the dominant culture through maintaining distinctive cultural and linguistic behaviors (e.g., stylized sulking and "doing steps") in defiance of school policy. The school used these culturally based behaviors to deny students access to programs that enhance literacy development. Social behaviors that demonstrated "alignment with if not allegiance to the school's ethos", (Gilmore:126) rather than cognitive levels, were used as the criteria to determine entrance to the higher tracks. Gilmore concludes:

> Thus, the underlying process involved seemed not to be the *acquisition of literacy*, implying a growing set of reading and writing skills. It appeared instead to be an exchange of appropriate attitudes for what can more accurately be described as an *admission to literacy*, a gatekeeping enterprise. (111)

In the data presented above, Elsa cannot understand why the school cannot build upon the students' "already culture." Social reproductionists theorize that one of the ways schools reproduce the stratification of the society along ethnic, class, and racial lines is through the validation of the "cultural capital" that middle-class White students bring to school and invalidation of the "cultural capital" of students from minority groups (Bourdieu, 1977). "Cultural capital" includes interactional styles, speech patterns, and life experiences. By incorporating the cultural capital of some into the content of the curriculum, schools give these students a head start. When others fail to see their cultural capital legitimized by the classroom, it puts them at a distinct disadvantage. The denial of access to a learning environment that is culturally congruent to the backgrounds of the students is highly political:

> Social/cultural control is tied directly to the structure of knowledge and symbols in schools and to the manner in which knowledge is presented in the schooling context. Schools, acting as agents for the culture, control the extent to which personal knowledge may enter into the public knowledge of school curriculum; they thus have a direct influence upon cultural continuity and change. (Roth, 1984:303)

Two studies of English literacy acquisition among second-language learners support the hypothesis that access to culturally familiar points of reference greatly enhance the process. Malik (1990) conducted a psycholinguistic analysis of the reading behavior of Iranian students at an American university. He selected two texts from the *Encyclopedia Britannica* dealing with Japanese and Iranian belief systems, respectively. Iranian students' reading comprehension and reading strategies such as predicting, confirming/correcting, and integrating were significantly enhanced when given the text that was culturally familiar, as compared to their performance when reading text about Japan. Malik cites the findings from other reading studies among both native and nonnative English speakers that have concluded that culturally familiar texts aid in reading comprehension, speed, and recall.

A more subtle dimension of literacy development in cross-cultural situations has been explored by Heath (1986) in her study of oral genres. Genres—such as stories, accounts, and recounts—exist among all linguistic communities; however, their frequency and the language associated with them vary cross-culturally. Discrepancies in sociolinguistic conventions may confuse both students and teachers unfamiliar with each other's genres. Heath cited the example of a Mexican-born child in her study: "In Mexico, he had been a reader; in his community he knew what stories were and he could tell them. In his new school setting, definitions of reader and storyteller do not include his ways of recognizing or telling stories" (174). These two studies point out the ways in which literacy development may be constrained by the schools' failure to take advantage of the cultural capital that linguistic minority students bring to school, the unwillingness of the school to build on what Elsa refers to as students' "already culture."

Student–Teacher Trust

A third theme to emerge from our data is the breakdown in the mutual trust between students and teachers. While the students differentiate between good and bad teachers, it is strikingly evident that in their experiences, many relationships with teachers show a clear erosion of trust and cooperation on both sides. According to the social learning theories of Vygotsky discussed earlier, this breakdown can have serious consequences for students' learning.

In earlier discussions of the first two themes—marginalization and cultural respect—some teachers are implicated. For example, students experience stigmatization by teachers as well as by their peers. This is recalled most painfully by a Puerto Rican boy who describes the time that a teacher

called me a spic right in the class. I didn't like that. Most of the
students didn't like that. I think they suspended the teacher for at
least a year. None of the teachers are supposed to say that to the
students.

And Alicia concludes bitterly that some teachers "think that just
because you don't have blond hair and blue eyes you're not honest. . . . And it really drives me up the wall."

Students also blame some of their teachers for creating a sense
of invisibility and exclusion. In Marla's view, teachers

have to welcome us before we can really respond. Cause right
now the teachers are looking away from us, they're saying, 'Oh,
they're Hispanics, they can't do as much as the other kids can
do.' They're saying that we're not good enough.

These examples and others cited earlier suggest that these Hispanic
students feel betrayed by what they see as the lack of caring, the
low expectations, and the blatant racism of some of their teachers.
Adding to their sense of betrayal is the perception that the adults in
the school have failed to use their positions of authority to dispel
the ignorant and racist misconceptions of the other students, a
failure that the Hispanic students see as an abdication of moral
responsibility.

The refusal of the school to incorporate students' language and
cultures, discussed earlier, also seems to weaken teacher-student
rapport. Elsa complains that "teachers don't learn from us, they
don't learn from anybody. They don't ask." According to the data,
ignorance of students' backgrounds contributes to the mutual
alienation of Hispanic students and their Anglo teachers. One Puerto Rican girl, for example, feels that teachers "should know
about our ethnic backgrounds before they start judging us." If they
did, she feels, teachers would "treat us the same as other people."

Another dimension of the theme is the students' expressed desire to establish more caring, supportive, even family-like relationships with teachers. One student discusses the costs:

I think that many Hispanic students are dropping out of school
because of support. You see, when we do something and we
don't understand, we need support from teachers.

Several students contrast the nature of teacher-student relations in
Latin American countries with those they find in the continental
United States, and they seem to yearn for relationships that are

more familiar, in both senses of the word. Elsa articulates a preference for the kind of support she had experienced in the Dominican Republic:

> [In the United States] we're playing a game in school, it's just them [teachers] and us. Teachers don't get together with us. And in our countries, teachers are part of the students, they're part of the body of the students. They're friends, families to the students. I think teachers should open up to us, and try to be our friends and our parents. And then everything will be much better.

Other research suggests that the experiences of these students are not unique. The educational anthropologist George Spindler (1974) has done extensive research on the unconscious bias that teachers tend to display toward students most like themselves. Further evidence was supplied in Ortiz's (1988) six-year study of ninety-seven classrooms, both bilingual and monolingual, containing Hispanic students. She found teachers repeatedly expressed negative attitudes toward Hispanic students' abilities, and when children proved them wrong, the teachers reacted with resentment and suspicion. In addition to negative comments, Ortiz documented teachers' avoidance of interaction and eye contact with Hispanic students, as well as a tendency to leave them out of classroom activities. An earlier study of four-hundred classrooms in the American Southwest by the U.S. Commission on Civil Rights (1973) found similar bias. Mexican American students were praised 36 percent less often, were 40 percent less likely to have their ideas developed, received positive responses from teachers 40 percent less often, and were asked questions 21 percent less frequently than were Anglos. Research on the impact of teacher expectations on student performance suggests the potentially disastrous academic consequences of such bias (Smey-Richman, 1989).

That some teachers are in fact racist seems indisputable. Some of the evidence cited by the students, such as a teacher's use of racial epithets, makes clear some of the reasons for Hispanic students' mistrust of Anglo teachers. Learning can be impaired when authority figures abuse students' trust, according to Erickson (1978):

> Learning what is deliberately taught can be seen as a form of political assent. . . . Assent to the exercise of authority involves

> trust that its exercise will be benign. This involves a leap of faith—trust in the legitimacy of the authority and in the good intentions of those exercising it, trust that one's own identity will be maintained positively in relation to the authority, and trust that one's own interests will be advanced by compliance with the exercise of authority. (344)

Apart from the question of teachers' "good intentions," there is another dimension that may explain some of the breakdown in student-teacher trust. Cultural differences may magnify students' problems with their teachers, particularly the cultural variations in role definitions and interactional styles. One of the students herself offers this possibility. Elsa contrasts the warm relations in the Dominican Republic, where teachers are "friends, families to the students," with the more impersonal style of American teachers:

> Here, the teachers are just "open the book, read from page 20 to page 30, answer the questions on page 35." They don't relate to us as much, they don't talk to us, they just shut us off.

She disagrees with her classmates' assertions that this is evidence of teachers' lack of interest in their Hispanic students, for she says: "Some people say it's because we're Spanish, and I don't think it's just Spanish. I think it's all the students." Elsewhere, she points out, "It's the stress that the teachers have in these schools, that everyone has, no one has time for anybody."

Other research that has explored the characteristics of relationships between Hispanic teachers and students corroborates the cross-cultural differences identified by Elsa. These relationships have been found to reflect the interdependent, nurturing, supportive values that characterize the extended family of the Spanish-speaking Caribbean (Nine Curt, 1984). Montero-Sieburth and Perez (1987) documented the personalistic, intimate tone of interactions between a Puerto Rican bilingual teacher and her adolescent students. Colon (1989) characterized the three central features of the student-teacher relationship in a Puerto Rican context as *respeto* (respect), *relajo* (relaxed kidding around), and *apoyo* (support). The data presented above suggest that Hispanic students feel let down by their Anglo teachers on all three dimensions. Furthermore, it is likely that the American cultural values of autonomy, self-motivation, and independence (Stewart, 1972), which contribute to a more impersonal approach to teaching, may result in behaviors that Hispanic students interpret as cold, unresponsive, and alienating.

Thus, one way of looking at the breakdown in trust between Hispanic students and their teachers is as a mismatch of expectations regarding the appropriate ways that teachers should act toward their students. This interpretation is congruent with ethnographic literature that has documented the cultural discontinuity between the homes of minority students and their school environments. Aspects of cultural mismatch that have been studied include values (Sindell, 1988), styles of learning (John, 1972), interaction (Kochman, 1981), discourse (Heath, 1983), motivation (Vogt, Jordan & Tharp, 1987), and methods of control (Ballenger, 1992). This research also points to the possibilities for turning around minority school failure by promoting pedagogical styles that are more culturally congruent with linguistic minorities' backgrounds. Several ethnographic studies have documented the ways in which effective teachers consciously guide their linguistic-minority students through the alienating cultural demands of the school (Abi-Nader, 1990; Macias, 1987; Montero-Sieburth & Perez, 1987). Anglo teachers can learn to use more effective, culturally congruent behaviors, according to Ballenger (1992). She documents her own experience of learning from Haitian coworkers how to adapt her [English] classroom language so as to be more culturally familiar in values and speech patterns to her Haitian students. Most encouraging, too, is the work of the Kamehameha Elementary Education Program (KEEP), which has trained Anglo teachers to teach reading to native Hawaiian students based on interactional styles and motivational systems that anthropologists observed in native Hawaiian families (Boggs, 1972; Vogt, Jordan & Tharp, 1987). The literacy implications of this project are particularly noteworthy, for KEEP was able to produce "significant gains in reading achievement levels for educationally at-risk Hawaiian children." (Vogt, Jordan & Tharp, 1987:278).

Such interventions hold much promise. It is unrealistic to expect Hispanic students such as those in our study to master English literacy in school environments that ignore cross-cultural differences in teaching and learning. As Trueba points out:

The literacy problems faced by LEP [limited English proficient] children are related to school personnel's inability to capitalize on children's different experiences, cultural knowledge, and values. (71)

SUMMARY AND CONCLUSIONS: RESTRUCTURING THE CONTEXT

The data presented and discussed here have illuminated three themes central to the experiences of the Hispanic students who participated in this study: their marginalized position in school, the lack of cultural respect shown by the school environment, and the breakdown in mutual trust with many teachers. The educational research literature that has been reviewed suggests some ways in which each of these factors may inhibit rather than promote the development of full English literacy. These findings imply that efforts to improve the English literacy skills of linguistic-minority students would benefit from restructuring the social, cultural, and psychological conditions identified as problematic by these students. Policy recommendations specific to each of the three themes follow.

Many of the complaints about their marginalized status voiced by the students fall within the realm known as "school climate." Traditionally, schools have tended to focus on improving intergroup relations only at times of crisis. The research presented here is consistent with other studies reviewed earlier, which suggest the importance of monitoring and improving race relations before they reach a boiling point. For, while not overtly hostile, negative intergroup dynamics in which linguistic-minority students participate may erode their academic achievement, contributing to drop-out rates, underachievement, and resistance to developing literacy skills in standard English. These findings suggest that effective prejudice reduction interventions such as those developed by Facing History and Ourselves (Strom & Parsons, 1982) must be adopted not just in the aftermath of crises. Multicultural education must be conceptualized to include antiracist education, as other researchers have advocated (Nieto, 1992; Sleeter, 1991). Alternatives to educational practices such as tracking, which have been found to have a particularly stigmatizing effect on minority students, should be encouraged (Wheelock, 1992). Instructional techniques can also play an important role in fostering intergroup harmony, and cooperative learning has been found to be particularly effective (Brubacher, Payne & Rickett, 1990; Cohen, 1986; Kagan, 1986).

The second area of concern raised by this study is the need to develop learning environments that incorporate students' home languages and cultures in respectful and meaningful ways. This means that attention must be paid to how bilingual programs are actually implemented, for the pressures on bilingual programs to use mostly English and to mainstream students into the English-only curriculum before they are ready may damage students' chances of acquiring full English literacy (Ramirez, 1991). The development of alternative bilingual program models such as integrated models and two-way programs, which raise the status of the native language, also show much promise in reducing the barriers that isolate linguistic-minority students from their peers (Brisk, 1991a; Genesee, 1987). Comprehensive multicultural educational programs that incorporate a multicultural perspective into every subject area and in which differences and similarities are an explicit part of the curriculum must be developed and implemented (Nieto, 1992). Pedagogical approaches such as whole language, which validate and allow students to build on their own experiences, should also be encouraged (Cummins, 1989). Many of these effective strategies are highlighted in the publications by California Tomorrow, which identify promising programs for the education of immigrant children (Olsen & Dowell, 1989).

The third theme that emerged in this study—the breakdown in trust between Hispanic students and some of their Anglo teachers—underscores the need to prepare and in many cases retrain teachers to be more effective with students who come from diverse backgrounds. Such training should include, in the words of one student, "how hard it is to learn another language and culture." The need for such training will be magnified by the demographic trends in American public schools, where it is predicted that one out of every three students will be from a minority background by the turn of the century (Banks, 1989). One promising development is the preparation of proposed professional standards for the preparation of bilingual/multicultural teachers (NABE, 1992). Efforts to retrain teachers have shown that changing behaviors toward minority students may be more difficult than anticipated (Sleeter, 1989). Training teachers to use pedagogical tech-niques that are culturally congruent with students' backgrounds, as demonstrated by KEEP in Hawaii (Vogt, Jordan & Tharp, 1987), hold much promise, however. Although that study is consis-tent with other research that indicates that teachers need not be from the same background as their students to be effective, it does not negate the importance of recruiting and retaining a far larger number of teachers and administrators who come from linguistic-minority backgrounds (Banks, 1989; Nieto, 1992).

In many states, increasing dissatisfaction with the public schools' success in producing students with the kind of academic skills, including English literacy, that will be demanded of workers in the next century has led to school reform initiatives of various kinds. Many of these "restructuring" efforts focus on solutions such as implementing more rigorous standards, increasing testing, and requiring greater teacher and administrator accountability for student performance. It is striking how few of the concerns voiced by the students in this study are addressed by the movement for school reform. If their perspectives are ignored, moves to increase the pressure to perform on standardized tests without first restruc-turing the learning environment may, in fact, be counterproduc-tive: more linguistic-minority students may be driven to drop out.

In contrast, researchers who have looked beyond test scores and used a qualitative approach to examine what is wrong with the schools, attempting to learn from the perspective of linguistic-minority students, have recommended that educational reform fo-cus on developing environments that foster high quality education (Nieto, 1992). Brisk (1991b) calls for moving toward the develop-ment of a school culture in which English-speaking and bilingual students see themselves as part of a bilingual, multicultural school-ing experience. The students in this study are very articulate about the need to restructure the mainstream, to transform it so that no one feels left out. With the creation of an inclusionary, multi-cultural learning environment, Elsa promises us, she and her peers "can be great students, we can be great people, we can be great leaders of this country." Let us not ignore her challenge.

NOTE

1. For consistency, the term "Hispanic" is used throughout this chapter because at the time when the study was conducted (1988), partic-

ipants used the term to identify themselves. Were they to be polled today, they might well prefer the term "Latino."

REFERENCES

Abi-Nader, J. (1990). A house for my mother: Motivating Hispanic high school students. *Anthropology and Education Quarterly, 21,* 41–58.

Ballenger, C. (1992). Because you like us: The language of control. *Harvard Educational Review, 62,* 199–208.

Banks, J. (1989). *Teacher education and ethnic minorities: Conceptualizing the problem.* Paper presented at the annual conference of the American Educational Research Association, San Francisco.

Beebe, L.M. & Zuengler, J. (1983). Accommodation theory: An explanation for style shifting in second language dialects. In N. Wolfson & E. Judd (Eds.), *Sociolinguistics and language acquisition* (pp. 195–213). Rowley, MA: Newbury House Publishers.

Bennett, A.T. (1983). Discourses of power, the dialectics of understanding, the power of literacy. *Journal of Education, 165,* 53–74.

Bogdan, R. & Taylor, S.J. (1975). *Introduction to qualitative research methods.* New York: John Wiley & Sons.

Boggs, S.T. (1972). The meaning of questions and narratives to Hawaiian children. In C. Cazden, V. John & D. Hymes (Eds.), *Functions of language in the classroom* (pp. 299–330). New York: Teachers College Press.

Brisk, M.E. (1991a). Toward multilingual and multicultural mainstream education. *Journal of Education, 2,* 114–139.

_____. (1991b). *The many voices of bilingual students in Massachusetts.* Quincy, MA: Massachusetts Department of Education.

Brubacher, M., Payne, R. & Rickett, K. (Eds.). (1990). *Perspectives on small group learning: Theory and practice.* Oakville, Ontario: Rubicon Publishing Inc.

Bourdieu, P. (1977). Cultural reproduction and social reproduction. In J. Karabel & J.H. Halsey (Eds.), *Power and ideology in education* (pp. 487–510). New York: Oxford University Press.

Clemant, R. (1980). Ethnicity, contact, and communicative competence in a second language. In H. Giles, W.P. Robinson & P.N. Smith (Eds.), *Language: Social psychological perspectives* (pp. 147–154). Oxford: Pergamon Press.

Cohen, E.G. (1986). *Designing groupwork: Strategies for the heterogeneous classroom.* New York: Teachers College Press.

Colon, N. (1989). *Understanding why Puerto Ricans drop out.* Keynote address delivered at "Abriendo Caminos" conference, Holy Cross College, Worcester, MA, sponsored by Hispanic Office of Planning and Evaluation.

Cummins, J. (1989). *Empowering minority students.* Sacramento: California Association for Bilingual Education.

Erickson, F. (1987). Transformation and school success: The politics and culture of educational achievement. *Anthropology and Education Quarterly, 18,* 335–356.

Ferdman, B.M. (1990). Literacy and cultural identity. *Harvard Educational Review, 60,* 181–204.

Freire, P. (1968). *Pedagogy of the oppressed.* New York: The Seabury Press.

Gardner, R. & Lambert, W. (1972). *Attitudes and motivation in second language learning.* Rowley, MA: Newbury House.

Genesee, F. (1987). *Learning through two languages.* Cambridge, MA: Newbury House Publishers.

Gibson, M.A. (1987). The school performance of immigrant minorities: A comparative view. *Anthropology and Education Quarterly, 18,* 262–275.

Giles, H. & Coupland, N. (1991). *Language: Contexts and consequences.* Pacific Grove, CA: Brooks/Cole Publishing Company.

Gilmore, P. (1985). 'Gimme room': School resistance, attitude, and access to literacy. *Journal of Education, 167,* 111–128.

Giroux, H.A. (1983). *Theory and resistance: A pedagogy for the opposition.* South Hadley, MA: Bergin & Garvey.

Gougis, R.A. (1986). The effects of prejudice and stress on the academic performance of Black-Americans. In U. Neisser (Ed.), *The school achievement of minority children.* Hillsdale, NJ: Lawrence Erlbaum Associates.

Heath, S.B. (1983). *Ways with words.* Cambridge, England: Cambridge University Press.

———. (1986). Sociocultural contexts of language development. In *Beyond language: Social and cultural factors in schooling language minority students* (pp. 143–186). Los Angeles: Office of Bilingual Education, California State Department of Education, Evaluation, Dissemination, and Assessment Center. [ERIC ED 304 241.]

Hoffman, D.M. (1988). Cross-cultural adaptation of learning: Iranians and Americans at school. In H.T. Trueba & C. Delgado-Gaitan (Eds.), *School and society: Learning content through culture.* New York: Praeger.

Jacobs, L. (1990). An ethnographic study of four Hmong students: Implications for educators and schools. In S. Goldberg (Ed.), *Readings on equal education: Critical issues for a new administration and Congress, Vol. 10.* New York: AMS Press.

John, V. (1972). Styles of learning–styles of teaching: Reflections on the education of Navajo children. In C. Cazden, V. John, & D. Hymes (Eds.), *Functions of language in the classroom* (pp. 331–343). New York: Teachers College Press.

Kagan, S. (1986). Cooperative learning and sociocultural factors in schooling. In *Beyond language: Social and cultural factors in schooling language minority students* (pp. 231–298). Los Angeles: Office of Bilingual Education, California State Department of Education, Evaluation, Dissemination, and Assessment Center. [ERIC ED 304 241.]

Kochman, T.C. (1981). *Black and White styles in conflict.* Chicago: University of Chicago Press.

Lambert, W. (1975). Culture and language as factors in learning and education. In A. Wolfgang (Ed.), *Education of immigrant students.* Toronto: O.I.S.E.

MacLeod, J. (1987). *Ain't no making it: Leveled aspirations in a low-income neighborhood.* Boulder, CO: Westview Press.

Macedo, D. (1983). The politics of emancipatory literacy in Cape Verde. *Journal of Education, 165,* 99–112.

Macias, J. (1987). The hidden curriculum of Papago teachers: American Indian strategies for mitigating cultural discontinuity in early schooling. In G. Spindler & L. Spindler (Eds.), *Interpretive ethnography of education: At home and abroad.* Hillsdale, NJ: Lawrence Erlbaum Associates.

Malik, A.M. (1990). A psycholinguistic analysis of the reading behavior of EFL-proficient readers using culturally familiar and culturally non-familiar expository texts. *American Educational Research Journal, 27,* 205–223.

Massachusetts Advocacy Center. (1990). *Locked in/locked out: Tracking and placement practices in Boston public schools.* Boston: Massachusetts Advocacy Center.

Matute-Bianchi, M.E. (1986). Ethnic identities and patterns of school success and failure among Mexican-descent and Japanese-American students in a California high school: An ethnographic analysis. *American Journal of Education, 95,* 233–255.

Moll, L.C. & Diaz, S. (1987). Change as the goal of educational research. *Anthropology and Education Quarterly, 18,* 300–311.

Montero-Sieburth, M. and Perez, M. (1987). *Echar pa'lante,* moving onward: The dilemmas and strategies of a bilingual teacher. *Anthropology and Education Quarterly, 18,* 180–189.

NABE (National Association for Bilingual Education). (1992). *Professional standards for the preparation of bilingual/multicultural teachers.* Washington, DC: NABE.

National Coalition of Advocates for Students. (1988). *New voices: Immigrant students in U.S. public schools.* Boston, MA: NCAS.

Nieto, S. (1992). *Affirming diversity: The sociopolitical context of multicultural education.* New York: Longman.

Nine Curt, C.J. (1984). *Nonverbal communication.* Fall River, MA: National Dissemination Center.

Oakes, J. (1985). *Keeping track: How schools structure inequality.* New Haven: Yale University Press.

Ogbu, J. & Matute-Bianchi, M.E. (1986). Understanding sociocultural factors: Knowledge, identity, and school adjustment. In *Beyond language: Social and cultural factors in schooling language minority students* (pp. 73–142). Los Angeles: Office of Bilingual Education, California State Department of Education, Evaluation, Dissemination, and Assessment Center.

Olsen, L. & Dowell, C. (1989). *Bridges: Promising programs for the education of immigrant children.* San Francisco: California Tomorrow Immigrant Students Project.

Ortiz, F.I. (1988). Hispanic-American children's experiences in classrooms: A comparison between Hispanic and non-Hispanic children. In L. Weis (Ed.), *Class, race, and gender in American education* (pp. 63–86). Albany: State University of New York Press.

Ramirez, J.D. (1991). *Final report: Longitudinal study of structured English immersion strategy, early-exit and late-exit transitional bilingual education programs for language-minority children.* (Contract No. 300-87-0156). Washington, DC: U.S. Department of Education, Office of Bilingual Education.

Rodriguez, R. (1975, February 8). Searching for roots in a changing world. *Saturday Review,* pp. 147–149.

Roth, R. (1984). Schooling, literacy acquisition and cultural transmission. *Journal of Education, 166,* 291–308.

Schumann, J.H. (1978). The pidginization hypothesis. In E. Hatch (Ed.), *Second language acquisition* (pp. 256–271). Rowley, MA: Newbury House.

Sindell, P.S. (1988). Some discontinuities in the enculturation of Mistassini Cree children. In J. Wurzel (Ed.), *Toward multiculturalism* (pp. 107–113). Yarmouth, ME: Intercultural Press, Inc.

Sleeter, C. (1989). *Multicultural education staff development: How much can it change classroom teaching?* Paper presented at the annual meeting of the American Educational Research Association, San Francisco.

_____. (1991). *Empowerment through multicultural education.* Albany: State University of New York Press.

Smey-Richman, B. (1989). *Teacher expectations and low-achieving students.* Philadelphia: Research for Better Schools.

Spindler, G.D. (1974). Beth Anne—A case study of culturally defined adjustment and teacher perceptions. In G.D. Spindler (Ed.), *Education and cultural process: Toward an anthropology of education.* New York: Holt, Rinehart & Winston.

Spradley, J. (1979). *The ethnographic interview.* New York: Holt, Rinehart and Winston.

Stewart, E.C. (1972). *American cultural patterns: A cross-cultural perspective.* Chicago: Intercultural Press.

Strom, M.S. & Parsons, W. (1982). *Facing history and ourselves: Holocaust and human behavior.* Watertown, MA: Intentional Education.

Trueba, H. (1987). Organizing classroom instruction in specific sociocultural contexts: Teaching Mexican youth to write in English. In S. Goldman & H. Trueba (Eds.), *Becoming literate in English as a second language.* Norwood, NJ: Ablex.

_____. (1988). *Raising silent voices: Educating the linguistic minorities for the 21st century.* New York: Newbury House Publishers/Harper & Row.

_____. (1989). *Empowerment and mainstreaming: Culture change and the integration of home and school values.* Paper presented at the annual meeting of the American Educational Research Association, San Francisco.

U.S. Commission on Civil Rights. (1973). *Teachers and students: Differences in teacher interaction with Mexican-American and Anglo students.* Washington, DC: U.S. Government Printing Office.

Vogt, L., Jordan, C. & Tharp, R. (1987). Explaining school failure, producing school success: Two cases. *Anthropology and Education Quarterly, 18,* 276–286.

Vygotsky, L.S. (1978). *Mind in society: The development of higher psychological processes.* M. Cole, V. John-Steiner, S. Scribner & E. Souberman (Eds.). Cambridge, MA: Harvard University Press.

Walsh, C.E. (1987). Language, meaning, and voice: Puerto Rican students' struggle for a speaking consciousness. *Language Arts, 64,* 196–206.

_____. (1991). *Pedagogy and the struggle for voice: Issues of language, power, and schooling for Puerto Ricans.* New York: Bergin & Garvey.

Weber, R. (1991). Linguistic diversity and reading in American society. In R. Barr, M.L. Kamil, P. Mosenthal & P.D. Pearson (Eds.), *Handbook of reading research, Vol. 2* (pp. 97–119). New York: Longman.

Wheelock, A. (1992). *Crossing the tracks.* New York: The New Press.

Zanger, V.V. (1987). *The social context of second language learning: An examination of barriers to integration in five case studies.* Unpublished doctoral dissertation, Boston University.

———. (1989). Chats in the teacher lounge are not enough: Preparing monolingual teachers for bilingual students. *Equity and Choice, 5,* 44–53.

———. (1991). Social and cultural dimension of the education of language minority students. In A.N. Ambert (Ed.), *Bilingual education and English as a second language: A research handbook 1988–1990* (pp. 3–54). New York: Garland Publishing, Inc.

CHAPTER 7

Literacy in the Loophole of Retreat: Harriet Jacobs's Nineteenth-Century Narrative

Barbara McCaskill

Moving between and beyond two worlds—one African, one American—is a subject that has riveted my fellow Black writers since they first sprang to their pens. Phillis Wheatley, Frederick Douglass, William and Ellen Craft, Maria Stewart, Sojourner Truth, David Walker, William Wells Brown—all are Blacks who had spoken in the decades before the Civil War of the twoness they experienced in a nation distant, hostile or indifferent, and strange. An encounter with one of my own writing students reminded me of these themes, and underscored the barriers that race and sex impose upon those whom we claim to be literate speakers and readers.

One hectic week while grading papers, shoveling snow, organizing lectures, fielding meetings, planning dinners, and reassuring my frazzled and woebegone cat, I missed my usual daily glances at the headlines. Then, during a tutorial, a student shared his reaction to the *Newsweek* that I had overlooked, an issue responding to the arrest of Marion Barry, then mayor of Washington, D.C. (Whita-

Much of the antebellum materials that I have cited were gathered from the antislavery Rare and Manuscript Collections of the Karl A. Kroch Library of Cornell University. I am grateful to the American Association of University Women Educational Foundation for a 1987–88 American Fellowship to research these materials for my doctoral dissertation. Also I most appreciate a Summer 1989 faculty assistance grant from the University at Albany, State University of New York, to continue this research.

199

ker, 1990). "Why This Isn't A 'Black Thing' " the bold-print head-lines ran: "Barry is a Victim of His Own Hubris, Not Racism."

"Why?" puzzled my student, White and male. Why were Blacks all over the nation raising their voices in angry response, picketing courthouses, phoning their mayors, accusing the detectives of sleight-of-hand entrapments and unjust, illegal lures? Why, as the *Newsweek* columnist himself had reported in direct and vivid terms, were hordes of Blacks "crying conspiracy" for one of their leaders? And why were we going to riot—again?

When my student showed me the article, I critiqued the reporter's language. A "crowd of supporters" had charged that Mayor Barry had been victimized and framed, but no one had counted the numbers of that "crowd"—hundreds, scores, singles, or twos—and no one had determined whether this so-called "crowd" had been solely Black people mustered to explain the definitive Black point of view. "[S]ome Blacks," the *Newsweek* writer had predicted, "will undoubtedly use the Barry case as an opportunity to vent some very real anger about some very real injustices." Again, I noted, the numbers were unclear. And the entire unclear statement, masqueraded as fact, merely speculated ("undoubtedly"), insinuated ("very real"), incited ("very real" for the second time), and stated no fact at all.

I sent the student back to the periodical racks to read the article again. And I wondered at how the periodicals themselves, the big-city dailies and the big-selling newsmagazines, have come to represent mainstream English literacy regardless of the double-talk inside them. How two readings had resulted in such different and contradicting interpretations! As a Black woman moving through a dominant culture not my own, I am always reading between the lines, inserting the unuttered phrase. And always I am writing—occasionally under the surface of what I say—what I really mean. For those of us who occupy two or more cultures, literacy presents to us opportunities to unpedestal authority and to call to attention the inadequacies of translation.

Incidents in the Life of a Slave Girl: Written By Herself announces the 1861 narrative of a Northern domestic—and former slave—named Harriet Brent Jacobs. Throughout her tale the author calls herself by the pseudonym Linda Brent, as if to underscore that she remolds herself for readers who may misunderstand her, that she refashions her tale or autobiography for a readership that speaks in words dissimilar to her own. It is a narrative that I have taught many times in my courses on nineteenth-century Black women writers. At first some of my students seem reluctant to discuss enslavement, reluctant to confront this nation's complicity and shame. And many students are ignorant of the history of abolition, not knowing of the Underground Railroad, or confusing Harriet Tubman with Sojourner Truth or with Harriet Beecher Stowe. I find myself murmuring "Give me strength," and pausing now and then to suck my teeth. Yet Harriet Jacobs's narrative inevitably awakens the class. Jacobs exposes them to complicated interactions of sex and race and class, and she allows them to connect her bondage to the psychological prisons our postmodern culture sustains.

Born in enslavement in Edenton, North Carolina, Linda in *Incidents* recalls a living hell from the tender age of six years. "I was born a slave," her story begins, "but I never knew it till six years of happy childhood had passed away" (5). Bereft of her mother before her seventh year, Linda is blessed enough to pass into the hands of an unusually kind White mistress who teaches her to read and write. When Linda reaches puberty, her agreeable owner dies, and the will bequeaths the hapless girl to the lecherous town physician, Dr. Flint.

With children by a prominent White lawyer to her name and her owners snatching at her heels, Linda soon initiates escape to the North, only to be waylaid for seven years as a fugitive in her free grandmother's home. When she finally arrives in Philadelphia, agents of her owners pursue her still with deeds of purchase, guns, and the Fugitive Slave Law supporting their underhanded schemes. The chase ends only when a kindly White editor's wife purchases the African woman's freedom.

Before she recalls one event of her story, the author underscores that she writes to an audience whose culture and circumstances differ radically from her own. "Rise up, ye women that are at ease!" she commands on her book's title page. "Hear my voice, ye careless daughters," she continues. "Give ear unto my speech." Like the Old Testament patriarch Isaiah, from whose prophecies she has borrowed this urgent appeal (Isaiah 32:9), Jacobs addresses an audience of Northern White women who more readily regard her as an outcast than as someone close to home.

Jacobs's narrative especially reflects the need to remove from enslaved female Africans the stigma of the sex-crazed "fallen woman." To justify the inhumanity of the auction block, slaveholders routinely described Black women as brutes with little interest in or affection for their children. Even some White abolitionists raised doubts that Black women could ever measure up to nineteenth-century standards of femininity and motherhood. "Unloving" Black mothers would draw disapproval from a White middle class that treasured the institutions of home and family.

Of course, the opposite was true. Less likely to be sold than their husbands, enslaved African mothers were active caretakers of their homes, and repositories as well of the family history (White, 1984:105–109). At the risk of being whipped or even shipped "down river," Black mothers stole food for their sons and daughters and snuck off in the dead of night to visit children on plantations miles away (Jones, 1985:29–41). As proof of this affection, Linda's anguish about her children's fates threatens to become her undoing. In fact, Linda flees her master to secure her family's bonds.

Usually, I find myself explaining here to my students how enslaved women like Linda could describe their anxieties and fears in tones that the class perceives as detached and calm. And how, my students wonder, could so many former slaves recite dimensions and lengths of chains, repeat the process of a flogging, or remember their loved ones' prices at the auction block with such clinical precision and depersonalized detail? In order to verify her story, a Black woman writer would often strike a dispassionate and journalistic pose. If she could reign her emotions in her writing, then surely she could offer even stronger proof that Blacks were not the impulsive brutes that Southerners made them seem. If sometimes she omitted the "low" vernacular from her prose, and replaced that language with sentences churned in what twentieth-century ears construe to be elliptical, convoluted style, then she convinced her readers that she had absorbed and emulated the texts that most literate middle-class Americans would have encountered. Much quoting of the Bible and of other "Master Texts" and much reticence about her own affections was the formula that the fugitive writer frequently adopted.

Jacobs rejects this formula and invents her own. She does remember lynchings and public harassments down to their minutest features, yet also she exposes more pleasant aspects of her private life. She challenges her readers to assume that she speaks of enslavement without hysterics and exaggeration. If anything, she omits the most gruesome details. And she questions why a literate Black woman writer is expected to speak authentically of enslavement with only a modicum of intimacy. Does the "public" voice really convey authority and literacy and truth, or does it assure a White readership of obedience and acculturation?

Midway through Linda Brent's adventures, these and other refabrications of literacy merge. Determined to free her two children, Ben and Ellen, Linda escapes from the lascivious Dr. Flint. She hopes that Flint then will sell her children to the trader's coffle, where their White father (Mr. Sands) has offered to purchase them clandestinely and secure their freedom. She initiates a seven-year hiding in the "loophole of retreat" (114), a coffin-sized attic in the home of her free grandmother.

Yet even as Linda's garret loophole is a prison, it is also the precursor of her liberation. Here, in her boldest and shrewdest maneuver, she posts mail to her owner Dr. Flint as if she has already arrived in the North. "I resolved," she writes, "to match my cunning against his cunning. In order to make him believe that I was in New York, I resolved to write him a letter dated from that place" (128). Directing all responses to be sent to Massachusetts, and dating her correspondence weeks ahead, Linda posts two letters through friends in the North: one to her free grandmother, whom she has apprised of the scheme, another to the villainous Flint.

Linda wields the pen as if to show that freedom and equality arrive when literacy is achieved. But she writes in language of doublecross, with a meaning that belies the words that appear on the page. She writes the truth to Dr. Flint: she reviles him for his abuses and reproaches him for his woe. Her letter to her relative rings equally sincere. To teach her children "to respect themselves" and "to set them a virtuous example" (129) are the thoughts, she confesses, that goaded her to flee. And through these letters, Linda castigates her White female readers in an indirect and canny way. Instead of saying bluntly what she means and risking indifference and disdain, Linda gently reminds her readers that they, like Flint, are complicit in the Africans' enslavement. They, as her grandmother does, must also come to understand the real love of African mothers.

The scorn that White Americans have cast upon her race and sex compels Linda to respond with language that does not state directly what she means. And Linda herself reads all replies for meanings that subvert what their writers intended. "[N]o place," she underscores, "where slavery existed . . . could have afforded . . . so good a place of concealment" (117). Linda reads and writes, she reminds her readers, always with the knowledge that survival means to read and write with the insight of the enslaved.

By christening her secret den the "loophole of retreat," Linda underscores her achievement of the dominant White culture's criteria for literacy. This phrase originates with the eighteenth-century English poet William Cowper, whose antienslavement verses were prized among abolitionists (Sypher, 1969:186–89). "Loophole of retreat" appears in the fourth book of Cowper's *Task* (1785), a blank verse celebration of home life and simple pleasures. In the lines from which the title for Linda's cell is gleaned, the poem's winter-weary speaker reclines before the fire and concludes:

'Tis pleasant through the loop-hole of retreat
To peep at such a world. To see the stir
Of the great Babel and not feel the crowd.
To hear the roar she sends through all her gates
At a safe distance, where the dying sound
Falls a soft murmur on the uninjured ear.
Thus sitting and surveying thus at ease
The globe and its concerns, I seem advanced
To some secure and more than mortal height,
That liberates and exempts me from them all.
(Lines 88–97)

Cowper's works had become a staple in nineteenth-century homes and schools on both sides of the Atlantic (Nicholson, 1960:5). Emerson, Bryant, Whittier—all had read and quoted him. He had contributed such sayings to the English repartee as "God moves in a mysterious way," "Variety's the very spice of life," "I am master of all I survey," and "How sweet, how passing sweet, is solitude!" And his abolitionist verses earned such favor that thousands of copies sold in Great Britain, and the verses were arranged for music (Sypher, 1969:19, 186).

Cowper's voice is everywhere in the abolitionist press, and in almost every captivity tale or narrative that I have researched, his name is one of the first to catch my eye. J. Olney confirms that quoting Cowper's lines went far to prove the literacy and truth of an African writer (1985:152). In *Running a Thousand Miles for Freedom; Or, The Escape of William and Ellen Craft* (1860), I have found a title-page allusion to Cowper's "Time-Piece," the second book of his *Task:*

> Slaves cannot breathe in England: if their lungs
> Receive our air, that moment they are free;
> They touch our country, and their shackles fall.
>   (Lines 40–43)

I have read these same lines in *The Liberator,* the point guard of the abolitionist press, in a column called "Guilt of New-England" (1832). In the 1879 memoirs of Maria Stewart (Richardson, 1987), a free Black woman of Boston, one page carries an unattributed poem on the trade in molasses and Africans. This poem, "The Negro's Complaint" (1788), is another that can be attributed to Cowper. And *The Non-Slaveholder* (1846) reprinted from his "Pity for Poor Africans" (1788), and it celebrated the fact that "more than half a century since," Cowper's verses "have lost nothing of their force." Cowper, as my grandmother would say, "had made his bed and laid in it," and the hotbed of abolition had provided a comfortable fit.

Of course, Cowper is not the only White writer to whom Linda Brent alludes. But her use of his words guarantees her a central position on the antislavery front. And mainstream English literacy, Linda demonstrates, accounts as much for the tools of the trade, for what one reads and writes, as it defines an entire process of reading and writing. Linda's familiarity with Cowper shows not only that she reads along the standards of America's middle-class Whites, but that she and her fellow Africans shall elevate America's culture, not undermine it.

And by quoting Cowper Linda shows antagonism and design. She suggests that the blissful netherland of Cowper's well-known phrase is a body-numbing nightmare for her. Neither "safe" nor "at ease" in her ramshackle surroundings, she lives in continuous fear of searches or accidental discovery. She is separated from her loved ones instead of sheltered with them, exposed to rather than shielded from corruption and injury. And she does not meditate vicariously upon freedom: she seizes it. She climbs up and down her cocoon to stimulate her muscles and to interact with friends bearing food, medicine, and messages. She borrows Cowper's phrase to bear the credentials of mainstream English literacy, but she utters his words with meanings that sting rather than praise.

When I discuss Linda's seven-year confinement with the under-graduates in my class, I often show engravings that underscore the tortures and the separations that had made the lives of the enslaved a living hell. Groans of disgust and sighs of disapproval at the tragedies these pictures reveal are soon replaced by interest in the pictures as weapons of liberation. Along with Scriptural pro-nouncements and the narratives of fugitive slaves, abolitionists had found pictures to be an effective way to undermine enslavement. Popular, low-cost items in the antislavery fairs and the churches' fundraising bazaars were scenes depicting the auction block, a coffle of manacled slaves, lynchings, kidnappings, detention houses and jails, or a fugitive's furtive escape. Portraits were distributed of Africans who had escaped the South and distinguished themselves abroad: Frederick Douglass, Henry "Box" Brown, William and Ellen Craft (Dumond, 1966:269–71). Booksellers often would fea-ture the sketch of a kneeling Black woman, her arms clasped up-ward in supplication, her wrists and ankles burdened by heavy chains (Yellin, 1989:12–26). The caption for this picture would read "An American Woman" or question "Am I Not a Woman and a Sister?"

Another stock representation compared enslavement to en-tombment and burial. My students usually find this connection "morbid," "depressing," or "weird." I find this a key to how Linda resists or calls into question Americans' definitions of liter-acy as moments of reading and writing. In "The Grave of the Slave," a poem circulated thirty years before *Incidents* went to press, Sarah Forten called this vision of burial to mind. Forten belonged to one of Philadelphia's most affluent and prominent free Black families. Using pseudonyms, she frequently contributed po-etry to Boston's *Liberator* (Sterling, 1984:121). Her "Grave of the Slave" became so popular that it was played aloud as well as printed. In it Forten proposed that physical death, rather than being a curse or an agony, was a blessed and beloved spiritual prospect to the enslaved:

The poor slave is laid all unheeded and lone,
Where the rich and the poor find a permanent home;
Not his master can rouse him with voice of command;
He knows not, he hears not, his cruel demand.

Not a tear, not a sigh to embalm his cold tomb,
No friend to lament him, no child to bemoan;
Not a stone marks the place, where he peacefully lies;
The earth for his pillow, his curtain the skies.

The captives did not fear death of the body. The captives did not dread the prospect of dying and leaving their family and friends behind. How could they regret to leave a "paradise" that was a lie? As Forten herself had written, the scene was a familiar one when a master would "with an unshaken hand, tear the unconscious husband from his tender wife, and the helpless babe from its mother's breast" (1831:50). In enslavement, Forten underscored, Africans' bodies had already endured the isolation, heartbreak, and loneliness of the grave. Song as well as printed page became a vehicle for communicating this distinction of flesh from spirit.

This view of multiple literacies is also suggested by the vivid descriptions of Linda's attic cell. As if sealed inside a crypt, Linda despairs of ever escaping "to draw in a plentiful draught of fresh air, to stretch . . . , to have room to stand erect" (121). At one point she literally becomes as stiff as a corpse, nearly dying from a bout of severe chills. "My limbs were benumbed by inaction," she recalls. "and the cold filled them with cramp. I had a very painful sensation of coldness in my head; even my face and tongue stiffened, and I lost the power of speech" (122). Sandwiched between ceiling beams and a wafer-thin roof, Linda describes her hideaway as a "living grave" (147). Her quarters are so narrow that she cannot turn with ease or sit erect, so dark that she finds it impossible to tell night from day. Gruesomely, as if she were a decomposing body, rats skittle over her flesh and insects puncture her skin. She swaddles herself like a mummy in her tissue-thin bedclothes and rags. And death commingles even with her thoughts on home. She describes her daughter Ellen as "a balsam to my heart" (142), a presence that rejuvenates and soothes, at the same time drawing upon "balsam" with its funerary meaning of "embalm." In exchange for her Ellen's freedom, Linda has plunged herself into a virtual death.

Whenever I read these descriptions from *Incidents,* I am struck by how they so clearly recall the songs and etchings and poems on the dead and buried slave. Linda's "grave of the slave" links to the popular culture of her day, to the handbills and penny prints of grief-stricken captives passed along the streets. It links to the illustrations in the antislavery press of men and women stacked upon each other like pence in the slave ships' lower decks. And it links to the stories told of other African captives who buried themselves in packing crates and entombed themselves in dark ships' holds in order to journey to freedom and release.[1] What is told and seen, Linda offers, can afford as much insight and knowledge as what is read. To declare oneself a literate person should *not* mean to discredit oral and visual expressions of creativity.

I have found that Linda's description of her attic cell also plays upon religious icons of the grave. In the evangelical poetry of eighteenth-century England, the grave suggested death and death's meanings as both a judgment and a release. No one could escape the final reckoning that awaited every soul upon death. In the grave the body rested until the final Rapture day, the day when every righteous soul would reunite with its earthly body, and every sinful soul would be consigned to fiery pits. To contemplate the grave while living meant to follow a moral path, to avoid the posthumous sentence of eternal Hell. And the grave, wrote poets such as Robert Blair (1743), made every woman and man the same. In death there existed an equality that earthly power struggles denied. Dissipated or virtuous, servile or aristocratic, affluent or poor—no woman or man could steal away from death. And no one in death could affect a rank higher than the rank or status of another.

For the Africans in an earthly "house of bondage" (Exodus 13:14), this assurance of ultimate and inherent equality proved compelling. And not with books but with spirituals, pictures, and prayers would most Africans manage to keep this assurance alive. Real-life contemplation of friends' and relatives' graves would substitute for an emblem or engraving. Literacy, as Linda's description of entombment once again admits, can be imagined as more than an alphabet and a pen. And when Linda suggests that mainstream English literacy must account for visual and oral expressions, I have found that she invests her own "visions" with as many meanings as she can uncover.

Linda's sequestration in her narrow attic cell underscores that a speaker may be branded illiterate merely because no words can translate how she responds to her world. For Linda the words of White culture cannot phrase how she as an enslaved African woman defines femininity and virtue. "Slavery," she remarks, "is terrible for men, but it is far more terrible for women. Superadded to the burden common to all, they have wrongs, and sufferings, and mortifications peculiarly their own" (77). Rape was this additional load imposed upon enslaved African women; rape was this burden that precipitated Linda's own fearful seven-year wait. Linda knew that it mattered very little what the Black woman's duties in the household might be. Whether she stooped over the ovens in the White family's kitchen, whether she ploughed and planted the aisles of cotton bursting in the fields, the enslaved African woman was not protected by law from the unsolicited charms of a Southern "gentleman." In fact, the stereotypes posed as fact that the Black woman always ignited the solicitations. Some Whites might have granted extra rations or overnight visiting passes to those enslaved Africans whose so-called easy virtue they compromised. Yet the African woman's obedience to the White man's authority was never contingent upon these favors. Instead, his will alone was to be her sole compulsion to submit.

Dr. Flint demonstrates that literacy can mean domination and control when he withholds Linda's letters to deceive her kin into telling of her true whereabouts. Even though he believes Linda's ruse that she has slipped into the "nominally free" North, Flint understands that the Fugitive Slave Law still sanctions her capture and identifies her as his property. So when Linda's letters arrive, he refashions her experience for an effect not far removed from the *Newsweek* column that my student uncritically swallowed as gospel. Flint writes his own version of Linda's message to home and shares that fraudulent correspondence with her free grandmother. He breaks the seal and reads a trumped up letter that bemoans "the disgraceful manner in which I left you and my children" and confesses "to have purchased freedom at a dear rate" (130). He recasts Linda as an irresponsible mother and a recalcitrant daughter, and writes her into the very same molds that her own writing tries to defy. And he stills her voice by defining her according to his terms, by disallowing her the right to translate her own version of the tale.

"What right have you," Dr. Flint had once growled to his slave,

". . . to talk to me about what you would like, and what you wouldn't like? I am your master, and you shall obey me" (75). Linda may write her way to authority in her temporary grave, but she still cannot talk completely because words cannot tell of all that she has undergone. How can she, an unwed mother, write herself as moral and good when her readers defined good women to be virginal until marriage? How can she, unmarried and orphaned, write an identity of her own when her readers turned to husbands and fathers for their names, their security, and their homes? Dr. Flint's phony letter underscores the resistance speakers can encounter when directing their thoughts from one culture to another. And it shows how the process of attaining mainstream English literacy is fraught with relationships the dominant White culture uses to its advantage. For Linda's creator, Harriet Jacobs, freedom and empowerment meant inscribing a place as a writer as well as a literal Northern home.

Jacobs sets this understanding in relief before she utters one sentence of Linda Brent's story. Immediately after the title page of Jacobs's astonishing tale follows a conventional apology and defense. Jacobs persuades her readers to pardon her for assuming a task much larger than she could bear, and she requests their patience with any imperfections. She assures her readers of her modesty and bashfulness, and she attests to her own sincerity and candor. To "excuse what might otherwise seem presumptuous" on the part of such a humble soul, Jacobs presents her book as merely proof of her moral desire to be "kind and considerate towards others." She had declined to write the narrative when initially advised. Only the persistence of enslavement had changed her mind. With "two millions of women at the South, still in bondage," with millions in the so-called Free States still unconvinced by testimonies of enslavement as it was, Jacobs did at last consent to publicize her experiences "in behalf of my persecuted people." Without this selfless motive, she confides, "it would have been more pleasant to me to have been silent about my own history" (1).

Such a preface had been formalized by well-known English writers to whom Jacobs occasionally alludes. The popular, didactic publications of Charles Dickens and Daniel Defoe had conventionalized the author's protest of deficiency and reserve and had featured the desire not to profit but to serve.[2] Dickens begins his *Christmas Carol* (1843) with the humble wish that his "little book" not "put my readers out of humour with themselves, with each other, with the season, *or with me* [emphasis mine]." He signs himself, demure and restrained, as a "faithful Friend and Servant." More than a century earlier, Defoe had told the story of *Robinson Crusoe* (1719) "with Modesty, with Seriousness, and with a religious Application of Events to . . . the Instruction of others by this Example."

Both *Crusoe* and *A Christmas Carol* would have occupied places of honor in many of the libraries of Jacobs's middle-class readers. Her appropriation of their prefatory techniques legitimizes and refines her in a manner similar to her use of Cowper's *Task*. Jacobs's preface echoes the tradition of Dickens and Defoe in order to authorize herself the literacy that she never was supposed to possess. And again she calls keen attention to one of her narrative's central themes: mainstream English literacy means understanding what sanctioned materials to read as much as it refers to the process of reading and writing.

When I place Jacobs's preface along that of an earlier Black woman writer, the class dimensions of literacy focus sharply. Phillis Wheatley, whom I think has been much unfairly maligned, provides for this comparison. In the preface to her *Poems on Various Subjects, Religious and Moral* (1773), Wheatley hoped that her verses, "With all their Imperfections," would not "be cast aside with Contempt, as worthless and trifling Effusions." Like Jacobs, Wheatley coupled these modest remarks with hopes that no reader would "severely sensure [*sic*]" her mistakes. Like Jacobs, Wheatley published not for vanity but to satisfy the urgings of "her best, and most generous Friends." And her leisure moments and privacy, like Jacobs's, might have been just as difficult to preserve. The darling of English aristocracy and a prodigy among New England's balladeers, Wheatley nevertheless was enslaved. Her duties were dictated by her master; her body and her name were not her own; her movements in the colonies were circumscribed by the strictest legal codes. Yet in her preface she feigns the autonomy of a wealthy, emancipated woman. She describes her poems as trifles and amusements and as "Products of her leisure Moments," as if these moments were usual and guaranteed. Wheatley herself declines to discuss the difficulties of the enslaved. Instead she directs her readers to "her Master's letter in the following Page."

The preface to Harriet Jacobs's tale overtly calls attention to differences of class between the author and her readers. Jacobs admits that she has concealed or altered details to protect her friends still in Southern bondage. And she blames any errors that she might have overlooked on the rigors of a fugitive life in the North. She remarks:

> Since I have been at the North, it has been necessary for me to work diligently for my own support, and the education of my children. This has not left me much leisure to make up for the loss of early opportunities to improve myself; and it has compelled me to write these pages at irregular intervals, whenever I could snatch an hour from household duties. (1)

Jacobs exposes the unspoken rule that Wheatley is prohibited from explaining: the literacy of the middle-class readership has balanced upon both leisure and solitude. The poor and the enslaved remain the illiterate and the oppressed as long as reflective moments and privacy prove unattainable dreams.

I can point to evidence in the abolitionist press that implicates class—and race as well—in a definition of mainstream English literacy. In this example *Incidents* is reviewed in *The Anti-Slavery Advocate* (Review, 1861), a London monthly. "We have read this book with no ordinary interest," the *Advocate*'s reviewer testifies, "for we are acquainted with the writer; we have heard many of the incidents from her own lips, and have great confidence in her truthfulness and integrity." The reviewer acknowledges Jacobs as another "coloured" product of enslavement, yet compares her to "a southern Spaniard, or a Portuguese." Jacobs, reads the *Advocate*, proved a woman of great cultivation, a woman whose "manners were marked by refinement and sensibility, and by an utter absence of pretence and affectation." And the *Advocate* heaps an irony upon the slaveholders of the South by noting Jacobs's "kind and pleasing countenance." The phrases "kind and pleasing" and "kind and considerate" had been stock descriptions of mistresses in Southern proslavery tracts! Cruelty and greed had been connected to the lowly slave.[3]

In the Spanish climes or the Southern States, an idealized White woman is the measure to which the "slave girl" must compare. And Jacobs is presented as one who demonstrates the ideal traits that a White middle-class woman aspired to display. Humility, candor, moderation, grace—these are the middle-class "manners" by which Jacobs is defined, and in turn they define the former fugitive as a writer both capable and true. The *Advocate* reviewer bleaches Jacobs's African ties and credits her talents to a nobler source than Ethiopian genes. No matter that Jacobs herself alludes to Black as well as White writers throughout her text. To pronounce that she can read and write means to place her in the White middle class.

Black writers and critics must still struggle to expose class- and race-bound notions of who and what is literate or not. I realized the urgency of this task when I began to pursue my own graduate studies. In many mainstream academic circles a simple analogy applied: as the toothpick was to the Sequoia, as the faucet drip was to the sea, so was the transcription of the autobiography to the writing of serious literature. Contemplating American autobiography was worse than purchasing *Cliffs Notes,* emulating Keats, reading romance novels, writing romance novels, understanding *Ulysses* and enjoying it, or aspiring to become a columnist for *Rolling Stone* magazine. The ones least worthy and least literate were the ones who had published their autobiographies. And the abundance of these works in local bookstores cast upon them further aspersion and shame. "Most critics, poets, and teachers," I learned, "are uncomfortable with the popular form. Since the language is unspecialized and the experience everyday, the critic and teacher are left virtually with very little to say, an embarrassing situation" (Harris, 1984:218–19). An "embarrassing situation," I learned, never suited one's final transcript well.

The comic book was accounted a misdemeanor, a paltry and a pardonable offense. Autobiography loomed as an abomination and a crime, a lurid, heinous curse, like the threat of nuclear war, that dimmed the lustrous accomplishments of humankind. To appeal the sentence was a futile task (and a headachy one at that!), for my accusers would assail me with wisdoms such as that extracted from the strains and elocutions of Carlyle. It was Goethe's autobiography, and Goethe's autobiography alone, that Carlyle had praised as "such, indeed, as few men can be called upon to relate, and few, if called upon, could relate so well. What would we give for such an autobiography of Shakespeare, of Milton, even of Pope or Swift!" (Carlyle, 1828:203). Perhaps some gifted Black writers had existed: Booker T. Washington, Frederick Douglass, Richard Wright. But a motley crew made up the rest of the scene:

entertainers, laborers, domestics, Black women, prisoners, radical
activists, religious converts, Black women. And Black women!

Thus warned, I proceeded to stuff my satchels and shelves with
every Black woman's autobiography I could find. I began to visit
bookstores that specialize in African, Caribbean, and African-
American literature. Always I could lose myself in scores of shelves
brimming with stories of real Black women's lives. Rebecca Cox
Jackson, Nancy Prince, Ida B. Wells, Mary Church Terrell, Anna
Julia Cooper, Zora Neale Hurston, Gwendolyn Brooks, Anne
Moody, Maya Angelou, Pearl Bailey, Pauli Murray, Assata Olug-
bala Shakur. Even among the novelists and poets I could always
find assurances that autobiography is seminal and alive. Margaret
Walker's historical novel *Jubilee* (1966) intertwines her research of
enslavement with the stories that she heard upon her own grandmother's knee. Both blood relationships and kissing-kin ties forged
by layoffs, lynchings, and enslavement are the fabric that Lucille
Clifton patterns and weaves into poetry for her *Good Woman*
(1987). Audre Lorde's *Zami: A New Spelling of My Name* (1982)
and Michelle Cliff's *Land of Look Behind* (1985) transform the
autobiography into what Lorde christens biomythography—
syncretisms of history, poetry, autobiography, telephone calls, epis-
tolary writing, journalism, and myth.

"Enough to smack you back into last Sunday," as my own
grandmother would say. In the Black woman's literary tradition, I
marveled, autobiography reigns supreme. This awakening refuted
the catechism of my academic years that the crowning achievement
of the literate was the novel or the epic poem. I discovered that such
scholars as W. Andrews (1986), S. Cudjoe (1984), N. McKay
(1990), and D.T. Turner (1982) had linked Black women's autobiography to distinctive styles of language, motifs, and tropes.
Because their life stories did not always fit West European paradigms, Black women autobiographers had seemed easily dismissed
as barely literate muddlers in a literarily bleak and barren mode.

Lucille Clifton frames this dilemma at the beginning of her
Generations (1976), an "autobiographical statement" that glosses
her personal poems.[4] This beginning connects oral histories to
powerlessness and erasure. It connects the written language to the
classes that hold money and property, and it connects the spoken
story to the classes that have none, that are deemed by extension
lazy and uninspired. It connects the books and poems and ge-

nealogies to Whites; the Blacks supposedly founder in their half-witted scraps of song and half-remembered geographies and names. Mainstream English literacy, Clifton suggests, often provides just another Jim Crow code to keep Blacks, childlike and contented, in their place. Mainstream English literacy privileges and empowers a certain kind of language—a "standard" written language—to the detriment and debasement of all others. Write this language and read it, or abandon all hope of obtaining the American Dream:

> Where are the records, Daddy? I would ask. The time may not be right and it may just be a family legend or something. Somebody somewhere knows, he would say. (35)

Childhood stories not written down but told and told and repeated had inspired Clifton to research her genealogy and post inquiries about her family's history. One day a stranger telephoned with information. Her voice was White. Her interest was high. The stranger had compiled and published a history of her family, the same Virginia family to which Clifton's father belonged. She and Clifton had to recognize each other as women of one blood, the last of the women to carry on the family line. Bibles and manuscripts and index cards loaned the White woman's comments authority, but Clifton could only corroborate with the names that her Daddy would say—Africans' names, Blacks' names, midwives' and mammies' names, names of the people in the cabins, names of slaves. All the information Clifton recalled was based on photographs and oral testimony. All the enslaved relations on her Daddy's side reposed in unmarked graves, no headstone or inscription to be found. "It's a long time after," Clifton had reassured her caller, "and I just wanted to know" (6). But enslavement, Blackness, classism, and denial were legacies that the White woman shrank from sharing. Her voice stopped jumping and devolved into a sigh. Her interest drained. And her class and race pretensions never sent her phoning Clifton again.

Clifton encourages her readers to see that mainstream English literacy has its limits. Designed to grant hegemony to the culture(s) of a White and privileged class, mainstream English literacy has never guaranteed the progress of the non-White, non-middle-class, non-reading-and-writing "Others." Yet the oral tradition has provided a tradition that nurtures Clifton and her children, while the

White woman's household—for all of its printed volumes—has waned. "I see," Clifton says, "that she is the last of her line. Old and not married, left with a house and a name" (7). For Clifton and her children, the stories and songs have provided crucial lessons they have practiced to survive. Clifton's conversation enables us to recognize that in our privileging of one definition of literacy, we overlook the applicability and usefulness of others. When we label the oral traditions of a group "dysfunctional" or "retarded," we overlook the creativity and centrality of those traditions.

In my own family's oral tradition, we have sayings about a Georgia dish called "spider pie." When my mother and my grandmother are fuming with someone else, straightaway they declare that they will "make a spider pie." As a child I envisioned Daddy Long Legs, centipedes, jellyfish, boa constrictors, and squids: creepy-crawlers wiggling and hunching slimey trails through the lattice-patterned dough. I thought of a forkful of webs and dead flies, washed down by a sloppy mug of sorcerer's brew. My Mom would assure me that nobody sane would fill a pie shell with spiders, and that the recipe itself had nothing in common with the name. My Mom would laugh; my own stomach would groan; my throat turn rubbery and dry. I was content with tiny portions of Mom's baked products for a while! Never, I would promise, would I misbehave so much that my antics would incur the spider pie.

My family's "spider pie," I now suspect, is a legacy of the period of enslavement. In the seventeenth, eighteenth, and nineteenth centuries, American cooks used frying pans called "spiders" for preparing dishes directly over the flames. The spiders, like most skillets, usually were made of iron. Like most skillets, they featured long handles so that cooks could move them in and out of the hearth without receiving burns. What distinguished the spiders, however, was that they were frying pans fashioned on tripods or bottom legs, three legs that could conveniently stand the pan in the fireplace. Spider pies, spider cakes, spider bread, and spider loaves—all were prepared in the sturdy three-legged pan (Carson, 1968:129). So when my female relatives threaten spider pies upon the folks they just can't stand, perhaps they are recalling an enslaved woman's act of resistance. As E. Fox-Genovese writes, "Plantation letters and diaries abound with references to poisonings, and testify to the uneasiness of the whites. Poison could not always be detected as the cause of death, but was frequently suspected" (1986:156). How many African cooks and mammies fried a spider pie for Master's plate and laced their creations with fatal roots and herbs?

From Harriet Jacobs to Lucille Clifton, Black women autobiographers have expanded notions of literacy with the same kind of subterfuge and self-determination that created the spider pie. We contemporary students and scholars of literature must revise our constructions of literacy so that this covert resistance need not be an automatic response. There is a middle ground, as Harriet Jacobs attempted to discover over a century ago. It is time that we started looking.

NOTES

Some summaries of *Incidents* have been taken from my dissertation, *To Rise Above Race: Black Women Writers and Their Readers*.

1. Still's *Underground Rail Road* (1872), the classic history of Blacks' antebellum resistance, documents numerous accounts of Africans in enslavement who were nailed into crates and shipped up North. Philadelphia was the usual destination in these extraordinary escapes. Well-known is the story of Henry Box Brown, a Virginia slave who mailed himself as overland freight to Philadelphia (81–86). Escaping aboard a steamer chest was Lear Green of Baltimore. Green endured eighteen hours as freight in order to unite with her husband-to-be and marry on Canadian soil (282–84). Susan Brooks was secreted below decks in 1854 on a steamship bound from Virginia to the North. Along with her traveled two other African men, William White and William Atkins (211–13). And in 1857 an anonymous young Black woman, unable to speak and faint from the cold, was retrieved from a box posted by rail from Baltimore to Philadelphia (608–610).

2. Linda alludes to Defoe's *Crusoe* (1719) early in her "loophole" section. She proclaims herself to be "as rejoiced as Robinson Crusoe" when she discovers a drill that she can use to create her tiny peephole (115). Linda is disguised in sailor's clothes and hides aboard a boat before confinement in the attic—additional connections to Crusoe's nautical life before he became marooned.

As Defoe produced many antislavery verses of his own (Sypher, 1969:157–59), it is not surprising that he is acknowledged in *Incidents*. And his fictional tale of isolation and abandonment found mention in other Africans' autobiographies, such as Gustavas Vassa's eighteenth-century narrative (1837).

With Dickens, Jacobs's allusion is more elliptical. To "those noble men and women who plead for us [African slaves]," Linda dedicates this prayer:

> God bless them! God give them strength and courage to go on! God bless those, every where, who are laboring to advance the cause of humanity! (30)

This is reminiscent of the famous dinner scene in Dickens's *Christmas Carol* (1843), when the cheery Cratchits gather round their table and exchange the holiday blessings (47).

3.   Still's *Underground Rail Road* provides an example of an African woman using this phrase in ironic reference to her mistress's indifference (114). In Chapter 6 of his *Narrative,* Douglass recalls a new mistress with "kind heart" and "cheerful eye" who, under slavery's evil influence, soon became a "demon." Jacobs uses this phrase herself in the Preface (1).

4.   I am borrowing from Nikki Giovanni's description of her autobiography. I like the phrase because it suggests a process, a state of becoming, rather than a completion. "What we remember is only a ripple in a pond," Giovanni says. "And where does the last ripple go and who sees it? You never see the end of your own life" (Tate, 1983:68). This stance is one that Clifton assumes when reflecting upon and remembering her genealogy and personal life.

REFERENCES

Andrews, W.L. (1986). *To tell a free story: The first century of Afro-American autobiography, 1760–1865.* Urbana: University of Illinois Press.

———. (1990). Toward a poetics of Afro-American autobiography. In H.A. Baker, Jr. & P. Redmond (Eds.), *Afro-American literary study in the 1990's* (pp. 78–104). Chicago: University of Chicago Press.

Aptheker, H. (Ed.). (1965). *One continual cry: David Walker's appeal.* New York: Humanities Press. (Original work published 1830)

Blair, R. (1973). *The grave.* Los Angeles: Augustan Reprint Society. (Original work published 1743)

Brown, W.W. (1847). *Narrative of William Wells Brown, a fugitive slave. Written by himself.* Boston: Anti-Slavery Office.

Carlyle, T. (1899). Goethe. In H.D. Traill (Ed.), *The works of Thomas Carlyle.* (Vol. 26, pp. 198–257). New York: Scribner's. (Original work published 1828)

Carson, J. (1968). *Colonial Virginia cookery.* Charlottesville: University of Virginia Press.

Cliff, M. (1985). *The land of look behind.* Ithaca, NY: Firebrand.

Clifton, L. (1976). *Generations: A memoir.* New York: Random House.

_____. (1987). *Good woman: poems & a memoir, 1969–1980.* Brockport, NY: BOA Editions.

Cowper, W. (1846, June). Pity for poor Africans. *Non-Slaveholder,* p. 95. (Original work published 1788)

_____. (1934). *Poetical works* (4th Ed.). London: Oxford University Press.

Craft, W. (1860). *Running a thousand miles for freedom; Or, the escape of William and Ellen Craft from slavery.* London: William Tweedie.

Cudjoe, S. (1984). Maya Angelou and the autobiographical statement. In M. Evans (Ed.), *Black women writers (1950–1980): A critical evaluation* (pp. 6–24). Garden City, NY: Anchor Press/Doubleday.

Defoe, D. (1975). *The life and strange surprizing adventures of Robinson Crusoe* (M. Shinagel, Ed.). New York: Norton. (Original work published 1719)

Dickens, C. (1954). *A Christmas carol.* In his *Christmas books* (pp. 1–77). London: Oxford University Press. (Original work published 1843)

Douglass, F. (1845). *Narrative of the life of Frederick Douglass: An American slave. Written by himself.* Boston: Anti-Slavery Office.

Dumond, D.L. (1966). *Antislavery: The crusade for freedom in America.* New York: Norton.

Forten, S.L. [pseud. Ada]. (1831, January 22). The grave of the slave. *Liberator,* p. 14.

_____. [pseud. Magawisca]. (1831, 26 March). The abuse of liberty. *Liberator,* p. 50.

Fox-Genovese, E. (1986). Strategies and forms of resistance: Focus on slave women in the United States. In G.Y. Okihiro (Ed.), *In resistance: Studies in African, Caribbean, and Afro-American history* (pp. 143–165). Amherst: University of Massachusetts Press.

Gilbert, O. (Ed.). (1884). *Narrative of Sojourner Truth, with a history of her labors and correspondence, drawn from her 'Book of Life'.* Battle Creek, MI: Author.

Giovanni, N. (1968). *Gemini: an extended autobiographical statement on my first twenty-five years of being a Black poet.* New York: Penguin.

Guilt of New-England. (1832, January 7). *Liberator,* p. 1.

Harris, W.J. (1984). Soft sweet essence of possibility: The poetry of Nikki Giovanni. In M. Evans (Ed.), *Black women writers* (pp. 218–228). (See Cudjoe entry)

Jacobs, H.A. [pseud. Linda Brent] (1987). *Incidents in the life of a slave girl, written by herself* (L.M. Child, Ed.). Cambridge: Harvard University Press. (Original work published 1860)

Jones, J. (1985). *Labor of love, labor of sorrow: Black women, work, and the family from slavery to the present.* New York: Basic Books.

Lorde, A. (1982). *Zami: A new spelling of my name.* Trumansburg, NY: Crossing Press.

McKay, N.Y. (1990). The autobiographies of Zora Neale Hurston and Gwendolyn Brooks: Alternate versions of the Black female self. In J.M. Braxton & A.N. McLaughlin (Eds.), *Wild women in the whirlwind: Afra-American culture and the contemporary literary renaissance* (pp. 264–281). New Brunswick, NJ: Rutgers University Press.

Nicholson, N. (1960). *William Cowper.* London: Longmans.

Olney, J. (1985). "I was born": Slave narratives, their status as autobiography and as literature. In C.T. Davis & H.L. Gates, Jr. (Eds.), *The slave's narrative* (pp. 148–175). New York: Oxford University Press.

[Review of *Incidents in the Life of a Slave Girl*]. (1861, May 1). *Anti-Slavery Advocate,* p. 1.

Richardson, M. (Ed.). (1987). *Maria W. Stewart, America's first Black woman political writer.* Bloomington: Indiana University Press.

Shakur, A. [JoAnne Chesimard] (1987). *Assata.* Westport, CT: Lawrence Hill.

Sterling, D. (Ed.). (1984). *We are your sisters: Black women in the nineteenth century.* New York: Norton.

Still, W. (1968). *The underground rail road.* New York: Arno Press and *New York Times.* (Original work published 1872)

Sypher, W. (1969). *Guinea's captive kings: British anti-slavery literature of the XVIIIth century.* New York: Octagon Books.

Tate, C. (1983). [Interview with Nikki Giovanni]. In C. Tate (Ed.), *Black women writers at work.* New York: Continuum.

Turner, D.T. (1982). Appendix one: Uses of the slave narrative in collegiate courses in literature. In J. Sekora & D.T. Turner (Eds.), *The art of slave narrative: Original essays in criticism and theory* (pp. 127–134). Macomb: Western Illinois University.

Vassa, G. (1837, December). *Anti-Slavery Record,* p. 4.

Walker, M. (1966). *Jubilee.* Boston: Houghton Mifflin.

Wheatley, P. (1988). *Poems on various subjects, religious and moral.* In J.C. Shields (Ed.), *The collected works of Phillis Wheatley* (pp. 1–128). New York: Oxford University Press. (Original work published 1773)

Whitaker, M. (1990, January 29). Why this isn't a "Black thing": Barry is a victim of his own hubris, not racism. *Newsweek,* p. 30.

White, D.G. (1984). *Ar'n't I a woman?: Female slaves in the plantation south.* New York: Norton.

Yellin, J.F. (1989). *Women and sisters: The antislavery feminists in American culture.* New Haven: Yale University Press.

CHAPTER 8

Literacy and Social Power

Joanne Devine

INTRODUCTION

While scholars may disagree about what precisely constitutes literacy (see Kaplan and Palmer, 1992, for a recent discussion) or how best to insure its development, there can be little controversy about the importance of being literate in the United States. In a society dependent on print, anyone who cannot read and write is at a tremendous disadvantage in the job market, in school, and in many types of personal interactions. Indeed, for an illiterate member of a highly literate culture, personal growth and self-fulfillment may be severely restricted. As Gee observes, "reading, writing and language interrelate with the workings of power and desire in social life" (1990:27). The fact that some groups within the United States suffer disproportionately high rates of illiteracy has critical social and educational implications and raises questions about usual definitions of literacy, as well as related questions about the problems, successes, and failures of literacy acquisition for members of linguistic and cultural minorities.

Recent explorations of the sometimes dramatically differing rates of literacy acquisition by various groups within the culture can be characterized broadly as being of two main types: *difference* and *dominance*, categories that are not mutually exclusive but rather represent differences in emphasis. Difference investigations of literacy attainment typically focus on identifying and describing culturally patterned *literacy practices*—see Scribner and Cole (1981) and Reder (this volume) for a discussion of this term—and on examining the impact of these practices on the attainment of

what might be termed "expected" literacy behavior within an educational context. This expected behavior has been described by
Gee (1986) and others as "essay-text" (see below for a description
of this term), a form of literacy behavior associated with "mainstream middle-class and upper middle-class groups" (731). Groups
and individuals who do not or cannot successfully engage in this
form of interaction with print are regarded as "literacy failures."

Dominance investigations have examined differential literacy
attainment by various cultural groups within the United States in
the context of patterns of social relations, dominance, and power
inequalities. Like studies of literacy acquisition within difference
models, these investigations have stressed the social dimensions of
literacy attainment and literacy failure; they have, additionally,
focused on the role of ideology and political structures in understanding differences in literacy attainment among various cultural
groups. Dominance models have called into serious question
simple definitions of literacy as a neutral technology (that is, without implications for power) and as involving reading and writing
as divorced from other aspects of social interaction.

The purpose of the following discussion is to explore the differing literacy attainments of groups within the population. The discussion ultimately focuses on *muted group theory*; this theory
emphasizes the impact of asymmetrical or uneven power relationships within a society on access to language forms. The following
section begins with a discussion of the social nature of literacy,
including a overview of the findings of difference studies. The third
section provides a very brief summary of dominance models of
literacy. The fourth section outlines muted group theory, placing it
in the context of dominance models described in the third section.
Finally, the fifth section is an attempt to apply muted group theory
to an understanding of differing literacy attainment of various
groups within the United States.

LITERACY AS A SOCIAL ACHIEVEMENT

As Reder (this volume) has observed, the wealth of research into
literacy in the past decade has provided convincing support for a
view of literacy as a cultural activity, reflecting a web of social
expectations, beliefs, and accepted types of interaction with print.
Reder suggests that the key questions for an understanding of

literacy acquisition and development are social ones: What are the important uses that the culture makes of the written word? What are the roles of reading and writing in creating new cultural practices? And how and to what extent is the written word an important vehicle of socialization within the culture? Scribner captures the spirit of this line of study in her observation that literacy must be regarded as "a *social* achievement" (1986:8).

There is not, however, universal agreement on the significance of the social context of literacy. Implicit in the work of such respected scholars as Goody and Watt (1968), Hildyard and Olson (1978), and Ong (1982) is what Street (1984) has dubbed "the autonomous model," in which literacy is studied largely divorced from social and cultural contexts and influences. This model assumes, according to Street, that literacy "is a neutral technology that can be detached from specific social contexts" (1); in other words, a set of skills that, once mastered, can be readily transferred to new encounters with print, exclusive of the social or cultural context in which that print is found.

When literacy is regarded as a set of specific, context-free skills (as in the autonomous model), then attaining those skills can be seen as a *personal* achievement; not attaining those skills must consequently be regarded as a *personal* failure. While it may be acquired by most members of a culture, and hence be regarded as a characteristic of that culture, literacy thus envisioned is a personal quality of the individual. It is, furthermore, a static quality: Literacy skills, once attained, become part of the individual's permanent repertoire. Ferdman (1990) provides a useful summary of the implications of this model of literacy:

> [L]iteracy is experienced as a characteristic inherent in the individual. Once a person acquires the requisite skills, she also acquires the quality of mind known as literacy, and the right to be labeled a literate person. Judgments about a person's degree of literacy are not dependent on the situation. Rather, because there is wide agreement on what constitutes a literate individual, a person carries the label regardless of whether or not she continues to demonstrate the behaviors that first earned her the designation. (186)

In stressing what they regard as the individual, context-free nature of literacy, proponents of the autonomous model tacitly suggest that literacy operates apart from values and attitudes embedded in social structures. They also, as Gee (1990) suggests, either inadvertently or deliberately obscure "literacy's connections to political power, to social identity and to ideologies" (49), issues that will be returned to in the following section. A wealth of recent research (Gee, 1985; Heath, 1983; Langer, 1987; Michaels, 1981; Scollon & Scollon, 1981; Scribner & Cole, 1981; Snow et al., 1991) casts serious doubt on the validity of an autonomous (or acultural) characterization of literacy. Scholars investigating literacy in a variety of cultures (and subcultures within the dominant culture) have amassed data that argue convincingly for the central role of social context in understanding literacy attainment and practices.

Heath (1985), for example, makes an important distinction between literacy *skills* and literacy *behavior,* or between skills (in the autonomous sense) for processing written material and the actual behavior of engaging in interactions with texts. Literacy behavior is possible not only because the individual is in possession of the requisite skills, but also by virtue of the individual's membership in social/cultural groups that determine attitudes about and set purposes for interaction with written texts. Heath's distinction grew out of her study of literacy attainment among three divergent socioeconomic groups in a rural community in South Carolina (Heath, 1983). She discovered that each of the groups acquired literacy skills (that is, each was able to decode written language) but that the groups made very different uses of the skills. Only one of the groups—the "mainstream" population—successfully engaged in the types of reading and writing assignments (the literacy behavior) demanded in a school setting. From the point of view of the mainstream—or dominant—culture, only this group became literate. The other two groups had not failed to acquire literacy skills, but rather to engage in appropriate literacy behavior as demanded in the classroom. Yet these groups were regarded as literacy failures.

The work of Heath and others argues that literacy "failures" (that is, failures to perform expected literacy tasks, especially in school contexts) in divergent or nonmainstream, non-middle-class populations, can only be understood by investigating the social and cultural contexts in which reading and writing take place. A number of other chapters in this volume address issues of social relations in literacy acquisition in an attempt to understand the literacy failures of subgroups within the mainstream culture. For example, Zanger's study of access to English literacy for Hispanic youths has as one of its principal focuses the role of intergroup relations—social and cultural—in determining the extent to which Hispanic youths will or will not develop the expected or mainstream literacy practices of the dominant culture. Her conclusion that schools' efforts to improve English literacy among Hispanic students need to take into account the interpersonal dynamics of the school—including such variables as students' linguistic and cultural background; the relationship of this background to the creation of a congruent learning environment; the attitudes of other literacy initiates (other students) towards the minority students; and the personal relationship of minority students to potentially validating members of the dominant group (their teachers)—underscores the need to give primacy to social context in the understanding of literacy generally and in the study of literacy within minority groups in particular. Reder (this volume) provides a very good summary of other research comparing literacy practices across cultural groups and communities.

LITERACY AND SOCIAL POWER

It is not just for divergent populations, of course, that literacy is a social achievement: All literacy behavior reflects attitudes, values and practices of particular social, cultural, and/or ethnic groups. As Gee (1986) observes, "Discourse practices are always embedded in the particular world view of a particular social group; they are tied to a set of values and norms" (742). Mainstream or dominant cultural groups' literacy practices, no less than minority groups', reflect a particular world view and are "but one cultural way of making sense among many others" (731). The fact that these practices are often regarded as the norm, the natural, or the universal has less to do with the particular forms themselves than with the fact that the consciousness they represent reflects the interests of the most powerful social groups within our society. Gee notes that the dominant culture in the United States most usually values, cultivates, and rewards "essay-text literacy," characterized by a heavy emphasis on explicit, decontextualized, impersonal language. The illiteracy of certain groups in this country can perhaps be best understood not as skills deficiencies but as failure (or refusal) to internalize the values and attitudes and to understand and adopt the essay-text literacy practices favored by the dominant cultural group within the society.

As Gee (1990) argues, the features that characterize this form of literacy behavior should be understood as socially preferred behavior reflective not of universal values but of the particular values of a limited—albeit socially very powerful—segment of the population. In the case of essay-text characteristic of explicitness, for example, Gee observes:

> How explicit one is in using language is a matter of convention. Certain cultures, as well as unschooled people in our culture, simply do not have, and thus do not use, the convention preva-lent in our schools that in certain contrived situations (like "show and tell time") one pretends that people do not know or see what they obviously know and see. . . . Show and tell time is early training for later essay writing, where the same assump-tions are made. . . . Such assumptions—that one should ignore what the hearer knows and explicitly say it anyway—are also the hallmark of many middle-class home-based practices with chil-dren. (60)

Not all groups within our society, however, participate in this form of what might be called "literacy socialization." Indeed, as Gee notes, "such explicitness may be seen as rude because it is distanc-ing, blunt, or condescending to the hearer's intelligence or relation to the speaker" (60). To include "explicitness" in a definition of literacy, then, is to privilege the values and practices of one group among many others within our culture and to grant those practices special status as natural and universal.

Street (1984) proposes an "ideological" model as a corrective to autonomous conceptions of literacy, as a way of understanding the political implications of adopting a view of literacy as a neutral, universal, and unitary phenomenon operating outside cultural val-ues and power relations. As he formulates it, this model focuses on "the specific social practices of reading and writing" and explores the

> ideological and therefore culturally embedded nature of such practices. . . . It treats skeptically claims by western liberal edu-cators for the "openness," "rationality," and critical awareness of what they teach, and investigates the role of such teaching in social control and the hegemony of the ruling class. (2–3)

Street finds in the work of such scholars as Graff (1979) and Clanchy (1979) examples of literacy in the service of social control and cultural hegemony. Graff, for example, provides a detailed study of the literacy acquisition of various ethnic and occupational groups in Canada in the 19th century; he argues that literacy, rather than broadening educational and job opportunities and bettering living conditions for members of ethnic minorities and the working class, functioned to inculcate prescribed middle-class values and to reinforce forms of social control. Street (1984) summarizes: "Particular approved forms of literacy were employed by a particular class as socializing agents for particular oppressed groups and as a means of imparting to them a specific moral code" (105). Further examples of the highly political and ideological nature of literacy acquisition are developed in Street's critical examination of UNESCO and adult literacy campaigns in the United Kingdom and the United States.

Framing investigations into the reading and writing acquisition of minorities in terms of social/cultural values and sanctioned discourse practices suggests that certain groups, by virtue of the mismatch between their literacy values and practices and those of mainstream culture, will suffer from unequal "access" to literacy as it is typically defined within the dominant culture and especially as it is practiced in educational settings. For middle-class students entering school in this country, the acquisition of literacy represents a reinforcement of the literacy values of their background and an extension and refinement of the literacy practices initiated in their homes, as with Gee's example of "show and tell time." (See Snow et al., 1991, for an excellent recent discussion of this point.) Very broadly speaking, literacy—as it is defined and practiced in school—is immediately accessible for these students. Obviously not all middle-class students acquire literacy skills with equal ease or engage in literacy behavior to the same extent and with the same success; but for most middle-class students the demands of literacy education do not represent a fundamental challenge to the literacy values and practices of their homes.

The same cannot be said for students who are members of minority groups in this country. For minority students, literacy education may well entail discovering through painful trial and error what the preferred behavior is (and since the value of the behavior is assumed rather than examined, this is no small task) and adopting the attitudes and values of the middle class that inform and underlie these behaviors. As the work of Heath, Snow et al., and others has shown, these attitudes and values may be at odds with those of the minority cultural group. The demand for dramatic shifts in literacy practice, attitudes, and values on the part of minority students makes literacy education a very different enterprise for them than for most middle-class students. The extent of these demands perhaps marks the degree to which literacy is accessible for minority students.

Reduced access to literacy restricts minority-group members' educational mobility and social power within the larger culture; Black, Hispanic, and other minority students represent a disproportionately high number of high school dropouts and suffer un- and underemployment at dramatically high rates. In an equally significant, but perhaps less obvious way, minority members' limited access to literacy reflects, reinforces, and recreates asymmetrical power relationships within the larger culture. By narrowly defining literacy to exclude values and practices of minority groups within the larger culture, the educational system has, in Gee's assessment,

> historically failed with non-elite populations and . . . thus replicated the social hierarchy, thereby advancing the elites in the society. . . . [Literacy education, as it is currently practiced, teaches minorities] school-based literacy practices that carry within them mainstream, middle-class values of quiescence and placidity, values that will ensure no real demands for significant social change, nor serious questions about the power of aging elites. (1990:31)

UNEQUAL ACCESS TO LANGUAGE: MUTED GROUP THEORY

Literacy failure on the part of minorities within our culture can be seen as a mismatch between divergent sets of literacy attitudes and practices—those of the socially powerful mainstream culture and those of minority cultural groups. This mismatch often results in unequal access to literacy by socially less powerful groups. To explore both the causes and results of this unequal access to literacy, it is profitable to examine the relationship between this line of inquiry and research into the differential access to language, both written and spoken, by women and men—an area of intense recent interest in the field of language and gender studies. This field, of course, encompasses a wide range of topics and theoretical approaches; of special relevance to the current topic are studies examining the different and unequal access by women and men to language generally, and to written language more specifically. Historical evidence (see Virginia Woolf, *A Room of One's Own*), research (Abel, 1980; Graddol & Swann, 1989; Kramarae, 1981; Penelope, 1990; Penfield, 1987; Spender, 1980; Thorne, Kramarae & Henley, 1983), and anecdotal evidence (see, for example, the appendix in Spender, 1989) have all suggested that language does not serve women and men equally well. A quick look at the canon of literary works currently taught in U.S. universities or at the debate over the question of what is meant by women's voice in literature (Bleich, 1986; Gardiner, 1980; Russ, 1983; Schweikart, 1986; Spender, 1989) or even at the relative silence of women in public forums (even when the subject at hand has special significance for women—e.g., abortion) suggests, at the very least, that women and men have different relationships to the written and spoken word. Muted group theory (see Ardener, 1975, for the original formulation of the theory) is especially useful in understanding some of these observed differences.

Muted group theory, simply put, suggests that the communication system does not serve all members of a culture equally, in large part because not all members have participated equally in its formulation, and hence the system (the language) does not reflect the practices and values of all members. Implicit in this discussion is a definition of language as social behavior, reflective of social values and status positions within a culture.

Muted group theory provides a way of conceptualizing two types of structures important for understanding the workings of language within a social context: the underlying *template structures* of a group (the mesh of beliefs, attitudes, prejudices, and categories that might be said to comprise their world view) and the *structure of realization* or the articulation of that world view—the spoken and written language (see Kramarae, 1981, for a full discussion). The underlying structures cannot be known; we can only know them indirectly through their reflections in language and other signs. Codified within the language that we use, then, are beliefs, values, and attitudes. However, since not all members of a culture have participated equally in the formulation of the language (that is, have not been sufficiently empowered to insure that their beliefs, values, and attitudes are codified) the language—the structure of realization—does not necessarily reflect all the world views held by its speakers; indeed as Spender (1980) and others have argued, it reflects a limited range of experiences and world views: those of the most powerful members of the culture.

Sociologist Edwin Ardener (1975) argues that groups that are on top of the social hierarchy determine to a great extent the dominant communication system of a society:

> [A] society may be dominated or overdetermined by the model (or models) generated by one dominant group within the system. This dominant model may impede the free expression of alternative models of their world which subdominant [minority] groups may possess, and perhaps may even inhibit the very generation of such models. . . . [T]here may be presumed to be a considerable degree of "fit" between the dominant model and their [the dominant group's] structural position in society. This gives them a great advantage over those in the subdominant groups for whom the "fit" might be very imperfect. As a result, the latter might be relatively more "inarticulate" when expressing themselves through the idiom of the dominant group, and silent on matters of special concern for them for which no accommodation has been made. (xii)

As Ardener suggests, dominant-group members are in a privileged position vis-à-vis the language since it is their world view that is reflected in the spoken and written word. As a result, their experiences and beliefs find easy expression and accommodation within the language. Members of nondominant or minority cultural groups, on the other hand, are often required to "translate" their beliefs, values, and experiences into the terms set in language by the dominant group; at times even this translation is impossible since some of the groups' experiences (perhaps the most significant ones?) are alien to the experiences and interests of the dominant group and hence find no expression within the language.

Subordinate or nondominant groups within the culture (including women, children, and minorities) are thus made "inarticulate" since the words and norms of speaking are not generated by nor necessarily suited to these groups' experiences. In this sense these groups are muted. Their experiences and values are not deemed significant or important; often these experiences are not even represented in the language, which is in itself an important form of validation. To gain access to the language, nondominant- or minority-group members must filter their experiences and values through those of the dominant group, the only acceptable means of expression available. The other option for women, children, and minorities is to develop alternative codes that reflect their experiences, attitudes, and values (see for example, Tannen, 1990, for an extended discussion on women's language and women's culture); when they do so, these groups run the risk of being further marginalized within and trivialized by the dominant culture.

It should be noted that this characterization of dominant and subordinate groups within a culture oversimplifies a complex situation. Participation in a cultural group—the sharing of values, attitudes, and practices—is hardly an all-or-nothing thing. Nor is the situation static in terms of group membership or of the values, attitudes, and practices of the groups. Hence, members of a dominant social group may vary considerably in the extent to which they adhere to values concerning language behavior and the frequency with which they engage in certain language practices; and, too, their values, attitudes, and practices may change over time as a result of contact with other groups, educational experiences, etc. The dynamic nature of cultural groups notwithstanding, the theory suggests that certain groups, broadly defined, are in a relatively privileged position with respect to socially rewarded language habits. Other groups, by virtue of their class, race, ethnic origin, or gender, may be categorically excluded from determining which language behaviors will be socially valued and cultivated.

Muted group theory suggests further that constant reference to the dominant model as a way of validating experiences threatens to undermine the nondominant groups' ability to separate their attitudes and experiences from those of the group in power, perhaps even to articulate their own attitudes and values other than in relation to the powerful group. Examples of the mismatch of dominant and nondominant models of reality and their impact on nondominant groups abound. Spender, for example, has argued persuasively that female sexuality has been defined, not in terms of the female experience, but from a male perspective, as minus sexuality; as a result, Spender concludes,

This allocation of sexuality to the dominant group—in the face of the evidence to the contrary—illustrates how dominance and mutedness are constructed. It is not just males who perceive the nonsexuality of women according to the dictates of the culture—females learn to perceive it as well. (1980:172)

As the above discussion suggests, muted group theory, with its emphasis on the implications of social power for access to language, provides a way of understanding the nature of the mismatch between minority groups' language and literacy values, attitudes, and practices, and those of the dominant group, explaining the frequent failure of members of these groups to successfully master prescribed language and literacy conventions.

LITERACY AND ASYMMETRICAL POWER RELATIONSHIPS

Muted group theory suggests that different access to language can best be understood in the context of asymmetrical or uneven power relationships. With respect to minority groups and their access to language (written and spoken), power relationships can be seen to affect literacy acquisition in the following way: Literacy is defined by the dominant group, which in this country is essentially White and male; it is typically equated with dominant group (essay-text) literacy, characterized (as mentioned above) by explicit, decontextualized, impersonal language. These features, in turn, are expressions of the values and norms of the dominant cultural group that has largely been responsible for the formulation of this essay-text definition of literacy (see discussions in Gee, 1985 and 1990). In this country, essay-text literacy is thus equated with "literacy." All other types of literacy behavior are regarded as derivative, lesser, marked, much in the same way that dominant group humor and logic are equated with "humor" and "logic"; hence, there is a special category for "women's humor" and "women's logic." Failure to acquire this specific type of literacy, as Heath (1983) noted, is regarded more generally as failure to acquire literacy at all. So, for example, from the mainstream perspective, the literacy practices of members of the Roadville and Trackton communities in Heath's study—expressions of the values and attitudes of those communities—do not qualify as true literacy. Literate behavior that does not conform to the definition of literacy set by the dominant group, while it may be recognized as acceptable, even cultivated, by other groups, has little or no positive status within the dominant culture.

The very importance of the dominant/marginal (of lesser value) distinction is likely to be a product of the dominant definition of social structure. Some features of the minority's experience, including literacy norms and practices, have not been encoded within the dominant language forms and hence cannot be expressed easily within this social structure, which validates and gives expression only to the experiences of the dominant group. The resulting failure of the minority group to participate fully in the language—that is, their "mutedness"—is a product of the asymmetrical or uneven power within a culture. A minority group's mutedness with respect to expected literacy behavior further aids in maintaining the status quo; by residing on the fringes of literacy, minorities are poorly positioned to initiate the very social changes that might ultimately result in broadening the definition of acceptable (desirable) literacy behavior. Minority-group members are thus consigned to relative unimportance in the culture by virtue of their mutedness with respect to the accepted forms of literacy.

Furthermore, literacy failures of minority-group members are regarded as personal failures, since within the accepted autonomous model literacy is regarded as a personal attribute. Repeated instances of literacy failure are thus considered failures of personal initiative by members of minority groups. Discussion focuses on minorities themselves, who are regarded as suspect—why *is it* that Blacks and Hispanics have such relatively high rates of literacy failure?—while the underlying assumptions about the nature of literacy and the role of literacy education in reinforcing and recreating the values and privileged position of the dominant group go unexamined.

When the definition of literacy is seen in the context of uneven social power, attempts by marginal groups to introduce alternative literacy values, norms, and behaviors (thus perhaps broadening the standard definition of literacy) can be understood to pose a serious threat to the dominant culture, for whom the ability to designate certain literacy forms as viable and others as unworthy is an important source of social power. Maintenance of power, in the form of what might be called possession of literacy, then becomes critical. If other forms of literacy are recognized, even valued, the dominant essay-text form must be regarded as one among a number of possible literacies. The social power—in the form of jobs, educational opportunities, status that accrues to those who define the acceptable formats and expressions of literate behavior—is at risk. Access to literacy must be in the terms set by the dominant group; to allow for variation is to accede power.

Members of the marginal group who participate in the dominant culture, then, must adopt the communication system of the dominant group—its encoded meaning, values, and attitudes. Minority-group members who adjust to the dominant definition of literacy may suffer severe social and personal displacement; those who are unwilling or unable to make this adjustment may well suffer literacy failure. The Hispanic students Zanger interviewed were clearly aware of the personal and cultural demands that accompanied success in school, which must be defined in part as the acquisition of accepted, dominant-culture literacy norms and practices. These students saw themselves as outside literacy, that is, as outside the group that defines the rules for participation in the dominant culture. The more successful of these students, of course, have acquired literacy, but we might ask at what price. They seem to understand why many of their fellow students might not have chosen to make similar concessions. A number of the statements by these students illustrate the extent to which they feel that their culture and cultural identity is not highly valued within the school and indeed plays no significant role in school literacy:

> [T]hey won't accept you if you're not like them. They want to monoculture (you).

> [T]hey (the schools) say they have programs for ethnic backgrounds, for multicultural communities, but that isn't really true, all the way. It's true to some extent [but] they only focus on certain ethnics, besides whites, but they don't really focus on ours. They ignore ours. They don't give us the respect that we deserve. They ignore our culture, our Hispanic culture.

> . . . and to let them [schools, other students] know that we can do as Americans do, that we can express ourselves and let them know that our culture is as good as their culture, let us unificate [sic] with them so they understand us and we understand them.

Zanger's discussion of the ambivalence of many members of the dominant group about full literacy (and resulting participation in the culture) for minority groups can be seen in terms of the threat of power realignment: a shift from a single conception of literacy defined by the dominant cultural group to a broader definition of literacy that includes forms of print interaction specific to nondominant groups within the culture. And the ambivalence that members of the minority group might themselves feel about full access to essay-text literacy can be seen as a reflection of their understanding of what they may have to sacrifice—cultural identity—in order to gain access to this literacy. One of the students ends by stating that "you don't need to change your culture to be American." Given the other observations the students have made, this sentiment seems naively hopeful. It seems that access to the dominant culture—and in a culture that is print dependent, this includes literacy—does indeed extract the very high price of giving up at least part of this cultural identity.

The above discussion suggests a number of challenging, interrelated topics that might be explored by educators involved in literacy education in this country. First, these educators might profit from a critical examination of the autonomous model of literacy, especially assumptions about the social functions of interactions with print. Secondly, discussions of this topic would ideally lead to investigations of the divergent literacy practices of the students served by this country's educational system as well as to fuller understanding—and, it is hoped, appreciation—of the cultural values that underlie these practices. Finally, both educators and students might well benefit from a thoughtful exploration of the connections between social power and the literacy practices cultivated and rewarded within this country's schools. Open discussion of topics such as these might help to reduce the cultural risks and enhance the personal rewards associated with acquiring literacy.

REFERENCES

Abel, E. (Ed.), (1980). *Writing and sexual difference*. Chicago: University of Chicago Press.

Ardener, E. (1975). The "problem" revisited. In S. Ardener (Ed.) *Perceiving women* (pp. 19–27). London: Malaby Press.

Bleich, D. (1986). Gender interests in reading and language. In P.P.

Schweickart & E.A. Flynn (Eds.), *Gender and reading: Essays on readers, texts and contexts* (pp. 234–266). Baltimore: Johns Hopkins.

Clanchy, M. (1979). *From memory to written record.* Baltimore: Edward Arnold.

Cook-Gumprez, J. (Ed.). (1986). *The social construction of literacy.* New York: Cambridge University Press.

Ferdman, B. (1990). Literacy and cultural identity. *Harvard Educational Review, 60,* 181–204.

Freire, P. and Macedo, D. (1987). *Literacy: Reading the word and the world.* S. Hadley, MA: Bergin and Garvey.

Gardiner, J.K. (1980). On female identity and writing by women. In E. Abel (Ed.) *Writing and sexual difference* (pp. 177–191). Chicago: University of Chicago Press.

Gee, J.P. (1985). The narrativization of experience in the oral style. *Journal of Education, 167,* 9–35.

_____. (1986). Orality and literacy: From *The Savage Mind* to *Ways With Words. TESOL Quarterly, 20,* 719–746.

_____. (1990). *Social linguistics and literacies: Ideology in discourse.* New York: The Falmer Press.

Goody, J. & Watt, I.P. (1968). The consequences of literacy. *Comparative Studies in History and Society, 5,* 304–345.

Graddol, D. & Swann, J. (1989). *Gender voices.* Oxford: Basil Blackwell.

Graff, H.J. (1979). *The literacy myth: Literacy and social structure in the 19th century city.* New York: Academic Press.

Heath, S.B. (1983). *Ways with words.* New York: Cambridge University Press.

_____. (1985). Literacy or literate skills? Considerations for ESL/EFL learners. In P. Larson, E. Judd & D. Messerschmidt (Eds.), *On TESOL '84* (pp. 15–28). Washington: TESOL.

Hildyard, A. & Olson, D. (1978). Literacy and the specialization of language. Unpublished manuscript, Ontario Institute for Studies in Education.

Kaplan, R.B. & Palmer, J.D. (1992). Literacy and applied linguistics. In W. Grabe & R.B. Kaplan (Eds.), *Introduction to applied linguistics* (pp. 191–212). Reading, MA: Addison-Wesley.

Kramarae, C. (1981). *Women and men speaking.* Rowley, MA: Newbury House.

Langer, J. (Ed.). (1987). *Language, literacy and culture: Issues of society and schooling.* Norwood, NJ: Ablex.

Michaels, S. (1981). "Sharing time": Children's narrative styles and differential access to literacy. *Language in Society, 19,* 423–442.

Ong, W.J. (1982). *Orality and literacy: The technologizing of the world.* New York: Methuen.

Penelope, J. (1990). *Speaking freely.* New York: Pergamon Press.

Penfield, J. (1987). *Women and language in transition.* Albany: State University of New York Press.

Russ, J. (1983). *How to suppress women's writing.* Austin: University of Texas Press.

Schweikart, P.P. (1986). Reading ourselves: Towards a feminist theory of reading. In P.P. Schweikart & E.A. Flynn (Eds.), *Gender and reading: Essays on readers, texts and contexts* (pp. 31–62). Baltimore: Johns Hopkins.

Scollon, R. & Scollon, S. (1981). *Narrative, literacy and face in inter-ethnic communication.* Norwood, NJ: Ablex.

Scribner, S. (1986). Literacy in three metaphors. In N.L. Stein (Ed.), *Literacy in American schools: Learning to read and write* (pp. 7–22). Chicago: University of Chicago Press.

Scribner, S. & Cole, M. (1981). *The psychology of literacy.* Cambridge: Harvard University Press.

Snow, C., Barnes, W., Chandler, J., Goodman, I.F. & Hemphill, L. (1991). *Unfulfilled expectations: Home and school influences on literacy.* Cambridge: Harvard University Press.

Spender, D. (1980). *Man made language.* London: Routledge and Kegan Paul.

———. (1989). *The writing or the sex.* New York: Pergamon Press.

Street, B. (1984). *Literacy in theory and practice.* New York: Cambridge University Press.

———. (1987). Literacy and social changes: The significance of social context in the development of literacy programmes. In D. Wagner (Ed.), *The future of literacy in a changing world* (pp. 49–64). New York: Pergamon Press.

Tannen, D. (1990). *You just don't understand.* New York: Ballantine Books.

Thorne, B., Kramarae, C. & Henley, N. (1983). *Language, gender and society.* Rowley, MA: Newbury House.

Trueba, H. (1989). *Raising silent voices: Educating minorities for the 21st century.* New York: Newbury House.

Woolf, V. (1963). *A room of one's own.* New York: Harcourt Brace Jovanovich.

CHAPTER 9

Value and Subjectivity in Literacy Practice

Mark Zuss

In an era in which a concern for cultural pluralism may have come
of age, educational philosophy, research, and practice urgently
need to attend to the origins and significance of varying forms of
self- and collective representation within cross-cultural encounters.
In order to initiate this task in the interest of a genuinely student-
centered pedagogy, I believe that it is vital for educators to reflect
critically upon the relations established by the modes of discourse
privileged in cross-cultural classrooms. This chapter will analyze
linguistic practices within classrooms and the premises that generate them to disclose how forms of value, or ideological processes,
are inherent to multicultural literacy practices, and are germinal in
the formation of student motives, interactions, and identities.

The concepts of value and subjectivity, the focus of this paper,
serve to describe processes by which implicit power relations usually function within cross-cultural classrooms. These forms of
power are embodied in language use, standards, and criteria for
linguistic transaction. The privileging of certain modes of discourse
and organization of knowledge involves institutionalized norms of
rationality, meaning making, and literate interaction—modes that,
unevenly at best, include as well as exclude salient varieties of
cultural expression. Individual students and distinctive ethnic and
subcultural groups enter cross-cultural sites with differentials in
"cultural capital" (Apple, 1982), or resources enabling them to
interact and perform successfully in academic settings. Their ability to establish autonomous unified selves or individual and group

subjectivities is often riddled with contradictions and difficulties, deriving in large measure from values immanent to imparted educational practices, forms, and uses of knowledge that are never neutral. These values are inculcated, however implicitly and indirectly, by well-intentioned teachers and administrators, through privileged forms of language and linguistic interaction.

While student empowerment and critical thinking are now shibboleths for many educators who wish to allow students to develop "voice" and negotiate the structure and content of curricula, fundamental inquiry into the intentions and values students attach to the acquisition of literacy skills and the forms of language use salient to them is all too frequently unknown. Ignorance or rejection by educators of the forms of language use and values pertinent to diverse cultural groups attempting to participate in Adult Basic Education (ABE) and English as a Second Language (ESL) classes can create and sustain some measure of the profound alienation experienced by both teachers and students within the cross-linguistic classroom. Many ESL students are confronted with the complexity of mixed cultural identities. They often find themselves faced with conflicting choices in their linguistic interactions with regard to their own and others' perceived expectations of oral and written performances. Students are placed in linguistic exchanges with teachers and peers that draw from their own unequal expertise within both their native and target languages. Students, when questioned, frequently express that their goal is to transform their personal and working lives and that they view adult education as one of the chief means of gaining access to the prevailing social forms of power and discourse. In hundreds of interview questionnaires[1] that I have gathered, students recurrently define themselves as outsiders to the forms of power embodied in speaking and writing skills and view education as the primary route toward mastery of the language skills through which they can gain or regain positive self-definition, overcome shame, and utilize their experience and intelligence as full and equal participants in society. Yet educators appear generally unaware of the texture of these aspirations and their implications for literacy development. The cost of keeping hidden the specific articulation of students' expectations and perceptions of education is the continuance of a "narrative of exclusion" (Spivak, 1989) by otherwise enlightened educators.

One example of how students define their motivations and expectations was manifested a few years ago in an adult literacy program in which I worked, when the budget did not allow for the purchase of new materials. During the initial months, existing materials were used and students began to bring in their own books, newspapers, notes, and compositions for analysis and discussion. At one point, students questioned why we could not petition public officials for educational materials. One class decided to write letters to the Governor. I think the following letter by a recent South American immigrant is an eloquent, if not idealized, voicing of many students' expectations of education:

> Dear Governor:
>   It is not easy for me to write a letter, any letter. But the reasons that make me write this one are very important. Reading and reading better opens the world and all its wonders to me and to be able to read about other people, their lives, their good times and their sad lets you know that you are not alone and all people share times of fun and times of tears. To be able to write is to be able to put what you are thinking into words that can be changed, to be made better and more powerful and is in a big way better than just talking to someone. For the above reasons, I asked that the gifts of reading and writing be given to as many of us who reach out for help. Please do not forget us for we need help to be more part of the world.

This chapter addresses issues relevant to the use of subcultural and historically specific forms of language use by *discourse communities* and the ways these patterns shape the linguistic resources of individuals, including the forms of relevance, meaning, and rhetoric within particular collective contexts and repertoires. I am especially concerned with the linguistic constitution of the notion of identity in socialization. I will discuss contexts of use as generally relevant to often divergent cultural and linguistic communities. The contrast between academic and nonstandardized linguistic registers and the notion of value attached to disparate forms and contexts of language use are the most important facets of this inherent linguistic tension.

In relation to cross-linguistic education, I present a critique of value and its functioning. My primary intent is to demonstrate that value operates as a determining influence within what I term a "linguistic economy." This economy includes literacy acquisition and is thus central to the linguistic construction of subjectivity in the socialization and enculturation practices of contemporary societies in which power is distributed unequally. To formulate this argument, I analyze culturally salient forms of making meaning through the discourse communities—or audiences—to whom a speaker or writer intends to communicate, and the privileging of certain forms of language and thinking. More specifically, I critique popular "process" oriented writing theory and practice and their implicit assumptions. As Wallerstein (1983) points out, "Many ESL texts teach a language of survival or of expressing an opinion or purpose. Few, however, teach language that goes beyond identifying or accepting a situation—language that leads to empowerment" (17).

In describing the contexts within cross-linguistic education in which value is contested and of significance, I discuss what I take to be a primary dialectical relation between linguistic value and the formation of identity and subjectivity. This discussion of value and subjectivity is premised on a social constructivist view in the social sciences. Bruffee (1986) defines the social constructivist view succinctly in ascribing to it the assumption "that the matrix of thought is not the individual self but some community of knowledgeable peers and the vernacular knowledge of that community. That is, social construction understands knowledge and the authority of knowledge as community-generated, community-maintaining symbolic artifacts" (777). A social constructivist view affords scrutiny of value and subjectivity within contexts of socio-historically derived symbolic activity. This approach can avoid psychological or social reductionism in examining the formation of, constitution of, and changes in such complex cultural practices as discourse communities or standard and marginalized linguistic registers.

In order to assess the complex social, historical, and psychological forces brought to bear on students, I believe it is vital to examine the experiential and cognitive resources individuals from diverse ethnic and subcultural origins bring to the cross-cultural classroom. Ethnographic description of classrooms alone, however, while essential, is not always sufficient to explain the uneven levels of literacy, or cultural capital, within and between first and second languages and their complex interplay within matrices of power, culture, and value. Language experience, types of exposure, and contexts of familiarity with English, as well as the particulars of gender, race, age, and class compositions, vary dramatically within most multicultural settings. It is not always possible or desirable to attain a sense of what literacy means through empirical and research methods alone. Also necessary is an appreciation of the functions and relations various forms of literacy serve within a culture. As Scribner and Cole (1981) have argued, an approach that concerns itself with "cultural practice" is invaluable in any attempt to ascertain the specific constellation of social and cognitive factors present within particular settings. From this perspective, analyses of both social dynamics and individual cognition must be conducted in order to provide a richly contextualized account of a cultural practice. The approach necessary for an appreciation of the internal dynamics of cultural practices like literacy is one that takes heed to "considerations of value, philosophy and ideology" (Scribner, 1984:8). Most relevant to my analysis are the questions that Scribner proposes in order to examine the specific activities, motives, and constitution of literacy practices. These include: "What activities are carried out with written symbols? What significance is attached to them, and what status is conferred on those who engage in them? Is literacy a social right or a private power?" (8). Asking these questions augments traditional empirical research by probing the complex relations of power and difference—on the group and individual levels of class, race, and gender filiation—within differentially distributed activities like literacy practice.

The cultural practice and social constructivist approaches that orient my analysis of the functioning of value naturally entail a concern for cultural "dissonance" in cross-linguistic encounters. Delpit (1988) raises this problem in her examination of the divergent philosophies and practices regarding the education of Black and minority primary school students. Delpit interprets the "culture of power" operating in classrooms as a reflection of the prevailing norms, interactional styles, embedded meanings, and forms of discourse dominant in American society. In addition to teacher authority this power is expressed through the principles and guiding premises of textbooks and curricula that serve as exponents of a specific world view and its maintenance through educational standards, methods, and contents. Most importantly, Delpit finds the culture of power embedded in codes or rules that "relate to linguistic forms, communicative strategies, and presentation of self: ways of talking, ways of writing, ways of dressing, ways of interacting" (1988:283). What must be emphasized and supplemented to this notion of power is its dynamic quality as an interactive relation in which students in cross-cultural encounters are not merely acted upon, but act in opposition or resistance to dominant forms of the culture of power. Discourse communities and subcultural group identities cohere; their resilience is based on shared experience and knowledge. Even the kind of voluntary subcultural groupings that may arise during the span of a semester—such as working women with children, or individuals studying together for civil service or academic testing—have the capacity, at least potentially, to act as autonomous agents in formulating their own standards, goals, and forms of value and power.

The discussion that follows is based on my experience as a teacher, researcher and administrator within several adult education institutions. In these capacities I have become aware of the forceful role of power relations in classroom dynamics emerging from the fabric of diverse linguistic usages and experiences. My work within these varied settings has furthered my commitment to adapting a Freirean-inspired pedagogy to urban American contingencies. This commitment rests in large measure on accepting that in the United States the politics of language use is almost always denied, and that urgent issues facing students in cross-cultural educational settings with regard to the value of what and how they learn and to their chances to genuinely gain access to forms of power are often obscured by technocratic or methods-oriented analyses. Freire and Macedo (1987) are explicit about this:

> [T]he intellectual activity of those without power is always characterized as nonintellectual. I think this issue should be underscored, not just as a dimension of pedagogy, but a dimension of politics as well. This is difficult to do in a society like that of the United States where the political nature of pedagogy is negated ideologically. (122)

Freire and Macedo claim that this denial of politics functions as the effect of an ideology that gives the "appearance that education serves everyone, thus assuring that it continues to function in the interest of the dominant class" (122). I accept their call for American educators to "assume a political posture that renounces the myth of pedagogical neutrality" (126). The following sections of the chapter provide an analysis that adopts such a Freirean perspective with regard to the social construction and conflicts inherent to the issues of value and subjectivity in literacy practice.

VALUE AND DISCOURSE COMMUNITIES

The notion of discourse communities derives from studies of the ethnography of communication (Gumperz, 1978; Hymes, 1974; Labov, 1972). Within the cultural practice and social constructivist approaches that inform my work, this notion is a valuable concept for examining literacy acquisition practices and socialization through language use. Hymes (1972) defines speech communities as cultural and subcultural collectives "sharing rules for the conduct and interpretation of speech, and rules for the interpretation of at least one linguistic variety" (54). In the concept's original formulation, the focus was on forms of dialect, standardized, and vernacular speech forms, with Black English being perhaps the most often scrutinized and cited. Applied to composition—a central concern of this chapter—the notion of discourse communities is necessary for an investigation of the dynamics of learning in relation to what can be regarded as linguistic forms of cultural stratification. It is especially helpful in addressing the tensions and more than occasional confrontations of linguistic registers that take place between students and educators who come from cultures that differ in what has often been loosely termed, and I think inappropriately, "cognitive style."

Chase (1988) claims that "discourse communities are organized around the production and legitimation of particular forms of knowledge and social practices at the expense of others" (13). Discourse communities structure expression by favoring and restricting particular forms and organization of language. For Freed and Broadhead (1987), discourse communities define the codes available within groups, generating institutional norms that determine decisions regarding rhetorical usage. These norms, whether "cultural," "generic," or "situational," govern the parameters of communicative competence. They constrain features of oral and written language by "regulating tone, style, content, and level of technicality" (163). Discourse communities' norms also influence text production, including "documentation practices (style), in-house format guides, and group or disciplinary injunctions such as 'do not use the first person'" (1987:157). Johns (1990) stresses the role of "participatory mechanisms" that provide the means for feedback and reinforcement, and points out how practices such as journal keeping, newsletters, and the selective use of certain genres serve to define and sustain them. Johns also observes how academic discourse communities establish "conventions for establishing the 'truth', for example, through developing hypotheses and analyzing data" (32). Distinct vocabularies and conventions, including such key features of "voice" as acceptance or rejection of figurative language and self-reference, are also common indicators of the practice of discourse communities. Johns cites the examples of students confronting the pressure to "talk like engineers" within academic specializations that require their "surrendering their own language and modes of thought to the requirements of the target community" (33).

Value, in my conception, operates as the underlying, and often unexamined, basis for evaluations of intellectual and literate activity. Determination of the interactive viability of specific discursive forms that students might utilize as natural resources for their second-language acquisition, such as the narratives of emigration and autobiography frequently recounted by ESL students, is done in accord with the values of the prevailing "culture of power." As both Delpit's (1986; 1988) and Giroux's work (1983) strikingly demonstrate, these dominant and hegemonic criteria and their attendant evaluations and norms—or instantiations of value—are reproduced in the classroom through discursive practices. Value is constitutive and inherent to many of the choices, selections, and standards governing language use, including forms of rhetoric, allusion, thematic and topic coherence, imagery, and the use or rejection of figurative language. This notion of value permits viewing linguistic tensions as reflective of unequal exchanges and distributions of power, particularly between subcultural communities and the dominant values of standardized and academic discourse.

Value, as the manifestation of dominant forms of power, including discursive criteria and norms for their exchange through negotiated language use between discourse communities, cannot be meaningfully examined without observing its impact on students' activity and on the choices confronting them. This effect includes the generation of forms for the expression of identity and self definition in and between groups and individuals. Value is implicit in the linguistic formation of identity, through specific, historical forms of linguistic socialization that structure forms of subjectivity that do not necessarily coincide with other aspects of students' lives outside the classroom. Value is materialized in practices that constrain or prohibit forms of nonstandardized, idiomatic, and figurative usage (Heath, 1983). It is also seen in the authority long granted to forms of rationality and argument privileged in Western education, such as the expository essay with its ordered thesis development and radical denial of voice. These forms— which also include top-down, deductive logical models, gists, summarization skills, use of titles, standards of citation, quotation, and other accepted standards of argumentation—have been accepted so thoroughly by generations of educators that they have become transparent and seemingly natural. This process serves to justify the implementation of certain forms of value as universal, and their use as guiding principles and unquestioned sources for the motivations of institutions and the students who come to assimilate them.

The dominance of a primary and constitutive value affecting all groups points to another crucial aspect of the dynamic of discourse communities in relation to cross-cultural literacy and activity, namely, their power to exclude. The norms established by the academic discourse community dictate the functional criteria for measuring cognitive development and legitimate what constitutes literate activity. Bizzell makes this clear in observing that academics frequently decide that

> a large number of students are incompetent in the form of literacy preferred in school. This "academic literacy," as I call it, entails the ability to use Standard English and think academically. Hence, to be an "academic illiterate" is to be unpracticed in Standard English and inept in "critical thinking." (Bizzell in Johns, 1990:29)

For observers like Bourdieu and Passeron (1977), discourse communities represent fundamental world views, inculcating members to "particular ways of life" that inaugurate and structure the use of specific values. In ESL and cross-cultural classrooms, academic conventions are especially instrumental in creating what Bizzell (1982) considers the "outsider" status relegated to students and, consequently, to disempowered discourse communities. Arguing that students from non–Standard English cultures face the difficulty of needing to develop their facility in "multiple literacies," Bizzell observes that these "outsiders" actually function within a larger linguistic and cultural repertoire than students enculturated with Standard English alone.

Divergences in cultural expectations frequently involve disparate forms of individual and group representation and standards of argumentation, persuasion, and organization. Gumperz (1982) claims that "where communicative conventions and symbols of social identity differ, the social reality itself becomes subject to question" (3). Gumperz describes the cross-linguistic miscuing and the asymmetry of power relations that can occur within problematic interethnic communication encounters, including courtrooms, hospitals, classrooms, and job interviews. He gives the example of an interview between an East Indian applicant and his Standard-English-speaking interviewers. Even what would seem to be such a basic and transparent encounter as the exchange of greetings can become problematic between teachers and students or between students of different cultures. English lacks many of the subtleties of address and pragmatic function available to speakers of languages like Japanese or Balinese. In Balinese, for example, an "elaborate repertoire" of labels and designations that includes "birth order markers, kinship terms, caste titles, sex indicators" (Geertz, 1984:129) is utilized in communication between individuals, allowing for complex and precise expression of formality, deference, authority, respect, or intimacy. A speaker of Balinese learning English could be confronted by fundamental differences in the available linguistic pragmatics. Integral differences of this kind between languages may result in conflictual linguistic exchanges that affect students' identities by interfering with culturally salient forms of interpersonal communication, resulting in silence or hindered second-language acquisition.

Gumperz (1982) details features of face-to-face encounters that can account for some of the qualities of an individual's "symbolic and social capital." Apple (1982), Bourdieu and Passeron (1977), and others use these terms to refer to differences in the cultural resources and linguistic repertoires that enable or disenable an individual to interact and perform in a given context. Culturally meaningful forms of signification can be conveyed bodily through microsignals such as facial and eye movements, through proxemic signals including poise and posture, and through handshakes, winking, and the direction or avoidance of an individual's gaze. These kinds of symbolic differences result from varying cultural assumptions regarding appropriate behavior, meanings, and forms of structuring information, as well as from distinctive linguistic pragmatics and patterning. Their recognition is a crucial starting point for a pedagogy that attends to value and subjectivity and their differential constitution and expression. Wallerstein (1983) emphasizes the need to observe cultural practices and differences that can easily be misinterpreted or ignored to the detriment of learning. Citing the interactional styles of two Asian groups— Cantonese and Laotian students—she observed that

> Cantonese students tend to sit upright, focus on the teacher, and repeat individually or as a group after the teacher. Laotian students are strikingly different. They tend to lean toward each other, talk under their breath as they point out the lessons to their neighbors and laugh at (and with) each other's attempts to speak English. (13)

Wallerstein also notes, for example, that many Indochinese students use nonverbal cues—such as the nodding of their heads toward teachers as gestures of respect—that do not necessarily indicate understanding.

Within multicultural classrooms, fundamentally different and culturally specific forms of signification are frequently transmitted and function during routine interactions. These activities include those essential to the exchange of knowledge and the formulation of meaning, such as culturally valid and familiar construals of evidence, exposition and development of topic, and the construction of salient and persuasive argument. Mishra (1982) describes how speakers of Indian English structure and maintain conversational cohesion through distinct forms of prosodic organization that include particular pitch emphases and markings that allow for indicating major arguments shared by various sentences, shifts in topic and perspective, and the sequencing of narrative events.

This discussion of discourse communities is premised on the notion that forms of value, criteria, and evaluation are, at least, implicit in cross-linguistic pedagogy. The imposition of homogeneity through dominant forms of value can mean a denial of cultural and linguistic diversity. Attention to the distinctiveness of cultural and symbolic capital that individuals and groups are capable of utilizing, and the alternate, heterogenous forms of value that they represent, provides an initial view into the formation of subjectivity and identity that is the focus of the next section.

SUBJECTIVITY AND LINGUISTIC ECONOMY

This inquiry into the entwining of value and subjectivity is premised on tenets of structuralism with regard to language and social relations. I borrow in particular the economic connotation of Saussure's (1959) designation of value to the linguistic signifier, or bearer, of meanings and reference. For Saussure, the notion of an economy of signifiers is arbitrarily established and maintained in the synchronic structure of given languages (*langue*) as well as in their actual historical use in all the manifold discourses (*parole*). The specific contexts of use, pertinent to the cultural-practice approach espoused here, can be observed in the dynamics of classroom conversations, the filling out of applications, role-playing, and oral or written student narratives. Within a given standardized national language, the making and preservation of meaning is maintained through equivalences and differences in signs. Comparing the precepts of linguistics with political economy, Saussure (1959) states that "as in political economy we are confronted with the notion of value; both sciences are concerned with a system of equating things of different orders—labor and wages in one and a signified and signifier in the other" (79).

This structuralist description, when augmented with a notion of the differential values established by specific cultures and discourse communities, offers a conceptual tool for examining how various signifiers of value function within cross-linguistic educational encounters. The focus here is on marginal individuals and groups—or "outsiders"—to Standard English conventions, whose particular class, gender, and ethnic specificity may be denied by institutionalized and normative forms of discourse, such as the composition and rhetorical techniques usually taught in adult basic education programs. For example, as noted below, topics are as culture-bound as are their structuring and rhetorical construction. In multicultural classrooms, the format of the expository essay, an academic bedrock, is often poorly understood by those students whose first-language skills have not familiarized them with it. The reappropriation of varying conversational styles in formalized, academic settings and the lack of salience of both genre and topic frequently mitigates against the powers of expression, knowledge, and fluency of many communicatively competent nonnative speakers.

A critical aspect of my analysis is the linkage in the maintenance of identity between the notion of value proposed here and socialization processes. Identity is a generalized term in common usage that requires closer scrutiny, and one that I believe is insufficient in addressing the complexities of cross-cultural education, particularly with regard to the relation between thinking and discourse. I would like to distinguish ethnic, gender, and class identity formation from subjectivity for the purposes of probing into some of the complexities facing students and educators. Giroux (1983) stresses this point cogently in stating that a "pedagogy of critical literacy and voice needs to be developed around a politics of difference and community that is not simply grounded in a celebration of plurality" (21). In contrast to a frequently invoked form of radical cultural pluralism that, as Giroux shows, considers linguistic practices as simply differing from each other, and one that considers a form of "cultural imperialism" (Labov, 1972) any educational reforms that attempt to resituate working class students (who comprise the majority in ESL classes), I argue that cross-cultural encounters represent not merely empirical differences but situate the inherent contestation of values encoded in discursive practices. Difference in relation to values must not be perceived as a quantitative issue of plurality or cultural relativism, but rather as a question of the commensurability and mutual compatibility of often very divergent linguistic, educational, and ideological practices on the part of educators and students alike.

The basis for this discussion of subjectivity stems from work by Foucault (1976), Spivak (1988, 1989), and others in which the self is considered "without ontological foundations" and as a "full nexus of forces" (Lentricchia, 1980:201). With the notion of "subject positions," Smith (1988) offers an apt description of the multiple and contradictorily constituted nature of consciousness. Subject positions is a useful term with which to provisionally locate the discontinuous or nonidentical nature of subjects, as distinguished from the sense of individuation of ego as a discrete, autonomous, or stationary entity. Multicultural classrooms are sites in which evidence supportive of the notion of subject positions can be observed and articulated. Discontinuous and often contradictory forms of subjectivity are formed in the interplay of divergent linguistic economies and differentials in value and cultural or symbolic capital attached to classroom discursive practices.

Gumperz (1982) corroborates this point with regard to identity in noting that ethnic, class, and gender distinctions are not constants. They do not provide an accurate delineation of individual communicative abilities, nor do descriptions of these categories fully afford the "parameters" of how individuals participate and interact within and between linguistic economies. It is the task of analysts of discourse to begin to identify how identities are "communicatively produced." Giroux, whose work documents the nature of the reproduction of ideology and knowledge within schools, considers one of the tasks of educators concerned with issues of identity formation to be to attend

> to the contradictory nature of student experience and voice and therefore establish the grounds whereby such experience can be interrogated and analyzed with respect to both their strengths and weaknesses. Voice in this case not only provides a theoretical framework for recognizing the cultural logic that anchors subjectivity and learning, it also provides a referent for criticizing the kind of romantic celebration of student experience that characterized much of the radical pedagogy of the early 1960s. At issue here is linking the pedagogy of student voice to a project of possibility that allows students to affirm and celebrate the interplay of different voices and experience while at the same time recognizing that such voices must always be interrogated for the various ontological, epistemological, and ethical and political interests they represent. (In Freire and Macedo, 1987:20)

The research that I believe to be necessary now is one that will permit careful appreciation of the complexities of both cultural diversity and linguistic use. Researchers and educators must give attention to how individuals represent and define themselves as they use language in the classroom. This requires recognition that each member of any given ethnic and cultural group is placed within a specific regional and national linguistic economy that allows for a certain latitude or field of subjectivity to emerge. Within the cultural, linguistic, and individual constellation of plurality and difference, the identities that are maintained and internalized in the classroom afford certain relative, if at times dramatically unequal, degrees of freedom for their development and expression. In order to conduct this type of research or educational practice, it is crucial that teachers and researchers reflect on their own self-representation in terms of the implicit values and forms of ideology implicated by the linguistic practices that they bring to their teaching or research and to the assessment of students.

Between and within discourse communities, the varieties of linguistic usage and value in disparate and unequal linguistic economies are also constitutive of often-divided senses of self or subjectivity of individuals whose identities are formed by the more inclusive designations and markings of ethnicity, gender, and class. Subjectivity can be defined for the present purpose as the specific, contextualized linguistic instantiation of power relations and dynamics that derives from differentials in value between and within discourse communities. Students in ESL classes, for example, bear at least two linguistic and cultural repertoires; for many of these students the language and culture in which they were socialized remains a primary referent. It is useful to raise again Bizzell's observation (in Johns, 1990) that these students negotiate multiple literacies and that their available linguistic resources or cultural capital are often considerably richer in diversity than that provided by Standard English. In addition, it is necessary to emphasize that a given student's competence and facility in each will vary and that each form of literacy may bear distinctive pragmatic rules of interpersonal performance, as illustrated in the Balinese and Indian English cases cited above. When confronted with the linguistic and cultural models utilized in educational and bureaucratic institutions, conflicts arising from students' status as linguistic "outsiders" and the constraints imposed on the range of their expression can occur.

These conflicts can be manifested in a number of ways that detrimentally influence student performance. They can include the physical and symbolic bodily forms mentioned earlier, expressive of a disparity in cultural expectations. While these kinds of conflicts are most likely to occur in cross-linguistic settings, they are also manifest within more homogeneous encounters. Most classrooms incorporate students with some degrees of divergence in academic and linguistic skills, especially in terms of their facility at using the different registers required for academia and specialized and increasingly technological workplaces. More importantly, the hegemonic values that set the prevailing criteria of modern educational and business performance require an assimilation and identity formation that is not often achieved without some resistance. Socialization does not uniformly and monolithically reproduce identity or ideological orientation within groups. It also involves disjunctures, splittings, and contradictions within the cognitive and affective realm of all individuals attempting to become full participants and communicative agents. These disjunctures develop along the fault lines of a dominant value imposed on individuals whose identities develop primarily from specific cultural, subcultural, and discourse communities and from the domains of knowledge, dialect, idiom, and reference germane to their everyday existence.

The kind of educational practice that I am concerned with is a critical pedagogy informed by both cognitive and cultural development. It is a reflective practice that attempts to examine its own premises considering the developmental origins, tensions, and possible expression of multiple self- and collective representations. In delving into these issues, it is concomitantly concerned with how subjectivity is sociohistorically and linguistically constituted. By defining subjectivity in relation to differential values employed in discursive practices, it becomes possible to observe how students in various contexts of activity contest the limits of a liberal educational and cultural pluralism that purports to be inclusive of all student identities yet often essentially disregards crucial forms of difference among groups and ignores those inherent to the subjectivity of individual students. With regard to the complexities faced by ESL students, Wallerstein (1983) observes that, "although the melting pot theory no longer predominates within American society, many students find that its replacement—cultural pluralism—is also a myth" (5). The multicultural, diversified classroom is a site of contestation and differential access based on varying and not necessarily compatible or commensurable discourse conventions. Cultural pluralism has become manifest in practices that claim to generate equal opportunities but fail—in such implementations as the writing process approaches like those of Calkins, Elbow and Murray discussed below—to acknowledge the differences in cultural capital (including the specific skills, linguistic competencies, and styles) with which students enter schools and that can determine their access to educational and social mobility.

It is in the forms of language use within classroom discourse, both oral and written, that the pivotal role of value in constituting the subjectivity of members of discourse communities must be acknowledged. The injunctions that emerge from particular theories and practices of literacy instruction and, in particular, composition techniques—even in 'freewriting' and expressivist process oriented modes—are not likely to be made explicit or formalized. As Freed and Broadhead (1987) point out, "they can exist as result of tradition and practice. Within the writing process, they reflect a writer's overall environment for thinking, composing and revising" (157).

The value-laden nature of composition theories and practices is discernible in the near ubiquity of "process" approaches. Process approaches such as those advocated by Elbow (1973), Murray (1982), and Calkins (1983)—all of which emphasize 'freewriting', non-directive teaching, and the use of journals for personal writing experience—are intended to permit self-expression and the generation of student-centered texts in nonauthoritarian contexts. In actual classroom practice, however, the process approach can serve to suppress the development of voice. Particularly in cross-cultural settings, emphasis on process over product, or "organism" over mechanism, while generative of writing, can disregard the salient cultural choices members of discourse communities are likely to use in self-representation and expression. As work by Reid (1990) and Michaels (1986) (discussed below) discloses, such basic notions as topic, narrative coherence, and self-description are very much dependent on a complex of cultural and linguistic values.

Process approaches as represented in ESL theory and practice have been particularly influenced by the cognitivist orientation. A focus on the mental operations, heuristics, and protocols of writers has dominated work of influential researchers like Hayes and Flower (1983) whose work stresses the individual and recursive nature of writing processes. Berlin (1988) describes this view as one in which it is assumed that the "structures of the mind are in perfect harmony with the structures of the material world, the minds of the audience and the units of language" (480). This form of universalizing process, or abstracting cognition and practice from the actual contexts of discourse use and community, prevails in the guiding premises of many multicultural educational settings.

Emphases on process, whether expressivist or cognitive in orientation, can act to deny the development of self- and community articulation by refusing to acknowledge the importance of differences between discourse communities and their relation to prevailing linguistic economies. Delpit (1988) quotes an African-American student's perception of a writing class that utilized a process approach:

> I didn't feel she was teaching us anything. She wanted us to correct each others' papers. . . . Maybe they're trying to learn what Black folks knew all the time, We understand how to improvise, how to express ourselves creatively. When I'm in a classroom, I'm not looking for that, I'm looking for structure, the more formal language. (287)

Delpit makes the important point that students do not always know what is expected of them in process-oriented sessions and that

> teachers do students no service to suggest, even implicitly, that "product" is not important. In this country, students will be judged on their product regardless of the process they utilized to achieve it. And that product, based as it is on the specific codes of a particular culture, is more readily produced when the directives of how to produce it are made explicit. (287)

We must remember that how we teach and how we read and interpret texts and the genres that appear to be natural and inherent to them are constructed in the context of unequal distributions of power. As Lentricchia (1983) argues, "all intellectual activity . . . is itself, from the start, a kind of praxis" (87) and is founded on various political, epistemological and aesthetic representations that express, if indirectly, collective wills to power.

Another example of the role that value plays in classroom discourse is provided by recent work in contrastive rhetoric, which proposes that different languages lead to variations in individual linguistic patterns and preferences in syntactic and textual organization. Work by Grabe and Kaplan (1989) and Reid (1990) focuses on forms of cultural variation and transaction in which dynamics of value can be traced. Reid's research is concerned with syntactic and lexical variation in topic types and tasks in the composition of Spanish, Chinese, Arabic, and English native speakers. Reid's work provides significant evidence for the contrastive rhetoric hypothesis, particularly in lexical features. For example, English speakers are found to use few coordinating conjunctions and a concurrently high percentage of passive-voice verbs and prepositions. In contrast, Arabic and Spanish texts evidenced more usage of coordinating conjunctions and significantly fewer passive-voice verbs and prepositions. These findings are important in elucidating how an apparently neutral area such as topic variation can involve linguistic differences and negotiation of meaning. Enculturation to specific syntactic and lexical preferences manifests itself in the organization of discourse within specific genres and contexts. Reid observes that "second language writers who are successful writers in their first languages often know what is socially and culturally appropriate in terms of writer roles, audience expectations, rhetorical and stylistic conventions, and situational or contextual features of written text in their native languages" (201), but that there is no basis for expecting these competent nonnative writers to be cognizant of the forms and conventions in a second language. These forms of lexical distinctiveness in the making and negotiation of meaning can be fundamental to conflicts of understanding in multicultural sites. While learning the conventions of a second language, ESL students are confronted with the possible humiliation of having their meanings appropriated and misconstrued through translations of intent that can involve a significant loss of personal and collective voice.

An example of tension and miscontrual from a developmental perspective also involves the issue of topic coherence and organization. Michaels (1986) observed crucial divergences in the discourse styles of Black children of working-class backgrounds and White English children from middle-class origins in "sharing time" storytelling sessions. Group differences were manifest in the organization and coherence of narratives. Almost uniformly, White middle-class children tended to present tightly organized, "topic centered," and thematically developed stories through linear ordering and lexical cohesion, resulting in direct resolutions. The Black children, on the other hand, evidenced a "topic associating style" that violated the White teacher's model of appropriate and adequate cohesion for storytelling sessions. This style was observed by Michaels to be constituted by a series of segments or episodes implicitly linked in highlighting some person or thing, shifts in both topic and temporal orientation, and intonational markings for shifts in topic. The topic centered children interacted rapidly with the teacher, synchronizing rhythms, showing a high degree of cohesion across turn takings. In contrast, the interactions of topic associating students with the teacher were marked by the teacher's mistimings, interruptions, and difficulty in discerning the topic.

This discussion of subjectivity is intended to emphasize the conjuncture of identity formation and linguistic enculturation. Drawing on research of several educators, I wish to convey a sense of the complex host of cultural, linguistic, and cognitive factors that are at play in the formation and expression of student subjectivity. This concern is premised on an appreciation of the unequal distribution of cultural resources that exist both inside and outside the classroom, as well as by a recognition that each individual subject is not reducible to any idealized notion of ideology or mechanical process of socialization. Multiply constituted, students as subjects in cross-linguistic settings function in specific constellations of plurality, difference, and agency.

EXCHANGE VALUE AND CLASSROOM DISCOURSE

There are certain correspondences or homologies that we can observe between specific intercultural educational practices and the larger complex of socialization to value and the reproduction of knowledge. These homologies, whose epistemic value only can be analyzed fully in specific contexts, include a correspondence between market values, standard language use, and propositional language and logic, on the one hand, and verbal play, figure, irony, idiom, and imagery on the other. The material form of these correspondences in discrete discourse communities, specifically in the salience of genre and cultural criteria for organization and interpretation, often reflects a subjectivity that is at times as much created by historical relations as it is an agent of its own creative process. These actual demarcated relations, functions of local linguistic economies, evince the affirmation and privileging of certain discourses, strategies, and forms of language use and their implicit ideological values over others. Most fundamentally, they represent a configuring of subjectivity in American educational settings.

Subjectivity is constituted within a matrix of discourses of unequal power that coexist with a prevailing hegemonic and hierarchic dominant form. This is the exchange value imparted to the social relations of individuals and collectivities within an international market economy. This claim is supported by the work of Buck-Morss (1975), Werstch (1988), and Collins (1988), who draw parallels between abstract reasoning and the ascension of capitalist relations of production and values. In Buck-Morss's analysis, abstract formalism must be distinguished from abstract reasoning, which is a cognitive function inherent to the repertoires of all forms of linguistic competence. Abstract formalism is the "ability to separate form from content, and the structuring of experience with that distinction. Its model is the supra-empirical, purely formal language of mathematics" (38). Her intent is to deconstruct Piagetian stage theory and its teleology in granting abstract formalism status as a universal structure of cognitive maturation. Buck-Morss identifies the processes by which abstract formalism came to be the "dominant cognitive structure with the emergence of Western capitalism which first made possible a shift in the mode of production from agriculture to industry" (39). An important feature of abstract formalism is its rejection of concrete experience, offering primary cognitive value to abstract propositional statements and a reliance on the ahistorical Kantian categories of space, time, and causality. These values, constructive of a prevailing historical episteme, or set of precepts, served as grounds for Western European modernism's claims to knowledge and rationality. They functioned as paradigms of consciousness during the rise of the industrial era and "parallel the capitalistic concern for abstract exchange value rather than social use value" (38).

Within classroom discourse, abstract formalism serves to function as an exchange value extracted from experiential relations, intersubjective contexts, and the particulars of cultural practices, including the specific uses and content of literate activity. Abstract formalism is the paradigm of an objective, expository discourse, most evident in scientific and academic argument and organization, a genre marked by the absence of narrators, personal voice, situation-specific reference, or other indications of subjectivity. Interpersonal and dialogic classroom discourse is vitiated in situations that require an almost exclusive adherence to these forms.

The metaphor of productivity in a linguistic economy provides a description of the process of enculturation through literacy practices that instantiate abstract formalism as a core and determining value. Such prevalent forms of literate practice, especially institutionalized methods that privilege decontextualized knowledge and discourse, can be seen as generative of exclusively "useful" curricula and relations to texts for the purpose of the labor market, standardized testing, and the maintenance of the existing social order. Reflective means for self-description, expression, and organization—those forms of literate practices that attend to the "code" or "poetic" axis, in Jakobson's (1971) terms—rather than the referential, directive or instrumental aspects of language use, become marginalized forms of articulation. In a historical review, Collins (1988) utilizes work by Graff surveying the relations between standardized language, social mobility, and literacy. Collins states that the "twentieth century confronts us with an increasingly 'technocratic economy of literacy' in which a persisting stratification of skills coexists with an ideology of literacy as technical capacity and marketplace worth" (1988:6).

Through analysis of students' writing and interviews in a large number of multicultural classes, I have found that students are frequently aware of the importance of the signifying values of their choices of language use. They are alert to linguistic differences reflected in the alternatives they confront when utilizing or rejecting certain familiar cultural patterns, indicating, as Delpit (1988) asserts, that those outside the "culture of power" are often those who are most conscious of its functioning.

The forms of linguistic friction that arise in the selecting, phrasing, emphasizing, and topic marking, as well as the figurative use of language cannot be attributed solely to constraints of classroom discourse, acculturation, or transfer problems in the acquisition of Standard English. It is my contention that the dominant and privileged discourse of abstract formalism, functioning as an incipient mode that favors decontextualized knowledge, reigns unchallenged in most educational practice and research. I believe strains of positivism still exert control in maintaining the criteria of fields like educational testing, forming the premises behind such common assessment tools as the Test of Adult Basic Education (TABE), the General Educational Development (GED) tests, and many college entrance examinations. The hegemony of propositional logics and their descendants in current formulations of the analytic philosophy of language in the Anglo-American world view (Austin, 1975; Kripke, 1972; Putnam, 1975; Searle, 1969) has, in part, been generative of a positivist impulse within formal and artificial intelligence models like those of cognitive science. Propositional and formal logics like those of computer simulated heuristics (often used as models of cognitive activity during writing "protocols") still thrive and are employed in learning models. A general debasement of figure and images has resulted in established conceptualizations of intelligence that rely predominantly on these formal and decontextualized models. Work by Siegler (1984), Case (1984), and Scardamalia and Bereiter (1982), stemming from a neo-Piagetian orientation in cognitive psychology, bears witness to the tenacity of this trend.

The traditional debate regarding orality and literacy can be considered in terms of issues regarding contextualization. Overall, within analyses of writing development, the dichotomy between oral and written discourse has been overstated. A cognitive divide between oral and written or literate forms was formulated by Vygotsky (1962, 1978) and Luria (1976) and continues to be supported in recent work (Olson, 1977; Ong, 1982). They are best appreciated, however, not as dichotomous activities indicating intellectual growth, but rather as socially constituted continua. As Rader (1982) points out, development does not proceed uniformly and unidirectionally toward increased autonomy and decontextualization. Tannen's (1982) concern for the interpersonal, as opposed to content oriented, character of both speech and writing expresses an appreciation for the functional overlapping between them. Writing cannot be considered to replace speech forms. Tannen makes the important observation that "when literacy is introduced, the two are superimposed upon and intertwined with each other" (3). Decontextualization is a relative state pertinent to the uses, setting, and genres to which it is applied. This perspective allows us to think more clearly about providing apertures in practice and theory through which they might converge and inform one another rather than being treated as a binary opposition overcome only through higher education.

I am especially concerned with the uses and misuses of figurative language. Metaphorical usage—including the significance of conversational discourse of particular dialects and ethnic, gender, and subgroup patterns as well as idiomatic and colloquial usages—requires more than recognition in the spirit of pluralism common to many cross-cultural settings. Features of first-language usage need to be emphatically foregrounded. They are one of the primary sources that educators must draw from to catalyze cognitive and linguistic development within intercultural educational sites. As Raymond Williams (1977) notes, these kinds of figurative language and thought give entry into the production and identity of discourse, elements he calls "complex notations of source" (170). Williams includes features such as "reported speech and dialogue; indications of explicit and implicit thought processes; indications of displaced or suspended monologue, dialogue, or thought; indications of direct or of 'characterized' observation" (171), all indications

> of the identity of the writer, in all its possible senses. Such notations are often closely involved with indications of situations, the combinations of situation and identity often constituting crucial notations of part of the relationship into which the writing is intended to enter. (170)

Through the conscious selection and use of subjective linguistic indices like these, students can affirm and mark themselves while signifying their own personal or collective values. Multicultural educators can explicitly emphasize the use of these indices, clarifying and structuring oral and written discourse on the basis of divergences and differences between the various forms of cultural and linguistic representation that students provide. Within and outside of the classroom, articulation of these variations are signifiers of alternative, even rival values to the dominant discursive practices. Their expression can assist in the formulation of individual and collective definition, becoming instances of reflective self-inscription.

Students in multicultural settings usually strive for flexibility and control of their capacity to switch between contextualized and abstract knowledge within their target language. School-based knowledge appears almost universally to stress abstract forms of knowledge and their removal from contexts and references in lived experience (Wertsch, 1988). Rather than encouraging the use of language richly informed by experience and the kinds of exchanges that utilize and draw from idiomatic, figurative usages in meaningful contexted usage, academic settings (including cross-cultural ones) generally function as generators of the forms of rationalist, abstract and decontextualized meanings and usage prevalent in the world of business, science and technology. Students justifiably perceive these forms as privileged and as often denying their own experiences and forms of linguistic expertise. The privileging given to certain forms of discourse and interaction is constitutive of the value granted to these forms in relation to others within a generalized economy of linguistic values. It is also pivotal in the constitution of the presentation of the self or subjectivity of the very students who are, consciously or not, appropriating these forms of value embedded in language use.

While standardized forms of language use have emerged throughout the world to produce the very processes defining national identities, the hegemony that results in the domination of certain discursive practices and their underlying values (Pecheux, 1982) over alternative or subaltern signifying practices is also historical and subject to tensions that can lead to transformations of structure and accepted usage. An ahistorical pluralism and concern for process reifies an existing linguistic economy, including its salient genres and, thereby, the social relations from which usages are articulated and given differential value. While it is a basic responsibility of cross-cultural educators to acknowledge and to impart the various existing structures and uses of socially accepted knowledge, organization, and coherence, since these can provide students some of the requisite skills necessary to gain access to employment, housing, and social mobility, I believe educators must also allow for the emergence of critique and reflection on the part of students in their own engagement with and relations to language use. This engagement, including critical evaluation by students of visual and oral forms of culture represents what Giroux (1983) considers "a view of human knowledge and social practice that recognizes the importance of using the cultural capital of the oppressed to authenticate the voices and modes of knowing they use to negotiate with the dominant society" (227).

In the context of specific discourse and classroom contexts, the next section brings into focus a concern for the linguistic formation of student subjectivity with the possibility and practicality of fostering the expression of alternative discursive practices to the historical reign of abstract formalism.

SUBCULTURAL NARRATORS

Cross-cultural education is a form of cultural production. It is a medium through which creative activity is possible through the appropriation and use of knowledge. Subjectivity is not simply reproduced and internalized by dominant discursive and ideological practices. Individual and collective self-formations can result from a critical pedagogy that allows students to situate themselves within the complex of linguistic, cultural, and value-laden practices in which they participate in schools. Critical reflection by students themselves on the practices, methods, materials, and underlying world outlook implied by classroom discursive practices allows them to objectify and restructure their participation in educational activities. Reflection of this kind signifies a genuine means to realize individual and collective aspirations and needs. Autonomous kinds of self- and collective representation and action will be generated through literacy practices that expose the facade of ahistorical formalisms, structures, and, in Freire's (1985) terms, "rhetoric of authority." Beginning in Recife, in northeastern Brazil, in the 1960s, the establishment of "culture circles" created programs in which members of the local peasantry could become, for the first time, full participants and agents in their acquisition of literacy. The goal of these culture circles in developing critical, reflective, and historically situated thinking through "problematizations" of the conditions of their lives by students remains relevant for contemporary American cross-cultural settings. Just as these culture circles focused on the making of narratives by formerly illiterate and landless peasants, who were thus able to scrutinize experiences that they previously passively accepted, an engaged approach sensitive to the dynamics of ideologically and power-riddled discursive practices applied to multicultural classrooms in the United States can also permit a "reinvention of power" and agency (Freire, 1985:179).

I draw from experience teaching and administering at the Veteran's Education Center of LaGuardia Community College in New York City. While veterans are a very disparate group, ranging widely in terms of academic experience, age, ethnicity, and skills, there are certain commonalities that allow for a subcultural identity to become evident and serve as a locus for instruction. Shared training and instruction in boot camp, and active- and postservice experiences all contribute to a cohesive identity. Among Vietnam veterans, who comprise nearly one-third of the total number of students served by the program, a cohesive subcultural identity is especially apparent. It is one frequently marked by a subjectivity constructed through adherence to, ambivalence about, or complete rejection of the imperatives responsible for America's military commitment, as well as through sharing of common combat experiences and often very similar physical, emotional, and economic hardships in the war's aftermath. Vietnam-era combat veterans, who comprise a large part of the nation's homeless,[2] also confront practical problems of reattempting an integration into society. Due to the demand for a massive infusion of troops in the late sixties, standards for entry were reduced to allow almost any physically fit individuals into service. These troops, largely composed of urban Blacks and Hispanics, but also of Appalachian and recent immigrant groups, dubbed "McNamara's 300,000", entered military service with extremely low academic skills. Frequently they are now individuals with the least chance of maintaining employment, lacking the skills to enter a changed workplace.[3]

A sense of the disenfranchisement experienced in the subculture of veterans' experience can be garnered from a journal entry a Hispanic-American veteran shared with me. Relating his attempts to integrate into the workforce after service, he writes:

> The desire to be a human being and search for knowledge is always interrupted by a simple word 'money.' If you work 40 hours a week you don't have enough to get educated and make your family comfortable. I have no money, officially a high school diploma that don't pay out, a DD214 (military service discharge) to keep in the records. Instead I lost my freedom the day the system didn't allow me to seek and discover the knowledge for sale that I cannot afford.

I have worked with homeless veterans who, though psychically scarred from either service or attempts to reintegrate into society, are nevertheless highly motivated in transforming their condition. As Rose (1989) observes, veterans often reenter the educational system with "magical" expectations to "reclaim" their lives. They are a vivid example of the kinds of subcultural discourse communities whose experiences, values, and aspirations educators must utilize and foster.

Cultural identities run the risk of being idealized or essentialized, that is, frozen into generalized theoretical orientations and practices that do not adequately address the divisions and differences among students. To avoid this tendency in teaching, for example, in the popular expressivist and process orientations in composition theory discussed above, we must allow for self-descriptions, definitions, and plural role-playing opportunities in classroom activities such as essays, autobiographies, storytelling, relevant problem solving analyses of social events, and group discussion and debate. These are among the methods that can be applied in multicultural classrooms in the interest of critical reflection and action by students through self-generated language use.

In attempting to formulate culturally salient material for a multicultural program, I sorted through autobiographical compositions students had written early in the course. Prospecting for features of personal significance and possibly social orientation led me to discern how cultural artifacts play a crucial role. Students were encouraged to describe their families as groups as well as the individuals composing them. They were asked to make verbal portraits of relatives, including any and all generations known to them. Most students' writing included some particular and distinctive feature of self-description and a willingness to disclose certain aspects of subjectivity. The initial compositions and accompanying "family trees" were complemented by students' self-chosen presentation of cultural objects, including clothing, tapes of traditional music and dance, maps, assorted condiments and dishes, and photographs. The writing and presentations of this class were prototypical of the expression of cultural signifiers discussed earlier. Individuals from very diverse cultural and linguistic communities—including Albania, Poland, Ethiopia, Ghana, Nigeria, Yemen, China, Korea, the Caribbean area, and Central America—were willing to exchange forms of self-representation, including language choices and styles, with considerable anecdotal, idiomatic, and descriptive detail, from which a unique sense of classroom community emerged. I believe this kind of intercultural, peer encounter exemplifies recognition and respect for differences between discourse communities and individuals without usurpation of their own choices, preferences, and experiences by a dominant form of value. The family and character portraits that were the initial basis of this assignment were given a framework that elicited the transmission and sharing of cultural and linguistic resources in a very heterogenous classroom. Family portraits were supplemented by the presentations of selected artifacts, thereby granted some semblance of their genuine cultural significance by incorporating students' own expression of linguistic and cultural value.

I wish to emphasize the need for the expression and development of a critical and reflective practice that includes an orientation to dialogue and revision, one that permits the figurative, gestural, and idiomatic features of discourse to emerge. This emergence may be recognized as a specific means by which writing mediates thought through a conjuncture of disparate realms of language use. The notion of voice is again valuable here. Freire and Macedo (1987) clarify the point that "critical mastery of the standard dialect can never be achieved fully without the development of one's voice, which is contained with the social dialect that shapes one's reality" (129). A point of origin for the kind of collective critical pedagogy called for here is recognition of the ideologically laden nature of all signifying practices and the means by which divergent dialects "encode" differing orientations toward knowledge and activity in the daily world. As Volosinov (1986) wrote over sixty years ago, "a sign does not simply exist as a part of reality—it reflects and refracts another reality. Wherever a sign is present, ideology is present, too. Everything ideological possesses semiotic value" (10).

It has been my concern in this chapter to assert the significance of continually posing questions regarding what is useful in the larger context of students' lives as they themselves frame and understand them. By extension, I wish to have called for the critical reexamination of assumptions held by adherents of cultural pluralism. Within a Freirean approach, the issues of value and subjectivity are, at root, questions of "reinventing power." For this notion to galvanize cross-cultural literacy in realistic, local frameworks, a practice is required that brings together all the vital elements and materials necessary for reconstructing core meanings and relations between individuals and groups; it implies newly emergent collective subjects and their objects of knowledge as well as the coherence of renewed and authenticated language use. The premises of this chapter are intended as suggestions for a critical literacy practice in which individual and community redefinitions will be realized. It is a project of partisan language use and value, one in which an individual and collective gaining and granting of selves will take place.

NOTES

1. A questionnaire was utilized in Adult Basic Education classes for two semesters. Students were asked to voluntarily describe their experiences with language both in their everyday life and within classroom interactions. Specific questions involved asking students what forms of communication proved difficult in everyday life, what problems of transfer and "code switching" occurred between languages, and what the various personal incentives and goals were that led them to Adult Education classes.

2. *New York Vets,* Fall 1988, Newsletter of the New York City Office of Veterans Affairs. According to this report, homeless veterans comprise over 3,000 of the homeless individuals in New York City shelters and, among them, 43 percent are Vietnam-era veterans.

3. *Legacies of Vietnam: Comparative Adjustment by Veterans and their Peers,* 1981, Center for Policy Research, New York City. Also, Veterans Administration Office of Controller for Reports and Statistics, 1980, states that 63 percent of Vietnam veterans sought hospital services for psychiatric assistance.

Of the thousands of Vietnam-era veterans who applied for Upward Bound educational services between 1980 and 1988, 60 percent were unemployed, and 94 percent reported zero income for the prior taxable year.

REFERENCES

Apple, M.W. (1982). *Education and power.* Boston: Routledge & Kegan Paul.

Austin, J.L. (1975). *How to do things with words.* Oxford: Oxford University Press.

Berlin, J.A. (1988). Rhetoric and ideology in the writing class. *College English, 50,* 477–494.

Bizzell, P. (1982). Cognition, convention, and certainty: What we should know about writing. *Pre/Text, 3,* 213–243.

Bourdieu, P. & Passeron, J. (1977). *Reproduction in education, society and culture.* Beverly Hills, CA: Sage.

Bruffee, K. (1986). Social construction, language, and the authority of knowledge. *College English, 48,* 773–790.

Buck-Morss, S. (1975). Socioeconomic bias in Piaget's theory and its implications for cross-culture studies. *Human Development, 18,* 35–49.

Calkins, L. (1983). *Lessons from a child: On the teaching and learning of writing.* Portsmouth, NH: Heinemann.

Case, R. (1984). The process of stage transition: A neo-Piagetian view. In R. Sternberg (Ed.). *Mechanisms of cognitive development* (pp. 19–44). New York: Freeman.

Chase, G. (1988). Accommodation, resistance and the politics of student writing. *College Composition and Communication, 39,* 13–22.

Collins, J. (1988). Hegemonic practice: Literacy and standard language in public education. In R. Parmentier and G. Urban (Eds.), *Working papers and proceedings of the Center for Psychosocial Studies* No. 21, Chicago.

Cook-Gumperz, J.C. & Gumperz, J.J. (1986). Language and the communication of social identity. In J.J. Gumperz (Ed.), *Language and social identity* (pp. 1–21). Cambridge: Cambridge University Press.

Delpit, L. (1986). Skills and other dilemmas of a progressive Black educator. *Harvard Educational Review, 56,* 379–385.

————. (1988). The silenced dialogue: Power and pedagogy in educating other people's children. *Harvard Educational Review, 58,* 280–298.

Elbow, P. (1973). *Writing without teachers.* Oxford: Oxford University Press.

Foucault, M. (1976). *The archaeology of knowledge.* New York: Harper and Row.

Freed, R. & Broadhead, G. (1987). Discourse communities, sacred texts, and institutional norms. *College Composition and Communication, 38,* 154–165.

Freire, P. (1985). *The politics of education: Culture, power and liberation.* South Hadley, MA: Bergin and Garvey.

Freire, P. & Macedo, D. (1987). *Literacy: Reading the word and the world.* South Hadley, MA: Bergin and Garvey.

Geertz, C. (1984). On the nature of anthropological understanding. In R. Shweder & R. LeVine (Eds.), *Culture theory: Essays on mind, self, and emotion.* Cambridge: Cambridge University Press.

Giroux, H. (1983). *Theory and resistance in education: A pedagogy for the opposition.* South Hadley, MA: Bergin and Garvey.

————. (1987). Introduction. In P. Freire & D. Macedo (Eds.), *Literacy: Reading the word and the world.* South Hadley, MA: Bergin and Garvey.

Grabe, W. & Kaplan, R.B. (1989). Writing in a second language: Contrastive rhetoric. In D.M. Johnson and D.H. Roen (Eds.), *Richness in writing: Empowering ESL students* (pp. 263–283). New York: Longman.

Gumperz, J.J. (1978). The conversational analysis of interethnic communication. In E. Lamar Ross (Ed.), *Interethnic communication* (pp. 13–31). Athens: University of Georgia Press.

———. (Ed.) (1982). *Language and social identity.* Cambridge: Cambridge University Press.

Hayes, J.R. & Flower, L. (1983). Uncovering cognitive processes in writing: An introduction to protocol analysis. In P. Mosenthal, L. Tamor & S. Walmsley, (Eds.), *Research in writing* (pp. 207–220). New York: Longman.

Heath, S.B. (1983). *Ways with words.* Cambridge: Cambridge University Press.

Hymes, D. (1972). Models of the interaction of language and social life. In J.J. Gumperz & D. Hymes, (Eds.), *The ethnography of communication* (pp. 35–71). New York: Holt, Rinehart and Winston.

———. (1974). *Foundations in sociolinguistics.* Philadelphia: University of Pennsylvania Press.

Jakobson, R. (1971). Shifters, verbal categories and the Russian verb. In R. Jakobson, *Selected writings* (Vol. 2, pp. 130–147). The Hague: Mouton.

Johns, A.M. (1990). L1 composition theories: Implications for developing theories of L2 composition. In B. Kroll (Ed.), *Second language writing: Research insights into the classroom* (pp. 24–36). Cambridge: Cambridge University Press.

Kripke, S. (1972). Naming and necessity. In D. Davidson & G. Harman (Eds.). *Semantics of natural language* (pp. 253–355). Dordrecht/ Boston: Reidel.

Kroll, B. (Ed.) (1990). *Second language writing: Research insights into the classroom.* Cambridge: Cambridge University Press.

Labov, W. (1972). Logic of non-standard English. In P. Giglioli (Ed.), *Language and social context* (pp. 179–215). Hammondsworth, England: Penguin.

Lentricchia, F. (1980). *After the new criticism.* Chicago: University of Chicago Press.

———. (1983). *Criticism and social change.* Chicago: University of Chicago Press.

Luria, A.R. (1976). *Cognitive development.* Cambridge: Harvard University Press.

Michaels, S. (1986). Narrative presentations: An oral preparation for literacy with first graders. In J. Cook-Gumperz (Ed.), *The social construction of literacy* (pp. 94–116). Cambridge: Cambridge University Press.

Mishra, A. (1982). Discovering connections. In J.J. Gumperz (Ed.), *Language and social identity* (pp. 57–71). Cambridge: Cambridge University Press.

Murray, D. (1982). *A writer teaches writing.* Boston: Houghton Mifflin.

Olson, D.R. (1977). From utterance to text: The bias in language in speech and writing. *Harvard Educational Review, 47,* 257–281.

Ong, W.J. (1982). *Orality and literacy.* New York: Methuen.

Pecheux, M. (1982). *Language, semantics and ideology.* London: Macmillan.

Putnam, H. (1975). *Mind, language and reality: Philosophical papers, Vol. 2.* Cambridge: Cambridge University Press.

Rader, M. (1982). Context in written language: The case of imaginative fiction. In D. Tannen (Ed.), *Spoken and written language: Exploring orality and literacy* (pp. 185–198). Norwood, NJ: Ablex.

Reid, J. (1990). Responding to different topic types: A quantitative analysis from a contrastive rhetoric perspective. In B. Kroll (Ed.), *Second language learning: Research insights from the classroom* (pp. 191–210). Cambridge: Cambridge University Press.

Rose, M. (1989). *Lives on the boundary.* New York: Free Press.

Saussure, F. de (1959). *Course in general linguistics.* New York: McGraw-Hill.

Scardamalia, M. & Bereiter, C. (1982). Assimilative processes in composition planning. *Educational Psychologist, 17,* 165–171.

Scribner, S. (1984). Literacy in three metaphors. *American Journal of Education, 95,* 6–21.

Scribner, S. & Cole, M. (1981). *The psychology of literacy.* Cambridge: Harvard University Press.

Searle, J.R. (1969). *Speech acts: An essay in the philosophy of language.* Cambridge: Cambridge University Press.

Siegler, R.S. (1984). Mechanisms of cognitive growth: Variation and selection. In R. Sternberg (Ed.), *Mechanisms of cognitive development* (pp. 141–162). New York: Freeman.

Smith, P. (1988). *Discerning the subject.* Minneapolis: University of Minnesota Press.

Spivak, G.C. (1988). *In other worlds: Essays in cultural politics.* New York: Routledge.

_____. (1989). *The post-colonial critic.* New York: Routledge.

Tannen, D. (1982). The oral/written continuum in discourse. In D. Tannen (Ed.), *Spoken and written language: Exploring orality and literacy* (pp. 1–16). Norwood, NJ: Ablex.

Volosinov, V.V. (1986). *Marxism and the philosophy of language.* Cambridge: Harvard University Press.

Vygotsky, L.S. (1962). *Thought and language.* Cambridge: MIT Press.

_____. (1978). *Mind in society.* Cambridge: Harvard University Press.

Wallerstein, N. (1983). *Language and culture in conflict.* Reading, MA: Addison-Wesley.

Wertsch, J.V. (1985). *Vygotsky and the social formation of mind*. Cambridge: Harvard University Press.

―――. (1988). Voices of the mind. In R. Parmentier & G. Urban (Eds.), *Working papers and proceedings of the Center for Psychosocial Studies*, No. 19, Chicago.

Williams, R. (1977). *Marxism and literature*. Oxford: Oxford University Press.

CHAPTER 10

Language and Literacy in Quebec: Exploring the Issues

Alison d'Anglejan

This chapter examines the complex issues surrounding language and literacy in Quebec against the backdrop of the province's language policy enacted in 1976. I will try to show how the province's preoccupation with the teaching and learning of French, defined in terms of the code, has, until recently, obscured the issue of literacy. The changing demographic patterns in Quebec and the demands of new technologies in the workplace are posing a challenge for policymakers. I propose that the state's mechanisms for language planning be adapted to address in more flexible and less bureaucratic ways the issues of both language and literacy.

SOME BACKGROUND INFORMATION

To understand the uniqueness of the Quebec situation, a few demolinguistic facts should be borne in mind. The first is that the Francophone group is the majority group in Quebec, representing 80 percent of the population, and French is the sole official language. The second is that given the linguistic dominance of English in the rest of Canada and in North America, the Francophone group perceives itself as a minority group threatened with assimilation. The protection of the group's majority group status in Quebec as a bulwark against assimilation is a primary societal goal, one that transcends and colors the formulation of policies in a variety of domains. Moreover, the province is moving politically toward a greater degree of sovereignty with respect to the rest of

Canada. (For a fuller discussion of these issues see Bourhis, 1983, and Levine, 1990).

Like many other industrialized societies, Francophone Quebec is undergoing rapid demographic change. The transformation of the French schools in urban Montreal from linguistically and culturally homogeneous institutions into ones struggling to adjust to a multilingual, multicultural school population has taken place over the past decade (Levine, 1990). While the phenomenon of cultural pluralism is not new in the urban areas of Montreal, only recently has it come to impact on the French-language school system. Prior to the enactment of language legislation in the 1970s, most immigrant children were enrolled in the province's English-language schools, while the staff and clientele of the French educational system remained dominantly Francophone and Roman Catholic.

A sharp decline in the province's birth rate in the 1960s and 1970s threatened the demographic advantage of the Francophone population. Indeed, demographers' projections suggested that if immigrants continued to integrate into the Anglophone community and to send their children to English schools, and if the current low birth rates were to prevail, Francophones could become a linguistic minority in Montreal, the economic heart of the province (Levine, 1990). This prompted the enactment of language legislation making French the sole official language of the province, and the language of the workplace, and mandated schooling in French for the children of immigrants. The impact of language policy changes (Laws 22, 1974, and 101, 1977, also known as the Charter of the French Language) on the ethnic composition of the majority-language schools has been extensive. Table 10.1 shows the shift in school enrollments according to the language of instruction over the ten-year period following the enactment of language legislation. The ethnic characteristics of more recent immigration have also changed. In contrast with the prior immigrant groups—Italians, Greeks, Portuguese—a larger proportion of today's immigrants are from the rural agricultural societies of Asia, Africa, or the West Indies (principally Haiti). Table 10.2 shows a breakdown of 1989–90 school enrollment figures in the French and English schools of Metropolitan Montreal according to mother tongue. According to Ministry of Education statistics, some 95 percent of allophone[1] children attend schools in the Montreal area.

TABLE 10.1
LANGUAGE OF INSTRUCTION OF ALLOPHONE* STUDENTS
IN QUEBEC FOLLOWING THE ENACTMENT
OF LANGUAGE LEGISLATION IN 1977

	1977–78 Law 101	1984–85	1986–87	1989–90
French-language instruction	30.0%	57.0%	64.4%	72.5%
English-language instruction	70.0%	43.0%	35.6%	27.5%

*The term "allophone" is widely used in Quebec to designate persons whose mother tongue is other than French or English.
Sources: • Paillé, M. (1986) Aspects de l'évolution de la situation linguistique du Québec, Conseil de la langue française, notes et documents, no 52. (Data for 1977/78–1986/87).
• Direction générale de recherche et développement. Ministère de l'Éducation du Québec, 1990 (Data for 1989/90).

In addition to its impact on schools, the language legislation placed new demands on the workplace. By law, French became the sole language of work, at all levels, from the production line to top management. It became incumbent upon public administrations, commercial establishments, and professionals to demonstrate their capacity to operate in French.

Thus, not only for immigrants, but for the province's Anglophone minority group (which includes many earlier immigrants who integrated into the English-speaking community), a sound working knowledge of spoken and written French is now an absolute necessity.

Language has long been a salient social issue in Quebec, as it is indeed in the rest of Canada. In the process of nation building that accompanied the growth of Quebec nationalism in the 1960s and 1970s, the Quebec government invested considerable resources in the bolstering of the French language. An "Office de la langue française" is responsible for the application of the Charter of the French language, which makes French the sole official language and the language of the workplace. An additional mandate of the Office is to assure the quality of French—the development of correct French terminology for all facets of life (an important focus is

TABLE 10.2

PRIMARY AND SECONDARY ENROLLMENT ACCORDING TO LANGUAGE
OF INSTRUCTION AND MOTHER TONGUE

MONTREAL * 1989–1990

Mother Tongue	French Instruction		English Instruction		Total	
French	121,325	70.0%	2,607	4.2%	123,932	52.7%
English	10,517	6.1%	41,972	68.2%	52,489	22.3%
Italian	4,632	2.7%	9,033	14.7%	13,665	5.8%
Greek	3,567	2.1%	1,535	2.5%	5,102	2.2%
Spanish	6,912	4.0%	416	0.7%	7,328	3.1%
Portuguese	3,151	1.8%	1,241	2.0%	4,392	1.9%
Arabic	3,527	2.0%	277	0.5%	3,804	1.6%
Creole	3,866	2.2%	19	0.0%	3,885	0.7%
Chinese	1,465	0.8%	265	0.4%	1,730	0.7%
Vietnamese	2,251	1.3%	53	0.1%	2,304	1.0%
Other	12,231	7.1%	4,109	6.7%	16,340	7.0%
Sub-total allophones	41,602	24.0%	16,948	27.5%	58,550	24.9%
Total	173,444	100.0%	61,527	100.0%	234,971	100.0%

* Source: Direction générale recherche et développement, Ministère de l'Éducation du Québec, 1990.

placed on technology) and to raise the public's consciousness about the need for good spoken and written French. Schools have set up special "welcoming classes" where the children of newly-arrived immigrants can spend ten months or more concentrating on the learning of French before entering the regular stream (d'Anglejan & De Koninck, 1992). Through special funding arrangements with the Federal government, intensive French language courses are available for adult immigrants to equip them with the language skills necessary for the workplace.

Quebec's English-speaking minority group—defined loosely in terms of those whose parents received their own schooling in English in Canada—has access to English schooling from kindergarten through university in addition to the option of sending their children to French schools. It is within the English school system that the very popular French immersion classes have developed. These are viewed as a practical means of equipping children with a good knowledge of French while at the same time assuring the sound development of English literacy skills and, not incidentally, ensuring the very survival of the English school system. Indeed, the decline in enrollment in the English schools caused by the implementation of the Charter of the French language (see Table 10.1), coupled with the tendency of some Anglophone parents to choose schooling in French for their children and the questioning of the legitimacy of English-language public education by some nationalist groups, has raised concern regarding the future of the English school system. In the 1989–90 school year, some 19,000 of the 103,000 children attending English schools in Quebec were enrolled in French immersion classes (Commissioner of Official Languages, 1990). In the "early" immersion programs, those beginning in kindergarten, initial reading instruction is given in French and English reading is introduced around grade 3. Thus the children's reading skills develop through instruction in reading and through exposure to written subject matter materials in both languages. In "late" immersion programs—those beginning instruction via French around grade 4 or even later at grade 7—literacy has already been established in the child's native language.

Over the past two decades these classes, in which children receive varying amounts of their schooling in a second language, have been the object of intensive research. Much of this research has focused on the school achievement of bilingually instructed students in comparison with control groups educated in their mother tongue and on the development of speaking and writing skills in French and English. (For a discussion of this research see Genesee, 1983, and Weber, 1991.) In general, the research has shown that in the context of Canada and Quebec, Anglophone children can develop the literacy skills required to handle subject matter presented via a second language at no apparent cost to the development of mother-tongue literacy. These findings provide evidence of the considerable contribution of the children's home environment—English speaking and generally middle class—to the development of English literacy skills. However, the research has provided few insights into the process of acquiring literacy in a bilingual setting. In early immersion programs the assumption is made that children will acquire literacy in French and transfer these skills to English. It may be equally plausible to hypothesize that in middle-class families it is the literacy skills acquired informally in English in the home that are transferred to the development of reading and writing abilities in French. An interesting topic for research would be to examine the acquisition of initial literacy in French, a second language, among children whose homes do not provide opportunities for access to literacy. This would help to establish more clearly the appropriateness of immersion programs for children from more diverse socioeconomic and sociocultural backgrounds. It would be important in such studies to follow the children's progress beyond the early grades since it is toward the end of primary school and at the high school level that higher level processing skills are called for.

THE NEED FOR A NEW THEORETICAL FRAMEWORK

My interest in the field of literacy dates back to the mid-1970s when, as a researcher in the area of second-language acquisition, I was invited by Quebec's Ministry of Immigration to investigate the problem of difficulties in the learning of French among adult immigrants graduating from government-supported language programs. More specifically, these preemployment programs involved 900 hours of instruction (6 hours per day for 30 weeks) and were designed to provide newly arrived immigrants with the language skills that would enable them to cope with everyday survival and to find employment. Immigrants received a stipend to cover living expenses during this period. The focus of instruction was, and still is, mainly on the development of oral fluency, and classes are housed in former public school buildings with few links with the surrounding community. While the program, according to data gathered by administrators at the time, appeared to be adequate for some learners, others seemed to learn *virtually nothing* during this 900 hour course of instruction, in spite of their instrumental motivation to do so. Our data (d'Anglejan & Renaud, 1985) revealed that a significant predictor of learning was the student's level of schooling. Indeed, students with low levels of schooling, who were marginally literate in their own language, and who had few personal contacts with mainstream Francophone society seemed to derive little benefit from second-language instruction in an academic setting, even when the approach was oral and did not draw explicitly on reading or writing. Many of the students who experienced learning difficulties were from societies where access to education is limited and where the important aspects of cultural learning are acquired in the context of everyday activities in a nonacademic setting. The language classroom provided few opportunities for this type of learning and their lack of metalinguistic and metacognitive skills made it difficult for such students to benefit from form-focused decontextualized instruction.

In the course of my research it became clear to me that theories of second-language acquisition that focused primarily on the code (e.g., Krashen, 1981; Gardner & Lambert, 1972) and that had provided the framework for my research with mainstream second-language learners were inadequate to deal with the situation of these learners with limited prior exposure to literacy. The issue of literacy needed to be taken into account.

Within the public school system, it is becoming apparent that children in these marginally literate families are also at risk and that disproportionate numbers drop out or are to be found in nonacademic streams (Québec, 1985). While the "welcoming classes" seem to provide a comfortable environment in which to acquire the spoken language, they do not deal with the development of literacy beyond the teaching of basic reading and writing skills. Little is done to socialize children to their roles as readers and writers or to stimulate independent literacy activities. The assumption is made for the older children in particular that they will transfer their native-language literacy to the second language.

The evaluation of children's readiness to enter the mainstream is based mainly on their mastery of oral French and mathematics appropriate to their age group. For the children of immigrants with strong family or societal traditions of literacy, the development of literacy in the second language may not be particularly problematic. Such seems to have been the case of the waves of refugees who came to Montreal from the countries of Central Europe in the 1940s and 1950s. And, as noted earlier, a similar pattern is found among the French immersion students who are introduced to literacy in their weaker language. However, those children who are not acculturated to academic literacy in the course of their everyday lives may not be in a position to progress beyond the mechanics of reading and writing in classrooms where the instruction is geared to the needs of mainstream children. Work by researchers such as Teale and Sulzby (1987) and Wells (1984) reveals the support for the development of literacy provided by mainstream families. The role of schooling appears to be considerably less important for children in such families than it is for children from families who participate in limited activities involving literacy.

My own understanding of what might constitute obstacles to the development of school literacy in traditional classrooms has been greatly enriched by readings in a variety of areas tangential to second-language acquisition. Work in the ethnography of communication by researchers such as Heath (1983) and Scollon and Scollon (1981) has helped scholars understand the very great difference in the way language is used in preliterate societies or ones in which the oral tradition prevails. Ong's (1983) book on the technologizing of the word points out the impact of literacy on speech itself—the gradual decontextualization that both written and oral discourse have undergone in post industrialized societies such as our own. Thus, for the young speaker of Haitian Creole from a nonliterate background, the learning of the school language in Quebec involves the acquisition not only of the code but of a totally different set of patterns of discourse. Indeed, the sociolinguistic rules that govern discourse in a language such as French and the cultural meanings associated with language may be in conflict with those that prevail in the student's home culture. Furthermore, the functions of literacy in a rural Haitian community are bound to differ from those in an industrialized setting such as Montreal.

Another body of research that I have found enlightening has been that which focuses on the early socialization of children to literacy in highly literate families. The gradual shift in focus from the pragmatic or context-bound mode of communication to one independent of the immediate context that is initiated by mothers and other caretakers, even before the child begins to attend school, has been shown in studies by researchers such as Snow (1983), Wells (1984), and Donaldson (1978). Parents read storybooks to their children, question them about the content, and draw their attention to language. Olson (1984) suggests that this focus on oral and written language provides the basis for the emergence of metalinguistic awareness and learning to read. These early experiences involving reading and storytelling are also thought to provide children with important schemas regarding the rhetorical structure of text as well as about their future roles as readers and writers of texts and members of a literate culture.

Heath's (1983) work in three Appalachian communities has shown how three very distinctive styles of discourse can coexist in close proximity to each other. Her study reveals important cultural differences between disadvantaged subcultures in their use of language and in their socialization practices, suggesting that social class or cultural membership alone is not an adequate predictor of children's socialization to literacy.

The studies cited above are but a few of the many that have shown the extent of cultural variation in the socialization of preschool children. They provide important insights into the way culture affects cognition. Before they even get to school, children in highly literate subcultures have been socialized to the culture of literacy and have had experiences that are prerequisites for the development of reading and writing. In most of our classrooms the cultural correlates of the development of literacy are taken for granted or ignored; yet as school populations grow increasingly diversified, the need to include this prereading preparation as part of the curriculum—or better still to incorporate it into a network of community services for families at risk—becomes more and more apparent. Ferdman (1990) argues convincingly that the connections between literacy and culture must be fully acknowledged and better understood by educators and policymakers if the goal of literacy for all is to be achieved in a multiethnic society. In many schools in Quebec the difficulties encountered by immigrant children are perceived to relate mainly to "cracking the code." Given the importance attached to the teaching and learning of French, the issue of literacy is often overlooked.

THE EMERGENCE OF LITERACY AS A PUBLIC ISSUE

As mentioned earlier, the priority of Quebec policymakers over the past two decades has been to improve the quality of spoken and written French and to extend its use to all facets of public life. The notion of "quality" has generally been operationalized in terms of the use of correct French terminology, spelling, and grammar and the elimination of Anglicisms. The focus thus has been primarily on the code itself. Until recently, the issue of literacy per se has not been salient in public perceptions. Adult literacy courses have received modest funding within the framework of general funding for adult education, but French, not literacy, has been Quebec's priority. It is interesting to note in passing that the French word for literacy is *alphabétisation,* a term that seems adequate to denote the acquisition of basic skills but which many Francophone specialists feel is inadequate to deal with the very much broader range of concepts dealt with in contemporary writings on literacy. An appeal has been made to the Office de la langue française, which is responsible for the development of French terminology, to find an equivalent for the English word *literacy* or to grant legitimacy to the neologism *littératie.* The appeal is still under study, but the word *littératie* is being used by university researchers in an attempt to extend the meaning and understanding of the concept of literacy beyond that conveyed by the term *alphabétisation.*

Until very recently there has been a noticeable difference in the priority placed on literacy in Quebec in comparison with the rest of North America. Since education is under provincial jurisdiction in Canada, the federal government's ability to intervene is limited. However, one factor that appears to have recently heightened Quebec's interest in literacy was the publication in 1987 of the results of a survey of literacy in Canada commissioned by the Southam Press (The Creative Research Group, 1987). The report was based on a questionnaire and a test of functional literacy administered individually to a sample of 2,398 adults across Canada.

The definition of literacy adopted was the following: "In this report, the term 'illiterate' refers both to adult Canadians who can barely read and write, called basic illiterates, and also to those whose reading and writing and numbers skills are not sufficient to get by in everyday life, called functional illiterates. The minimum standard for functional literacy was determinated with the aid of a jury panel."

The survey instruments were developed in cooperation with the National Assessment of Educational Progress (NAEP) in Princeton, New Jersey, and a panel of Canadian experts. The NAEP materials selected for use were adapted to Canadian standards, translated into English and French, and, finally, reviewed and edited by an outside consultant to the project. A detailed description of these instruments is provided in the report (The Creative Research Group, 1987).

The results of the study revealed several findings possibly relevant to the issue of literacy in a second language:

- The percentage of illiterates was significantly higher among Francophone Canadians (29 percent) than Anglophone Canadians (23 percent), a divergence noted even among the 18–34 age group.
- The percentage of illiterates in Quebec (28 percent) was significantly higher than the national average (24 percent).
- Illiteracy in either of Canada's official languages was higher among immigrants (35 percent) than among native-born Canadians (22 percent).

While at first glance, Quebec's higher than average rate of functional illiteracy might appear to be attributable to a language factor, a closer look at the facts reveals that the issue is more complex. The highest illiteracy rate in Canada (44 percent) is found in Newfoundland, an essentially English-speaking province. Illiteracy in Canada appears to be related more to being economically disadvantaged and to lower levels of schooling than to linguistic factors per se. Although since confederation in 1867 Quebec has had its own French-language school system, which now provides education from kindergarten through university, there is ample evidence that historically Francophones have been the targets of social and economic discrimination even in their home province. Furthermore, certain cultural characteristics of the Francophone group, which were conducive to protecting it from the forces of assimilation—notably the province's unusually high birth rate—are ones also associated with lower levels of formal schooling and lower income levels. Both of the latter indices are, of course, correlates of illiteracy, and they were the prime targets of Quebec's "Quiet Revolution," the movement undertaken in the 1960s to modernize the state and to use the powers of the state to shift the control of the economy from Anglophone to Francophone hands. (These issues are discussed at length by Bourhis, 1983, Esman, 1987, and Levine, 1990.)

The fact that relatively higher levels of functional illiteracy continue to prevail in Quebec in spite of the availability of quality education in French, of rigorous policies to democratize education, and of economic policies that have served to all but eliminate the discrepancy in income levels between French- and English-speaking Quebecers underlines the urgency and the complexity of the problem. Indeed, the findings of the Southam survey prompted a further joint study by the Federation of Francophones outside Quebec and the Canadian Institute for Adult Education to examine the implications of the survey for Francophones across Canada and to study the provisions for adult literacy training in Quebec and in minority Francophone settings. The report (Boucher, 1989) notes the relationship of illiteracy to socioeconomic and cultural factors. However, there is no mention of the issue of access to literacy in French for immigrants to Quebec nor for Quebec's Anglophone population.

As immigration from third world countries increases, the need to better understand the complex relationship among factors such as culture, language, literacy, and pedagogy becomes more acute. For Quebec policymakers, concerned as they are with the integration of immigrants into the Francophone group, literacy is only beginning to emerge as a distinct yet vitally important issue.

SECOND-LANGUAGE AND LITERACY PROGRAMS

One salient characteristic of both literacy programs and second-language programs in Quebec is the extent to which, until recently, most have been removed from the everyday life of the community and the workplace. According to Chalom (1988) and Boucher (1989) some community-based literacy programs do operate—

often within the Haitian community—and these tend to take into account the specific needs of their clientele. However, funding for community-based activities is erratic. Other literacy programs are administered by local school boards under provisions for adult education; little is known about the extent to which these programs make a distinction between the needs of the local Francophone population, those of the established allophone groups, and those of the more recent immigrants. Some do, however, offer literacy instruction in languages other than French or English.

Earlier in this chapter, mention was made of the French language requirements stipulated in the Charter of the French Language for the certification of professionals such as doctors, lawyers, nurses, etc. The information provided to the public regarding the nature of the written French requirement is instructive:

- Written COMPREHENSION: A French text is presented and the candidate must answer a series of multiple choice questions based on the text.
- Written EXPRESSION: The candidate's competence in French grammar and sentence structure is tested in this section. A typical question in this section would require the candidate to construct a sentence with a series of words or convert a question into a statement (Alliance Québec, 1990).

It is interesting that when the tests were put into place, one particular group of candidates showed a disproportionately high failure rate in these subtests. These were the nursing candidates, whose training requires only a community college level of education. A study conducted by Martin and Pires (1979) suggested that the problem was possibly related to the relatively restricted levels of literacy of some of the candidates, only some of whom were immigrants from third world countries. The problem faced by such candidates is thus related to both knowledge of the second language and to the development of adequate literacy skills. At the present time these two needs are rarely addressed simultaneously.

As mentioned earlier in this chapter, it is the centers operated by Quebec's Ministry of Cultural Communities and Immigration, known as COFIs (Centre d'intégration et de formation des immigrants), that offer most courses specifically designed for recent immigrants. Their focus is primarily on the development of functional spoken French and there is no recourse to teaching-languages other than French. Written French, when it is taught, is viewed as an additional skill, complementary to listening and speaking (cf. the definition of written expression used in the language tests for professionals). Over the years, the range of courses offered, in terms of scheduling and duration, has expanded in response to the varied needs of a highly heterogeneous clientele. However, according to Chalom (1988) and Gilbert (1990) the approach is very much geared to teaching the general oral language skills viewed to be required for social integration. Both authors note that the immigrants attending COFI classes tend to have very little contact with the host community and are dependent on the COFI classes for the development of language skills. Chalom questions the ability of the COFIs to promote effective second-language learning or the development of literacy, given their isolation from the Francophone community in general and the workplace in particular. Opportunities for the informal acquisition of French and of literacy are limited. Reder's chapter in this volume stresses the need for such opportunities.

The scarcity of community-based second-language or literacy programs geared to the specific needs of immigrants and the almost total absence of the type of workplace programs found elsewhere in North America and in Europe is difficult to understand. I believe that two factors help to explain this institutionalization or bureaucratization of second-language and literacy teaching, for immigrants in particular. First, the phenomenon may be a reflection of the high level of government intervention in virtually all aspects of social life, which has characterized the process of nation building in Quebec over the past three decades. Social engineering has been successful in Quebec in such fields as education, health, and language. This may have given rise to the expectation that the financing, setting up, and regulating of language courses by the government will produce the desired results. Secondly, since immigration, education, manpower, and social services come under different administrative jurisdictions and in some instances involve the federal as well as the provincial governments, there has been little cross-fertilization among these various bodies. Administrative priorities seem to have taken precedence over pedagogical concerns.

Gilbert (1990) notes that the only workplace programs in

Quebec truly designed for the needs of a specific clientele are those in sectors mainly occupied by women: nursing and the garment industry. Programs for nurses, housed in hospitals, were set up at the request of the professional association in response to the failure (noted above) of significant members of nursing candidates to pass the French language tests required for certification. Language courses for women in the garment trade are a recent development in response to pressure from feminist groups.

It is noteworthy that there has been relatively little pressure on the part of trade unions for the setting up of language or literacy programs in the workplace. Only recently have these groups seemed to become aware of the increasing demand for literacy in the workplace, which is anticipated as a consequence of rapid technological change (Economic Council of Canada, 1987).

Two years ago, I was invited by the Quebec Ministry of Education to help design and experiment an alternate program for newly arrived marginally literate or preliterate adolescent immigrants—a group truly at risk of dropping out of school and facing subsequent unemployment owing to their lack of language and job skills (Employment and Immigration Canada, 1990). For a variety of reasons, these young people, aged 12–15 years, have not yet acquired literacy or have minimal literacy skills in their mother tongue. Normally they would spend ten months or more in "welcoming classes" concentrating on spoken French and would then enter the regular stream. The welcoming classes for the target age-group are geared for students who have acquired literacy in their mother tongue. Instead, in our experimental classes we have placed the focus on literacy—both on the reading and writing process and on the socialization of these youngsters to their role as readers and writers. They are also working on social sciences, natural sciences, and mathematics.

Whereas the usual program for the welcoming classes extends over one academic year, we are experimenting with a two-year period. This allows the students to have the same teacher for language arts and the content subjects, apart from mathematics, which is taught by math specialists. The content subjects provide an excellent context for the development of the second language and school-related literacy. It is our hypothesis that this potential will be more fully exploited when such subjects are taught by homeroom teachers who are more familiar with the students and their needs than by a series of subject specialists as is generally the case at the secondary level.

The study is being carried out as an action research project. In collaboration with school board personnel, teachers, and specialists from the Quebec Ministry of Education we have developed a theoretical framework, program objectives, and classroom approaches designed to help the students develop and use literacy as they acquire increasing competence in the second language. Quantitative and qualitative (ethnographic) techniques are being used to follow the students' development and to evaluate the program. It is proving a challenge to provide secondary teachers who had no specialized background in the teaching of literacy with the necessary theoretical underpinnings for understanding the pedagogical innovations we are attempting to introduce through the program. In particular, we are trying to broaden the working definition of *alphabétisation* to include sociocultural considerations in addition to basic skills and to help students recognize the importance of literacy both inside and outside the classroom.

In terms of research, we are trying to document the innovation as fully as possible through the gathering of quantitative and qualitative information. We have chosen, in this instance, not to work with the usual experimental model involving control groups since the program is still in the developmental phase. We plan to follow the students when they enter the mainstream in order to monitor the effects of the program over a longer period.

One weakness we perceive in the program is the inadequate involvement of the families despite the fact that involvement was one of our original priorities. Since they are dispersed geographically, many are not in the neighborhood of the school in the course of their everyday lives. They have attended a parents' night and responded very positively to our explanation of the program, but the isolation from the community, which I referred to earlier in connection with the COFIs, seems to be perpetuating itself against our will in this project. We hope to discover a way to respond to this critical challenge in the near future.

CONCLUSION

Here I will summarize some of the issues I have touched on in this chapter. Whereas for sociopolitical reasons the teaching/learning of French as a second language has long been a high priority in

Quebec, literacy is only now beginning to emerge as a distinct issue. Within the framework of Quebec's language policy, concern for language in the workplace has focused on the application of the provisions of the language legislation to make French the normal language of work—translation from English of documents, forms, and manuals and the promotion of French-speaking personnel. It is interesting that very little if anything is known about the actual ability of workers—be they immigrants or native born—to deal with the French language and literacy requirements of the workplace. Furthermore, there is little systematized information available about what those requirements actually are in various occupational settings, despite the fact that such information might be quite accessible owing to the work carried out in compliance with the Charter of the French Language—e.g., the translation of documents and development of specialized terminologies for the workplace.

Provisions for the teaching/learning of French as a second language can be characterized as highly institutionalized and defined in terms of criteria perceived by these institutions as required for social integration. We know that the type of students most in need of language and literacy programs are those not generally attracted to, nor successful in, traditional academic settings. The results of the Southam Literacy Survey (The Creative Research Group, 1987) indicate they are likely to be individuals for whom limited literacy may be but one of a cluster of disadvantages including low levels of income and formal schooling and an inadequate knowledge of the predominant societal language. I believe that if these students are to be reached and helped, strategies must be provided to integrate language and literacy development more closely with other community services such as health, welfare, and employment. As mentioned previously, this is not the case at the present time given the isolation of the COFIs from the community and the lack of language and literacy programs in the workplace. Furthermore, there does not appear to be widespread appreciation for the amount of time required for the development of second-language and literacy skills beyond the levels required simply for survival. The successful development of language and literacy must be viewed as long-term goals, as aspects of personal and professional development and social integration that will require regular maintenance and upgrading.

For researchers the situation is a challenging one: we need to bring to bear on policymakers and program developers the new insights into the culture of literacy that we have gained from the recent surge of research and thinking on literacy. We need to convince educators, employers, and trade union officials to adopt a broad long-term perspective on the development of literacy. In the case of Quebec, we should be particularly well equipped through our experience with language planning to address the issue of literacy. To do so, policymakers should be encouraged to view literacy as an essential factor in language planning and be willing to explore less bureaucratic approaches in the allocation of resources.

NOTES

1.   The term *allophone* is widely used in Quebec to denote speakers of languages other than English or French.

REFERENCES

Alliance Québec (1990). *A guide to French second-language courses in Quebec.* Montréal: Office de la langue française.

Boucher, A. (1989). *En toutes lettres et en français: l'alphabétisation des francophones au Canada.* Montréal: Institut canadien d'éducation des adultes.

Bourhis, R. (1983). *Conflict and language planning in Quebec.* Clevedon, England: Multilingual Matters.

Chalom, M. (1988). *L'alphabétisation et l'intégration des immigrants adultes à la société québécoise.* Unpublished doctoral dissertation. Département de psychopédagogie et d'andragogie, Université de Montréal.

Commissioner of Official Languages (1990). *Annual Report 1989.* Ottawa: Minister of Supply and Services.

d'Anglejan, A. & De Koninck, Z. (1992). Educational policy for a culturally plural Quebec: An update. In B. Burnaby & A. Cumming (Eds.). *Socio-political aspects of ESL* (pp. 97–109). Toronto: Ontario Institute for Studies in Education.

d'Anglejan, A. & Renaud, C. (1985). Learner characteristics and second language acquisition: A multivariate study of adult learners and some thoughts on methodology. *Language Learning, 35,* 1–20.

Donaldson, M. (1978). *Children's minds.* Glasgow: Fontana.

Economic Council of Canada (1987). *Innovation and jobs in Canada.* Ottawa: Supply and Services Canada.

Employment and Immigration Canada (1990). *Youth—A national stay-in-school initiative.* Ottawa: Author.

Esman, M.J. (1987). Ethnic politics and economic power. *Comparative Politics, 19,* 395–418.

Ferdman, B. (1990). Literacy and cultural identity. *Harvard Educational Review, 60,* 181–204.

Gardner, R.C. & Lambert, W.E. (1972). *Attitudes and motivation in second language learning.* Rowley, MA: Newbury House.

Genesee, F. (1983). Bilingual education of majority language group children: The immersion experiments in review. *Applied Psycholinguistics, 4,* 1–46.

Gilbert, L. (1990). *Formation et intégration des allophones au Québec français.* Unpublished manuscript. Département de sociologie, Université de Montréal.

Heath, S.B. (1983). *Ways with words.* Cambridge: Cambridge University Press.

Krashen, S. (1981). *Second language acquisition and learning.* Oxford: Pergamon Press.

Levine, M.V. (1990). *The reconquest of Montreal: Language policy and social change in a bilingual city.* Philadelphia: Temple University Press.

Martin, A. & Pires, J. (1979). *L'échec massif des infirmières à l'examen de connaissance du français: élément d'une problématique générale de la question.* Montréal: Office de la langue française.

Olson, D.R. (1984). "See! Jumping!" Some oral antecedents of literacy. In H. Goelman, A. Oberg & F. Smith (Eds.), *Awakening to literacy* (pp. 185–192). Exeter: Heinemann.

Québec (1985). *L'école québécoise et les communautés culturelles.* Québec: Gouvernement du Québec.

Ong, W. (1983). *Orality and literacy: The technologizing of the word.* London: Methuen.

Scollon, R. & Scollon, S. (1981). *Narrative, literacy and face in interethnic communication.* Norwood, NJ: Ablex.

Snow, C. (1983). Literacy and language: Relationships during the preschool years. *Harvard Educational Review, 53,* 165–189.

Teale, W.H. & Sulzby, E. (1987). Literacy acquisition in early childhood: The roles of access and mediation in storybook reading. In D. Wagner (Ed.), *The future of literacy in a changing world* (pp. 111–130). New York: Pergamon Press.

The Creative Research Group. (1987). *Literacy in Canada.* Ottawa: Southam News.

Weber, R.M. (1991). Linguistic diversity and reading in American society. In R. Barr, M.L. Kamil, P.B. Rosenthal & P.D. Pearson (Eds.) *Handbook of reading research* (pp. 97–120). New York: Longman.

Wells, G. (1984). *Language through interaction: The study of language development.* Cambridge: Cambridge University Press.

PART 4

Reflections

CHAPTER 11

From Coercive to Collaborative Relations of Power in the Teaching of Literacy

Jim Cummins

EMERGING ISSUES IN THE LITERACY DEBATES

A number of themes have emerged in the preceding chapters of this volume. Most chapters, for example, deal with aspects of the sociocultural dimensions of literacy. This focus on cultural diversity is becoming increasingly salient in view of the rapidly changing demographic context in western industrialized countries and the fact that members of historically subordinated cultural groups are strongly overrepresented in the so-called functionally illiterate category (Kirsch & Jungeblut, 1986). The implications of these demographic changes have been discussed most explicitly in the chapter by d'Anglejan.

Many of the chapters highlight issues of empowerment and/or critical literacy for subordinated groups (e.g., Delgado-Gaitan, Zanger, McCaskill, Devine, Zuss). Dimensions or criteria of literacy are explored in several papers, most explicitly by Hornberger and Zuss. Finally, instructional issues are taken up in the chapters by Reder and Ramírez. In some chapters, the focus is primarily on children in schools, while in others the major focus is on issues of adult literacy (e.g., Zuss).

I believe that it is important to put these academic discussions into the context of the public debate on literacy issues. Many issues are intertwined in complex ways in the public debate on literacy, and, in an important sense, this public debate illustrates some of the central theoretical issues surrounding, in Freire's terms, reading the word and the world (e.g., Freire & Macedo, 1987). I shall argue in this chapter that the public focus and apparent political commitment to improving the ability of students (and adults) to "read the word" represents a facade that obscures an underlying structure dedicated to preventing students from "reading the world." Schools (and adult literacy programs) under the guise of imparting literacy and numeracy skills have acted (in concert with the media) both to control access to information and define the boundaries of "reasonable" interpretation of information, with the goal of limiting the possibility of action to challenge the societal power structure. I shall try to trace the manifestations of this discoursal pattern in several current debates on issues related to the North American "literacy crisis." Among the literacy-related issues that are currently high on the public agenda in Canada and the United States are the following:

- The relationship between worker literacy and business "competitiveness"; specifically, the argument that the relatively low literacy levels of North American workers (in comparison to workers from some Asian and European countries) is a major cause of the decline in the "competitiveness" of North American industry.

- Related to this issue is the perceived failure of North American schools to develop adequate levels of literacy and numeracy among their students and to prevent student drop-out prior to graduation. The failure of North American schools to be "accountable" to the public that funds them is perceived as a direct contributor to the crisis of "competitiveness" that business is currently undergoing.

- Within schools, a major culprit to emerge in the perceived decline of student literacy and numeracy is the proliferation of "progressive" "child-centered" teaching methods and the unwillingness of educators to teach "basic skills" and content in a direct no-nonsense fashion.

- When applied to reading instruction, this issue manifests itself in the perception that schools have virtually abandoned systematic instruction in phonics in favor of "whole language" methods that eschew direct instruction in the subskills of reading; since students are denied access to the building blocks of reading, it is hardly surprising (according to this view) that they don't learn to read very well.

- Although it has been less prominent in the public debate, a parallel argument is beginning to be heard against "process" approaches to writing instruction. Since process writing instruction has abandoned direct systematic instruction of vocabulary, spelling, and grammar in favor of allowing students to "discover" these aspects of literacy in the process of writing, it appears hardly surprising to critics of this approach that students have meager vocabularies and that their grammar and spelling are substandard.

- With respect to content instruction, there is a common perception (and some evidence [Ravitch & Finn, 1987]) that American students are profoundly ignorant of their own culture and history. This is usually attributed to the failure of American educators to transmit to students what Hirsch (1987) has termed "cultural literacy"; in other words, the essential shared knowledge base necessary to participate effectively in American society. The inference drawn by both academic and media commentators is that educators should desist from their permissive and "progressive" ways and start to *teach*.

- The relationship between equity issues and literacy has been prominent in U.S. educational debates since the 1960s. In recent years, there has been grudging acknowledgement that minority-group educational underachievement is related to the "literacy crisis" since it is difficult to avoid the fact that minority groups are massively overrepresented in the "functionally illiterate" category. However, in a somewhat ironic twist, the public discourse has shifted to absolve schools and society from responsibility for minority-group underachievement and once again to attribute school failure to minority students' own deficiencies (lack of academic effort), deficiencies of their families (parental inadequacy manifested in antisocial activity such as drug use), or to cynical manipulation by minority-group politicians (e.g., Hispanic "activists" forcing schools to implement ineffective bilingual education programs that deny children access to English). Thus, while schools are castigated for their failure to promote adequate literacy and academic "excellence" and for their cavalier attitude to "accountability," it is minority students and their communities that are largely to blame for their poor school performance. If broader societal institutions are at all responsible for minority-group underachievement, it is only to the extent that politicians and educators have caved in to "ethnic demands."

- Finally, the issue of "competitiveness" is occasionally linked in the North American media to the need for schools to better instruct students in "foreign" languages. Since global economic, scientific, and environmental interdependence is clearly a reality, cross-cultural sensitivity and the ability to communicate in international languages is seen by some business and educational leaders as desirable. These abilities could be viewed as dimensions of a "global cultural literacy," the lack of which is seriously hampering North American "competitiveness" in a shrinking global economy. However, with the exception of advocates for bilingual education, this issue is seldom related in the media to the possibility of promoting minority students' literacy skills in their first language (L1) by means of bilingual programs in school. The focus of groups such as U.S. English and most business leaders tends to be on teaching "foreign" languages more effectively as part of the movement for academic "excellence" rather than developing the "home-grown" linguistic resources of the country.

The relevance of these debates is that they form a framework of discourse that constrains, and is intended to constrain, the role definitions that educators can adopt and the consequent interactions that they engage in with students. The interactions between educators and students form an interpersonal space (Vygotsky's [1978] zone of proximal development) where minds and identities meet and where possibilities for social engagement are collaboratively explored. I argue that the public discourses of literacy sketched above have the effect of reinforcing the societal power structure by limiting students' power of critical thinking, constricting their options for cultural identity formation, and eliminating their capacity for transformative social engagement.

In outlining this thesis, I will first define the distinction between *coercive* and *collaborative* relations of power and then sketch the evolution of the "literacy crisis" and its relation to current demographic trends and subordinated group status. Then criteria of "literacy" will be critically examined and applied to the issues of public debate sketched above. Finally, I will outline a framework for conceptualizing the development of literacy in cross-cultural contexts as a function of the *microinteractions* between educators and students and the *macrointeractions* between societal institutions and minority communities. These interactions reflect the relations of culture and power in the society but they also *constitute* these relations and, as such, embody a transformative potential. In other words, the framework posits explicitly that participants (e.g., students, communities, and educators) in micro- and macrointeractions have the potential to resist and challenge coercive relations of power and to transform these into collaborative relations of power, thereby undermining oppressive structures.

COERCIVE AND COLLABORATIVE RELATIONS OF POWER

Coercive relations of power refer to the exercise of power by a dominant group (or individual or country) to the detriment of a subordinated group (or individual or country). The assumption is that there is a fixed quantity of power that operates according to a balance effect; in other words, the more power one group has, the less is left for other groups. Coercive relations of power usually involve a definitional process that legitimates the inferior or deviant status accorded to the subordinated group (or individual or country). In other words, the dominant group defines the subordinated group as inferior (or evil), thereby automatically defining itself as superior (or virtuous). The inherent inferiority of the subordinated group legitimates the treatment accorded to it by the dominant group. Coercive relations of power have constituted the predominant mode of intergroup contact since the beginnings of human history at the level of both international and domestic relations.

Collaborative relations of power, on the other hand, operate on the assumption that power is not a fixed predetermined quantity but rather can be *generated* in interpersonal and intergroup relations, thereby becoming "additive" rather than "subtractive." In other words, participants in the relationship are *empowered* through their collaboration such that each is more affirmed in her or his identity and has a greater sense of efficacy to effect change in his or her life or social situation. Thus, power is created in the relationship and shared among participants.

In educational contexts, the benefits of collaborative relations of power are clearly seen in the additive empowerment that results from cooperative learning activities in the classroom and in the global sister class networks documented by Sayers (1991). They are also evident in the family literacy projects documented by Ada (1988b) and Delgado-Gaitan (this volume).

I argue that the so-called literacy crisis can be adequately conceptualized only as a consequence of the operation, and in fact escalation during the 1980s (Barlett & Steele, 1992), of coercive relations of power. Furthermore, coercive relations of power will, in the long term, result in disempowerment of both dominant and subordinated groups, whereas a shift from coercive to collaborative relations of power has the potential to empower both groups. In other words, continuation of structures that create educational failure, functional illiteracy, and impoverishment among subordinated groups will also disempower the dominant group as a result of the increased costs for social and physical structures—such as welfare and prisons—necessary to protect itself from what it has created through the exercise of coercive relations of power. The riots in Los Angeles in the spring of 1992 vividly illustrate the mutually destructive potential of long-term coercive relations of power. In the context of the literacy crisis outlined above, coercive relations of power, manifested in the disinvestment in education and other social programs, are contributing directly to the functional illiteracy that is being blamed for the lack of competitiveness of American industry.

THE "LITERACY CRISIS"

The literacy crisis that has come to prominence during the past decade in western industrialized societies has evolved from three phenomena that have become increasingly intertwined during the past thirty years: (a) the persistent educational underachievement of students from certain minority groups in western societies and the consequent lower literacy levels and economic status among the adult members of these minority groups; (b) the rapid growth in cultural and linguistic diversity in western societies brought about by increased immigration and refugee resettlement programs; and (c) the perception that educational institutions have failed, and are failing, to provide the general population with adequate literacy and numeracy skills to function effectively in an economic environment that is becoming more technologically complex and internationally competitive by the day.

Until the 1960s, few policymakers in western countries considered illiteracy to be a major problem for their societies. The focus of international organizations such as UNESCO was predominantly on reducing illiteracy in underdeveloped nations and considerable progress has been made in this regard. UNESCO has estimated, for example, that between 1950 and 1985, illiteracy among the world's adult population decreased from 44.3 percent to 27.7 percent (Bhola, 1989). However, despite the fact that 98 percent of the world's illiterate population lives in underdeveloped countries (Newman & Beverstock, 1990), illiteracy in western countries has assumed crisis proportions according to many policymakers. Recent national data from Statistics Canada (1990), for example, suggest that while a majority (62 percent) of Canadians between the ages of 16 and 69 were judged to have adequate reading skills, a substantial number (38 percent) had either very limited reading skills or some degree of difficulty in reading when the task became more complex (see d'Anglejan, this volume). In the United States context, Stedman and Kaestle (1987) synthesized the findings of seven national studies to conclude that about 30 percent of the adult population have either minimal or marginal functional literacy skills.

These data may seem paradoxical in view of the fact that educational levels in western countries have increased steadily during the past fifty years. Baril and Mori (1991:17), for example, in reporting Statistics Canada data, note that:

> Canadians are better educated than ever before. Steady improvements in levels of educational attainment occurred over the past few decades. More younger Canadians today have university degrees and fewer have less than a Grade 9 education than did earlier cohorts.

What has changed, of course, is the nature of our society and particularly the nature of the workplace. Just as, over the long term, the Industrial Revolution in the 1800s created the need for a much broader range of literacy and numeracy skills than had hitherto been the case, the technological changes associated with the current "Information Age" require that workers employ literacy skills that are far beyond what their parents needed. Mikulecky (1986), for example, reported that workers read between 1.5 and 2 hours a day and much of what they need to read falls between the tenth- and twelfth-grade levels on a readability scale. From an economic point of view then, the "literacy crisis" refers to the gap between the significantly increased literacy demands of the workplace and the perceived literacy attainments of the workforce.

It is appropriate to introduce some terminological "caveats" at this point. The use of terms such as "functional illiteracy" implies that there is a phenomenon or a state of existence called "functional illiteracy" that characterizes people independently of the way in which, and the purposes for which, it has been defined. In fact, all notions of "illiteracy" (and, conversely, "literacy") are social constructions that are not in any sense neutral from a sociopolitical point of view. Furthermore, terms like "illiteracy" are potentially pejorative in that they are employed by "literate" individuals and groups to highlight perceived deficits in others. Individuals with limited reading and writing abilities seldom define themselves as "illiterate" and thus the sociopolitical functions served by terms such as these must be analyzed.[1]

While terms such as "functional illiteracy" may be problematic, it is clear that social mobility will increasingly depend on high levels of literacy skills. The gap between educational and literacy achievements and workplace demands is particularly apparent among members of minority or subordinated groups in western societies.[2] The focus on equality of educational and social opportunities during the 1960s and beyond was occasioned by considerable data demonstrating the widespread social and educational disadvantages experienced by members of subordinated groups. Subordinated groups such as Aboriginal Canadians and Francophone Canadians showed significantly lower levels of educational attainment and economic status than did Anglophone Canadians. A similar pattern of "underclass" status characterized Latin-, African-, and Native-American populations in the United States.

In more recent years, literacy surveys have consistently shown these subordinated groups in both Canada and the United States to be significantly overrepresented in the "functionally illiterate" categories. For example, a survey by the National Assessment of Educational Progress (NAEP) in the United States (Kirsch & Jungeblut, 1986) shows a direct relation between ethnic status and literacy. At each of the three literacy levels (basic—score of 200; intermediate—score of 275; and advanced—score of 350), Whites performed better than Hispanics, who in turn performed better than Blacks. Newman and Beverstock (1990:77) suggest that "[t]his division implies an alarming trend, considering the fact that minorities who have been economically and educationally disadvantaged comprise an increasingly large percentage of the population." They also note that literate skills involving thinking and problem solving at the 275 level and above on the NAEP scale will be increasingly required in the workplace of the 21st century:

> The scales of difficulty also demonstrated that complex and demanding tasks—those that are expected to characterize work in coming years—may be beyond the current skills of many young adults. For example, workers often will be expected to use information on computer screens, make calculations, consult documentation, and then type new instructions. (1990:77).

These activities reflect skills at or above the 275 level on the NAEP scale, a level that only 78 percent of White, 57 percent of Hispanics, and 39 percent of Blacks attained.

Thus, the educational underachievement and consequent marginal levels of literacy among subordinated groups contribute disproportionately to the broader problem of societal illiteracy. Furthermore, up to this point societal and educational structures have ensured that the "underclass" status of these groups has been transmitted from one generation to the next. As Newman and Beverstock (1990) note, the proportion of "minority" students is rapidly increasing in North American urban centres. To illustrate, the National Coalition of Advocates for Students (NCAS) estimates that by the year 2001, minority enrollment levels will range from 70 to 96 percent in the nation's fifteen largest school systems. In California, by that time, so-called minority groups (e.g., Latinos, African-Americans, Asian-Americans) will represent a greater proportion of the school population than will students from the so-called majority group.

Many minority students in the United States experience a much higher secondary school drop-out rate than do majority students and are frequently streamed into low ability groups. According to the NCAS report,

> inflexible assessment practices can lead to very low expectations of immigrant students by school personnel. Many young newcomers are placed in low expectation tracks or ability groups, where inadequate educational experiences may result in alienation from school, dropping out, and the impossibility of attaining higher education. (1988:48)

In summary, linguistic and cultural diversity is the norm in an increasing number of urban school systems in western industrialized societies. The historic and current overrepresentation of certain minority groups in low educational and "functionally illiterate" categories reflects the operation of the societal power structure. This reality has a direct but largely unacknowledged relationship to the current "literacy crisis" in North American societies.

In the next section, the social construction process involved in defining criteria of literacy is further examined and placed in the context of the current public debates on literacy.

CRITERIA OF LITERACY

While different theorists have distinguished a variety of forms of literacy, for present purposes it is sufficient to distinguish *functional, cultural,* and *critical* literacies (Williams & Snipper, 1990). Functional literacy implies a level of reading and writing that enables people to function adequately in society and, as such, is defined relative to changing societal demands. What is implied by functional literacy is a set of cognitive skills that permit individuals to function in social and employment situations typical of late-twentieth-century industrialized countries.[3]

Cultural literacy emphasizes the need for shared experiences and points of reference within an interpretive community in order to adequately comprehend texts. In contrast to functional literacy, where the emphasis is on *skills,* cultural literacy focuses on particular content or knowledge that is basic to meaningful text interpretation in particular cultural contexts. For example, many recent immigrants may lack the cultural literacy to fully interpret typical situation-comedy programs on American television, just as many middle-class White adults may lack the cultural literacy to interpret rap music. Cultural and functional literacies are related in the sense that the acquisition of the cognitive skills of literacy will be facilitated to the extent that the content of texts reflects a familiar cultural context.

Critical literacy, as expounded in Paulo Freire's work, focuses on the potential of written language as a tool that encourages people to analyze the division of power and resources in their society and work to transform discriminatory structures. For example, from the perspective of critical literacy, it is important to inquire who defines criteria of "adequacy" with respect to functional and cultural literacies and what social purposes are achieved by such definitions.

As is clear from the preceding chapters in this volume, there is increasing consensus among researchers and theorists that literacy must be defined in relation to particular cultural and social contexts that go beyond the usual conceptions of functional literacy. Functional literacy has often been viewed as a fixed inventory of skills and operationally defined in terms of particular grade-level abilities in reading and writing, as though it were an autonomous, culturally neutral phenomenon that could be assessed outside of particular contexts of application. Most theorists currently regard such views of literacy as very much oversimplified and educationally unproductive. The extensive range of literate behaviors that go beyond functional literacy is well illustrated in Hornberger's chapter (this volume). As many theorists have pointed out (e.g., Reder, this volume; Cumming, 1990), ways of using literacy may differ dramatically from one society to another, and even within the same cultural and linguistic group immense differences may be apparent in the uses to which literacy is put.

Along the same lines, Ferdman (1990) views literacy as intimately related to cultural identity and suggests that:

> In a culturally heterogenous society, literacy ceases to be a characteristic inherent solely in the individual. It becomes an interactive process that is constantly redefined and renegotiated, as the individual transacts with the socially fluid surroundings. . . . To be literate it is not enough, for example, to know how to sign one's name. One must also know when and where it is appropriate to do so. (187)

Ferdman defines cultural identity as the behaviors, beliefs, values, and norms that a person considers to define himself or herself socially as a member of a particular cultural group and the value placed on those features in relation to those of other groups. Thus, particular literacy behaviors that affirm the individual's sense of cultural identity will be acquired more easily and with more personal involvement than those that serve to deny or devalue his or her cultural identity. By the same token, the acquisition of certain forms of literacy may eventually require the individual to redefine his or her cultural identity.

As one example, Fordham (1990) discusses Black students' adoption of "racelessness" or "acting White" as a strategy for academic achievement or vertical mobility. Thus, for subordinated groups the acquisition of higher levels of literacy (or academic achievement) is enmeshed in a complex array of sociohistorical relations between their group and the dominant group in the society, as McCaskill's chapter in this volume illustrates. The microinteractions between educators and students are embedded in the macrointeractions between dominant-group institutions and historically subordinated communities. As Fordham's analysis makes clear, this nested pattern of interactions constitutes a process of negotiating identities:

> . . . within the school structure, Black adolescents consciously and unconsciously sense that they have to give up aspects of their identities and of their indigenous cultural system in order to achieve success as defined in dominant-group terms; their resulting social selves are embodied in the notion of racelessness. Hence, for many of them the cost of school success is too high; it implies that cultural integrity must be sacrificed in order to "make it." For many Black adolescents, that option is unacceptable. For the high achievers identified in this paper, achieving school success is not marked only by conflict and ambivalence . . . but with the need to camouflage efforts directed at behaviors that the group identifies as "acting White." (1990:259)

The relationship between literacy and cultural identity has implications for the ways in which literacy is defined. For example, Langer (1989:1) defines literacy as "the ability to think and reason within a particular society" and suggests that "there is no right or wrong literacy, just the one that is, more or less, responsive to the demands of a particular culture." While in an absolute sense there may be no right or wrong literacy, one must ask, however, who determines the demands of a particular culture or society? In culturally diverse societies, what counts as appropriate or valued knowledge is clearly more likely to be determined by the dominant group than by subordinated groups. A good example of this is Hirsch's (1987) attempt to specify what counts as "cultural literacy" in the U.S. context. Knowledge and ways of thinking that are culturally specific to subordinated groups are notably absent from Hirsch's specifications for "cultural literacy."

In this sense, as suggested above, the social construction process involved in defining functional and cultural literacies must be critically examined. What constitutes "adequate" functional literacy is determined by the dominant group in relation to the requirements of the system of production (i.e., the workplace). As illustrated by the public debates on literacy discussed below, this is equally so today as it was at the time when it was illegal in the United States to teach slaves to read. From the perspective of the dominant group, critical literacy among workers or students is no more welcome today than it was in the era of slavery.

Similarly, the construct of "cultural literacy" cannot be isolated from historical and current intergroup power relations in particular societies. What constitutes valued knowledge or "cultural literacy" (in Hirsch's sense) in a particular society is socially constructed and, not surprisingly, the dominant group plays a greater role in the construction process than do subordinated groups.

What this perspective implies within the present context is that the literacy of minority cultural and linguistic communities must be analyzed in relation to the cultural identity of these communities. Hirsch's attempt to define "cultural literacy" in the U.S. context is an attempt to further privilege the knowledge and values of the dominant group and to institutionalize the exclusion of subordinated group identities from the mainstream of economic and cultural life.

This analysis suggests that, in the case of subordinated groups, literacy programs that focus only on functional literacy to the neglect of cultural and critical literacy are unlikely to succeed. The process of reversing low levels of literacy among subordinated groups must acknowledge the sociopolitical dimensions of the phenomenon in addition to its technical dimensions. A remedial focus only on technical aspects of functional illiteracy is inadequate because the causes of educational underachievement and "illiteracy" among subordinated groups are rooted in the systematic devaluation of culture and denial of access to power and resources by the dominant group.

From this perspective it is possible to examine the ways in which the issues in the public debate on literacy have been framed to reinforce dominant-group hegemony.

THE PUBLIC DEBATES ON LITERACY

Worker Literacy, Education, and "Competitiveness"

Although low-paying jobs in the service sector represented the fastest growing segment of the job market in western industrialized countries during the 1980s, many employers have raised educational standards required for even such low-level positions (Rubenson, 1989). This trend appears to be related to the perception that the "trainability" of workers is essential for businesses to adapt in a flexible manner to a rapidly changing economic environment. As Rubenson points out, human resources are central to business success in an information economy:

> The combined effects of recent technological breakthroughs in microelectronics and telecommunications have had profound structural impact on the economy and pushed it toward an information economy. Consequently, human resource investments are being viewed as critical to the whole process of economic development. A nation's competitiveness on the world market is to a large degree expected to depend on its resources in terms of knowledge, learning, information and skilled intelligence. (387)

Many of the educational reform reports of the 1980s in the U.S. explicitly related the difficulties of American industry in competing against Asian countries to the inadequacies of the "human resources" that American industry had to draw on, specifically the low levels of worker "functional literacy." The low literacy of workers was, in turn, attributed to the failures of American schools to transmit basic literacy and numeracy skills in an organized and sequential way. In fact, the "imperative" for reform has been sparked by the widespread perception that educational standards in the United States have been in decline for a number of years and, as a result, American business interests are placed in jeopardy in an increasingly competitive world economy. As expressed in *A Nation at Risk:* "Our once unchallenged preeminence in commerce, industry, science and technological innovations is being overtaken by competitors throughout the world" (National Commission on Excellence in Education, 1983:1).

The recommendations of *A Nation at Risk* and most subsequent reports have focused primarily on raising standards and graduation requirements, eliminating the "curriculum smorgasbord" of "soft" subjects in favor of a common core curriculum for all students, and increasing the amount of time that students are expected to spend learning the "basics." The thrust is towards "getting tough" with students and teachers in order to increase the rigor in curriculum materials and instruction.

It can be argued that this discourse of "competitiveness" and "functional illiteracy" serves to make workers and educators scapegoats for the lack of competitiveness of North American industry in the 1980s and 1990s and the prodigious waste of human and economic resources by government and business during that period. As Hodgkinson (1991) has suggested, the American educational reform movement diverts attention from the failure of government to allocate resources to the social infrastructure essential for healthy human development. The lack of "competitiveness" of the "products" of American schooling in comparison to the "products" of schools in other countries has far more to do with the increase of poverty in American inner cities and the underfunding of inner-city schools than it does with the quality of American education in any absolute sense (see Kozol, 1991, for a vivid picture of the results of this selective underfunding).

Some of the data presented by Hodgkinson (1991) in support of this conclusion are the following:

- 23 percent of preschool children (birth to age 5) in the United States live in poverty, the highest rate of any industrialized nation.

- About 350,000 children annually are born to mothers who were addicted to cocaine during pregnancy.

- The United States ranked 22d in global rankings for infant mortality with a rate of 10 deaths per 1,000 live births (1988 statistics).

- The number of reports of child abuse or neglect received annually by child protection agencies tripled between 1976 and 1987 to 2.2 million.
- Young males in the United States are five times as likely to be murdered as are their counterparts in other nations.
- A Black male in the United States was about five times as likely to be in prison as a Black male in South Africa (1988 statistics).
- More than 80 percent of America's one million prisoners are high school drop-outs, and each prisoner costs taxpayers upwards of $20,000 a year.

Hodgkinson points out that while America's best students are on a par with the world's best, "ours is undoubtedly the worst 'bottom third' of any of the industrialized democracies" (10). He summarizes the situation as follows:

> about one-third of preschool children are destined for school failure because of poverty, neglect, sickness, handicapping conditions, and lack of adult protection and nurturance. There is no point in trying to teach hungry or sick children. (1991:10)

He goes on to point to the strong correlations among educational levels, income, and crime reduction. He notes, for example, that "every dollar spent on a Head Start child will save taxpayers $7 in later services that the child will not need" (15) (see Schweinhart, Weikart & Larney, 1986). Despite the fact that education is a far better public investment than prisons, the level of K–12 educational expenditures of the United States is considerably lower than that of other industrialized countries (4.1 percent of gross domestic product compared to a non–United States average of 4.6 percent).

The point I want to make here is that, while there is certainly considerable need for educational restructuring, to attribute the lack of competitiveness of American industry to the functional illiteracy of American workers and the failures of American schools serves to divert attention from the fact that the policies of government and business have significantly increased the gap between the wealthy and impoverished in the United States during the 1980s (Barlett & Steele, 1992), thereby contributing directly to the numbers of students who experience educational failure and drop out of school prematurely. The costs of more adequate social and economic programs designed to combat poverty (and by implication "illiteracy") are usually viewed as "prohibitive" by the same politicians who, with minimal dissent or even debate, bailed out $157 billion of taxpayers' money to "resolve" the Savings and Loan scandal (Waldman, 1990) and whose trillions of dollars of wasted military expenditures never required justification.

It is clear that while the rhetoric of combatting functional illiteracy flourishes, there is little interest in helping students and workers to make the transition from "reading the word" to "reading the world." In other words, the focus on functional illiteracy remains in the service of coercive relations of power despite the increasingly apparent costs of this focus for the dominant group itself.

Literacy Instruction in Schools

It is clearly beyond the scope of this chapter to review even a fraction of the vast amount of documentation on this topic. Each of the issues mentioned in the first section of the chapter (general orientations to pedagogy, phonics versus whole language reading instruction, traditional versus process approaches to writing, and the teaching of "cultural literacy") is complex from both educational and sociopolitical perspectives, and the pendulum of educational discourse has swung frequently between the extremes of these debates. The major point that I want to make, however, is that the current "back-to-basics" focus in literacy instruction associated with the educational reform movement is not a neutral stance based on educational research but rather part of the same sociopolitical agenda designed to limit the extent to which "reading the word" might lead students to "read the world." In other words, I argue that the unstated goals of this conservative discourse are (*a*) to promote sufficient functional literacy to meet the needs of industry in an increasingly technological work environment; (*b*) to promote cultural literacy and cultural identities that are in harmony with the societal power structure so that what is in the best interests of the dominant group is accepted as also being in the best interests of subordinated groups; and (*c*) to limit the development of critical literacy so that students do not develop the ability to deconstruct disinformation and challenge structures of control and social injustice.

The transparency of the sociopolitical agenda of the education-

al reform movement is apparent from even a superficial scrutiny of
its premises. Stedman and Kaestle (1985) point out that the apparent test-score decline in the 1970s that so concerned educational
reformers was due to a variety of factors other than educational
quality (e.g., the fact that more minority students were staying in
school rather than dropping out) and by the late 1970s the decline
in standardized test scores had ended, well before "the reformers
issued their reports, and before the legislatures passed their
post-1980 reform bills" (209). Thus, they argue that the alleged
decline in educational standards that precipitated the reform
movement was actually a fabricated crisis.

The alleged cause of the educational/literacy crisis was also
fabricated for sociopolitical reasons. Many of the educational critics of the 1980s attributed the alleged fall in academic standards to
the child-centered permissiveness and social unrest of the late sixties. However, as Stedman and Kaestle point out, the greatest student protest took place between 1968 and 1971, whereas the
greatest decline in standardized test scores occurred between 1971
and 1978:

> Blaming the decline on the effects of social unrest in the schools
> may be fashionable, but the middle to late 1970s were years of
> educational retrenchment, characterized by a renewed emphasis
> on the basics, the spread of statewide competency testing and
> moves to end social promotion. We can hardly blame the test
> declines of the 1970s directly on activist educators who, frus-
> trated by their inability to change schools, had effectively aban-
> doned their efforts by the mid-1970s. (1985:208)

A further point is that virtually all the empirical data (e.g., Goodlad, 1984; Sirotnik, 1983; Sizer, 1984) show that instruction in
schools has changed very little over the course of this century. The
process of teaching and learning, according to Sirotnik's (and
Goodlad's) analysis of more than one thousand elementary and
secondary classrooms, "appears to be one of the most consistent
and persistent phenomena known in the social and behavioral
sciences . . . the 'modus operandi' of the typical classroom is still
didactics, practice, and little else" (Sirotnik, 1983:16–17). He
notes that teacher lecturing or total class work on written assignments continue to emerge as the primary instructional patterns
and suggests that "navigating back to the basics should be easy. We
never left" (26).

In other words, while arguments for child-centered or experience-based pedagogy have been prominent in the academic literature for a considerable period of time (in fact, long before the term "whole language" was coined), actual practice in U.S. schools has remained relatively unaffected by such arguments. However, despite their relatively minimal impact, child-centered pedagogies have frequently been made a scapegoat for the perceived failings of American education (e.g., Rickover, 1959).

In a similar vein, Shannon (1989) points to the fact that basal reading programs have dominated the teaching of reading for most of this century. More than 90 percent of elementary school teachers rely on teacher's guide books and basal readers during 90 percent of their instructional time. As Durkin (1987) points out, the terminology and marketing strategies used to sell basal reading programs have changed over the years to reflect current pedagogical fashions, but the programs themselves have remained essentially the same. Shannon's analysis suggests that school systems require teachers to use the basal materials and teacher's guidebooks as a means of controlling the production of literacy "outputs," which will be assessed by means of standardized achievement tests. Within this "production management" model of reading instruction,

> teachers teach students what, when, where, how, and why to use the skill listed as next in the basal scope and sequence. . . . Questions asked during practice should be factual, encourage choral response from the group, and be carefully sequenced to lead students successfully to the goal without diversion. (Shannon, 1989:90)

Rosenshine and Stevens (1984), who summarize the research supporting this approach, suggest that high-level cognitive questions are inappropriate during reading lessons because they are not correlated with reading-test scores and there are no generic rules that students can use to answer them. The lack of correlation with standardized tests is hardly surprising in view of the fact that a large majority of such tests fail to assess higher-order cognitive skills.

As Shannon (1989) points out, the argument that such approaches to reading are more effective than whole-language approaches that substitute children's literature for basal readers and "reading management systems" is ironic in view of the fact that whole-language approaches are used almost universally in New Zealand, the most literate country in the world, with very low rates of reading failure and minimal use of standardized tests. Similarly, the attribution by media commentators of high drop-out rates and adolescent "illiteracy" to whole-language approaches in elementary school fails to take account of the fact that whole-language approaches have been implemented in only a fraction of schools and seldom in any sustained way beyond the early elementary grades. Furthermore, while the implementation of whole-language approaches has increased significantly in Canadian urban elementary schools during the past five years, a large majority of students who have dropped out would not have had the benefit of such approaches.

In short, the attribution of test score declines to "progressive" educational practices is pure scapegoating, since traditional teacher-centered instruction continues to predominate in classrooms across North America.

This teacher-centered transmission of information has the effect of limiting the possibility of any kind of critical thinking on the part of either teachers or students. Such deviations from rote transmission are penalized since they are "off-task" with respect to what is assessed on standardized tests. The image of our future society implied by this type of education is a society of compliant consumers who passively accept rather than critically analyze the forces that impinge on their lives. Sirotnik (1983) similarly points to the hidden curriculum being communicated to students in the typical classroom that emerged from his analysis; this classroom contains

> a lot of teacher talk and a lot of student listening . . . almost invariably closed and factual questions . . . and predominantly total class instructional configurations around traditional activities—all in a virtually affectless environment. It is but a short inferential leap to suggest that we are implicitly teaching dependence upon authority, linear thinking, social apathy, passive involvement, and hands-off learning. (29)

Hirsch's (1987) insistence on just one version of "cultural literacy" clearly fits into this vision of societal realities and goals. Curricula based on "cultural literacy" will continue to sanitize historical and current realities so that deviant thoughts are rendered "unthinkable" and "truth" is assured through the consensus of unified perspectives. Thus, to take a current example, Columbus's "discovery" of the Americas will continue to be regarded as "truth" and students' "intelligence" will continue to be defined in relation to their "ability" or inclination to regurgitate such "truths" on IQ tests (such as the Information subtest of the Weschsler Intelligence Test for Children—Revised, which explicitly asks "Who discovered America?").[4]

In summary, the common thread that runs through the conservative discourse about literacy in schools is the intense effort to exclude from pedagogical practices any collaborative quest for meaning on the part of teachers and students. The only meanings that are appropriate to "discover" are those that have been predefined and sanitized. This hierarchical control of the instructional process dictates the current pedagogical focus on passive reception rather than active exploration, the focus on out-of-context phonics rather than meaning, the focus on spelling and grammar rather than creative writing, and the focus on ingesting the "cultural literacy" of the dominant group rather than developing a critical literacy grounded in students' personal and cultural experiences. In other words, typical literacy instruction has the effect of preventing students from "reading the world." The perpetrators of these forms of instruction are locked into preserving coercive relations of power. A shift to collaborative relations of power in the classroom would require that educators also learn from their students and together negotiate possibilities for reading the world. Educators' fear or inability to engage in a critical literacy process themselves means that this potential for reciprocal empowerment usually remains unrealized.

Literacy and Subordinated Group Status

In view of the fact that subordinated groups experience disproportionate academic failure, one might have expected educational reform efforts to be predicated on a causal analysis of this phenomenon. Unfortunately, however, most media commentators do not move much beyond an analysis that blames the victim and exhorts teachers to be more effective. The educational reform movement, the effective schools movement, and the movement to combat "functional illiteracy" have all paid only lip service to the fact that historically subordinated minorities form the bulk of the students in the underachieving groups. One obvious contributor to the pattern of subordinated group underachievement is poverty, a phenomenon that has increased dramatically during the past decade (Barlett & Steele, 1992). However, in addition to factors associated with poverty and economic discrimination, an additional contributor appears to be a set of factors that derive from the sociohistorical relations between dominant and subordinated groups. These macrointeractions often appear to result in the internalization by the subordinated groups of a sense of ambivalence with regard to the value of their cultural identity and a sense of powerlessness in relation to the dominant group (Cummins, 1989; Ogbu, 1978). Wagner and Grenier (1991), for example, in an analysis of literacy among minority Francophones in Ontario, Canada, claim that there is a specific phenomenon of *subordinated group illiteracy* (*analphabétisme de minorité*), which represents the cumulative effect of generations of economic, educational, and psychological subjugation such that members of the subordinated group internalize the inferior status attributed to them by the dominant group. They distinguish two distinct forms of subordinated group illiteracy that have no counterpart in dominant groups. They term these two phenomena *illiteracy of oppression* and *illiteracy of resistance*. Both derive from the basic problems of access to appropriate schooling and contact between minority and majority languages. They describe these two forms of subordinated group illiteracy as follows:

> L'analphabètisme de résistance, quoique suscité par l'oppression, est en quelque sorte provoqué par le groupe minoritaire lui-même qui, voulant sauvegarder sa langue et sa culture, craignant l'assimilation, se replie, refuse l'école de la majorité. À la limite, on préférera demeurer analphabète plutôt que de risquer de perdre sa langue. On cultivera la parole parlée, on se rabattra sur la tradition orale et sur les autres constituants de la culture du groupe. À l'opposé, l'analphabètisme d'oppression est un effet direct du processus d'intégration/assimilation à l'oeuvre dans l'école publique et dans l'ensemble de la société; il résulte de la destruction lente de l'identité et des moyens de résistance de la collectivité minoritaire; il est provoqué, par conséquent, par l'action offensive de la société majoritaire. (44–45)
>
> [Illiteracy of resistance, although caused by oppression, is to some extent instituted by the minority group itself who, wishing

to safeguard its language and culture, and fearing assimilation, turns in on itself and rejects the form of education imposed by the majority group. At the extreme, the minority group would prefer to remain illiterate rather than risk losing its language. The group will cultivate the spoken word and fall back on the oral tradition and other components of its culture. By contrast, illiteracy of oppression is a direct consequence of the process of integration/assimilation at work in the public school and in the entire society; it results in the slow destruction of identity and of the means of resistance in the minority community; thus, it is brought about by the oppressive action of the majority society. (Translation, J. Cummins)]

This analysis has important implications for the promotion of literacy among subordinated groups. Approaches that focus only on technical skills of reading and writing (in either L1 or L2) are unlikely to be successful. If the root causes of illiteracy are associated with a collective sense of ambivalence in regard to the group's cultural identity, resulting from the internalization of dominant group attributions, then to be successful, literacy instruction must address these root causes. In other words, intervention must encourage students to challenge dominant group constructions of the cultural identity of the subordinated group and critically deconstruct the ways in which this devaluation of identity has been affected. A focus on functional literacy will have minimal success in these contexts if it is not closely integrated with cultural and critical literacies, as papers by Delgado-Gaitan and Zuss make clear in this volume.

In a similar vein, Stedman (1987) has pointed out that much of the effective schools literature fails to focus specifically on schools that achieved and maintained grade-level success with low-income students. His reanalysis of the literature from this perspective highlights two aspects of effective schools that are omitted from most other accounts. The first of these is a focus on *cultural pluralism*— specifically, effective schools reinforce the ethnic identity of their students. The second is a focus on *academically rich programs* in which students are actively engaged in learning through tasks that can be related to their own experience. Similarly, Lucas, Henze, and Donato (1990) emphasize a focus on *empowerment* as a central characteristic of high schools that were effective in educating Latino/Latina students in California and Arizona.

The vigorous opposition to bilingual education in the media and by groups such as U.S. English illustrates the reluctance by the dominant group to address the real causes of underachievement by bicultural students. The institutionalization of bilingual education would provide access to jobs and upward mobility for members of subordinated groups. In addition, the valorization of minority languages and subordinated group identities in the microinteractions between educators and students would challenge the historically entrenched pattern of macrointeractions in the broader society. As I have argued elsewhere (Cummins, 1989), the perceived potential of bilingual education to threaten the societal power structure has given rise to a campaign of disinformation designed to prevent educators, parents, and policy-makers from "reading the world." Under the guise of helping minority students to "read the word" (i.e., achieve academically in English), opponents of bilingual education have sought to mystify research findings so that subordinated groups will acquiesce in the perpetuation of educational structures (e.g., English-only instruction) that constrict the possibilities for students' personal and academic development.

In short, one of the reasons why educational reform and literacy promotion efforts have attained only limited success is that typical interventions do not address the fact that historically subordinated groups constitute a disproportionate number of educational underachievers. The microinteractions between educators and learners in these interventions tend to focus on decontextualized functional literacy skills (in English) and leave unchallenged the pattern of macrointeractions that represent a major cause of the students' underachievement. When such interventions, focused on functional literacy in isolation, fail to reverse educational underachievement, this is often taken as further proof of the inherent inferiority of the subordinated group (e.g., Jensen, 1969) and used to reinforce coercive relations of power.

One final aspect of the public literacy debates is worth noting. It is remarkable that despite all the discussion of "globalization" and the need to adapt to an increasingly competitive international economic environment, there has been minimal advocacy by the business or educational communities for bilingual education programs that would promote effective conversational and literate knowledge of international languages (for minority *and* majority students). Instead, the educational focus continues to be on eradicating the "home-grown" linguistic resources that children bring to school. In light of the discussion above, a reasonable hypothesis is that this apparent absence of good business sense is due to the dominant group's antipathy to reinforcing the cultural identity of bicultural students. To acknowledge that their bilingualism is a valuable cultural and economic asset would effectively reverse the historical pattern of devaluation of identity. The internal logic of the "international competitiveness" discourse might suggest that in an increasingly interdependent world, it is the mono-lingual/monocultural individual who is "culturally illiterate" and ill-equipped to prosper economically in "the new world order." Two-way bilingual programs for both majority and minority students illustrate very well the obvious potential of transforming coercive relations of power into collaborative relations. These programs develop bilingualism and biliteracy for both groups and significantly amplify the possibilities for knowledge generation and identity formation. By contrast, the present coercive structures attempt to render both groups "culturally illiterate" and deny minority students the possibility even of "functional literacy" in either of their languages.[5]

In summary, the public debates on literacy and educational underachievement are orchestrated to build public support (or in Chomsky's [1987] terms "to manufacture consent") for educational structures that exert increased hierarchial control over the interactions between educators and students. The content of instruction is prepackaged, the options for gaining access to and interpreting information are predetermined, and the possibilities for critical thinking and transformative action are stifled. In addition, educational success and upward mobility for members of subordinated groups is extended only to those who bring their identities into conformity with dominant group prescriptions.

A FRAMEWORK FOR INTEGRATING FUNCTIONAL, CULTURAL, AND CRITICAL LITERACIES

In previous sections, I have argued that in the microinteractions between educators and students many subordinated group students are rendered "voiceless" (Giroux, 1991) or silenced (Fine, 1987; Walsh, 1991) in very much the same way that their communities have been disempowered (often for centuries) through their macrointeractions with societal institutions. The converse of this proposition is that students from communities that have historically been subordinated will succeed educationally and amplify their "voice" or their expression of personal identity to the extent that the microinteractions in school reverse the macrointeractions that prevail in the society at large. The ways in which educators attempt to orchestrate the pattern of interactions with students will reflect the role definitions that they have assumed with respect to societal power relations.

The development of both identities and academic knowledge in school can be viewed within the framework of Vygotsky's (1978) notion of the the *zone of proximal development* (ZPD). Vygotsky viewed the ZPD as the distance between children's developmental level as determined by individual problem solving without adult guidance and the level of potential development as determined by children's problem solving under the influence of, or in collaboration with, more capable adults or peers. Expressed simply, the ZPD is the interactional or interpersonal space where minds meet and new understandings can arise through collaborative interaction and inquiry. Newman, Griffin, and Cole (1989) label this interpersonal space *the construction zone.* Moll (1989:59) points out that central to Vygotsky's notion of the ZPD are "the specific ways that adults (or peers) socially mediate or interactionally create circumstances for learning," and he emphasizes that the child is not passive but "an active organism helping create the very circumstances for his or her own learning."

The historical pattern of dominant–subordinated group interactions has been one where educators have constricted the zone in an attempt to sanitize deviant cultural identities. For educators to become partners in the transmission of "knowledge," minority students were required to acquiesce in the subordination of their cultural identities and to celebrate as "truth" the "cultural literacy" of the dominant group. The construction of the ZPD by educators reflected a process whereby they defined their role as "civilizing," "saving," "assimilating," or "educating" students whose culture and values they viewed as inherently deficient. Through this exercise of coercive power they reproduced the pattern of societal macrointeractions and limited students' possibilities to define and interpret their own realities and identities.

A starting point in constructing an alternative interactional

process is to recognize that educator-student interactions constitute a process of negotiating identities. Through our interactions
with students (and colleagues) we are constantly sketching an image not just of our own identities and those we envisage for our
students, but also of the society we hope our students will form.
Our actions and interactions reflect our identities and also contribute to their formation. This implies that identity is not a static and
fixed construct but rather encompasses multiple voices striving
toward coherence and harmony. Identity is constantly being
shaped through experiences and interactions, and different facets
of identity find differential possibilities for expression depending
on the institutional and interpersonal context (Laing, 1969; Simon, 1987; Walsh, 1991).

To illustrate, Zanger (this volume) describes very clearly the
dynamics of identity negotiation from the perspective of Lati-
no/Latina high school students. Students see very clearly the ways
in which teachers and peers ignore their contributions and attempt
to define them as inferior. In the words of one student describing
what happens to many of her Spanish-speaking peers:

> They just feel left out, they feel like if no one loves them, no one
> cares, so why should they care? No one wants to hear what they
> have to say, so they don't say anything. (177)

It is clear from the examples cited by Zanger that the process of
identity negotiation is closely tied to academic success and literacy
development in the school language. Although the students who
comment in Zanger's chapter managed to develop academically
despite devaluation of identity by teachers and peers, they represent a minority. One gets the impression that their insights into the
process of identity devaluation to which they were being subjected
was an important factor in helping them resist the devaluation
without sacrificing academic development. In fact, it is possible
that for these students, academic development represented a form
of resistance, a way of refusing to live down to their teachers'
expectations, or an expansion of the ZPD in response to the constricted possibilities proffered by teachers.

In short, the ZPD represents a useful metaphor for describing
the dual process of reciprocal negotiation of identity and collaborative generation of knowledge. Educators whose role definition
encompasses challenging discriminatory institutional structures

will attempt to create conditions for interaction that expand students' possibilities for identity formation and critical inquiry as part of knowledge generation. Rather than constricting the ZPD such that the voices of many students are silenced, educators who adopt this type of role definition will attempt to constitute the ZPD initially in such a way that students' voices can be expressed, shared, and amplified within the interactional process. Under these conditions, the ZPD will then be co-constructed by students and educators as, through their interactions, they script their own identities and that of the society they envisage. Many examples could be given of this process, ranging from the oral histories and "cultural journalism" of the *Foxfire* projects (Wigginton, 1989) to Regnier's (1988) account of student-scripted dramas in the Saskatoon Native Survival School in Canada.

An essential condition for educators who wish to amplify students' possibilities for identity formation is to view students as cultural resource persons and to *listen* to their *self*-expression. Educators must learn from their students if they are to expand their cultural knowledge and sensitivity. In the context of culturally diverse school systems, educators who are not constantly expanding their cultural knowledge in the process of interacting with students and parents are rooted in "cultural illiteracy." Concrete strategies for co-constructing zones of proximal development through critical literacy have been outlined by Ada (1988a, 1988b) and Shannon (1989), among others. Similarly, in the context of family literacy programs, Weinstein-Shr (1990) has articulated characteristics of promising programs that involve a shift from coercive to collaborative relations of power:

> With recognition of the strengths that multilingual families bring to programs, with collaborative work, with attention to traditional forms of knowledge, and with deliberate investigation of literacy and its uses, it becomes possible to imagine schools that understand and respond to families and communities; families that cooperate with schools toward agreed-upon goals; and generations who find in one another the resources to remember their past and to take on their present and future with confidence and joy. (3)

The framework outlined above is sketched in Figure 11.1. Societal macrointeractions determine the educational structures that

COERCIVE RELATIONS OF POWER MANIFESTED IN
THE MACROINTERACTIONS BETWEEN SUBORDINATED
GROUPS AND DOMINANT GROUP INSTITUTIONS

↙   ↘

EDUCATOR ROLE DEFINITIONS ↔ EDUCATIONAL STRUCTURES

↘   ↙

MICROINTERACTIONS BETWEEN EDUCATORS AND STUDENTS

forming a

ZONE OF PROXIMAL DEVELOPMENT

within which
knowledge is generated
and
identities are negotiated

EITHER

REINFORCING COERCIVE RELATIONS OF POWER
OR
PROMOTING COLLABORATIVE RELATIONS OF POWER

FIGURE 11.1
COERCIVE AND COLLABORATIVE RELATIONS OF POWER
MANIFESTED IN MACRO- AND MICROINTERACTIONS

frame the microinteractions between educators and students. The macrointeractions and educational structures also influence but do not completely determine the ways in which educators define their roles in relation to subordinated group students and communities. For example, societal attitudes and their reflections in the media towards subordinated groups (e.g., "immigrants are taking our jobs") are likely to influence the attitudes of many teachers towards teaching these students. Negative attitudes may be reinforced through discriminatory structures in the school. For example, subordinated group students may perform more poorly both in class and on biased IQ and achievement measures. Failure to address issues related to cultural diversity in preservice or in-service courses also represents a set of structures that reflect broader societal priorities and that will influence educator role definitions.

However, educators, both individually and collectively, have opportunities to become aware both of patterns of disinformation and of the effects of discriminatory structures and thus to challenge the process of "manufacturing consent" within the educational system. There are many examples of this process of challenging racist educational practices and structures (e.g., Ada, 1989b; Shannon, 1989). Thus, educator role definitions can affect specific educational structures, at least in local contexts.

Similarly, students and communities also have the possibility to actively resist the operation of the societal power structure as it is manifested in educational settings (see, e.g., Skutnabb-Kangas, 1988). While for some students, resistance may contribute to academic development (as Zanger's chapter suggests), in many situations resistance has severe costs with respect to academic success and upward mobility (e.g., Fordham, 1990; Willis, 1977).

The role definitions adopted by educators will determine the ways in which they attempt to orchestrate patterns of microinteractions with students in the school context. These microinteractions are limited by the educational structures that are in place at national and local levels. For example, the requirement to administer standardized achievement tests that do not reflect teachers' curriculum objectives (e.g., appreciation of literature, creative writing, critical thinking, etc.) may inhibit teachers' pursuit of these objectives. In other cases, the contradiction between the test and the educational objectives will provoke educators to actively challenge the assessment structure.[6]

The microinteractions between educators and students form a ZPD or *construction zone* in which possibilities for the generation of knowledge and formation of identity are negotiated. As outlined above, the ZPD is actively constituted by both students and educators, and the interactions within the ZPD script an image of the envisaged relations of culture and power within the society. The microinteractions either reinforce or challenge particular educational structures within the school or school system. Since these structures stand in a clearly defined relation to the power structure in the wider society, it follows that the microinteractions between educators and students are always either reinforcing coercive relations of power or, alternatively promoting collaborative relations of power in the wider society.

CONCLUSION

The framework outlined above integrates functional, cultural and critical literacies. Within the context of the framework, typical interventions to increase functional literacy or improve the teaching of literacy for subordinated group students fail because they do not attempt to challenge the societal power structure and attempt to teach functional literacy in isolation from students' lives. The message to students is "Read the prescripted word but don't even think of reading the world." In other words, functional literacy comes in a package that requires students to abdicate any pursuit of genuine cultural literacy or critical literacy. As such, most literacy programs for adults, and efforts at school reform, perpetuate the coercive relations of power that helped create low levels of literacy in the first place. By contrast, microinteractions between educators and students that focus on critical inquiry and negotiation of identity require the integration of functional, cultural, and critical literacies. As such, these interactions represent a shift from coercive to collaborative relations of power. Power is created and shared within the interpersonal space where minds and identities meet in defiance of societal prescriptions.

Thus, in line with the conclusions of several of the preceding chapters, this analysis suggests that in cross-cultural contexts, literacy instruction is intertwined with issues of empowerment and can never be regarded as neutral. Literacy instruction is always either an element of coercive relations of power or alternatively part of a challenge to the power structure, contributing to a shift from coercive to collaborative relations of power. The fact that in conditions of unequal power relations helping students to "read the world" is a subversive act helps explain why so much effort is devoted to sanitizing literacy instruction in schools by predefining cultural literacy and eradicating critical literacy.

NOTES

1. While some groups of learners may employ terms such as "illiterate" or "*analphabète*" as a means of focusing political action, it is noteworthy that the mission statement of the Learner Action Group of Canada recommends that "the term 'illiterate' not be used in reference to any

citizen or group of citizens" (Canadian Commission for UNESCO, 1991:51).

2. I am using the term "minority" to refer to groups whose members are numerically fewer than those of the "majority" group in the society. I will also use the term "bicultural" (as suggested by Darder [1991]) to offset what some people see as the pejorative connotations of the term "minority." The term "subordinated" is being used in a sociological sense to refer to groups that have been subordinated economically, politically, and educationally by the dominant group in the society. Thus, black South Africans historically have been a subordinated group despite being the majority group in the society. The status of women in the vast majority of countries historically and currently also illustrates the difference between "minority" and "subordinated."

3. It is worth noting that functional literacy is also sensitive to changes in the status of languages in a particular society. For example, the strengthening of the status of French within Quebec institutions and in the workplace during the past fifteen years has made it considerably more difficult for those with limited literacy in French to function adequately within Quebec society. Whereas before, high levels of literacy in English may have been sufficient for competent functioning and advancement in the workplace, that is clearly no longer the case. In other words, the changing status of French has rendered "functionally illiterate" a certain proportion of non-Francophones whose literacy skills may have been better developed in English than in French.

4. It should not be assumed that this conservative discourse has gone uncontested. Many school systems are attempting to inject a multicultural focus into their curricula (see, for example, New York State Social Studies Review and Development Committee, 1991) and both sides of the issue are hotly debated in educational policy journals (e.g., *Educational Leadership*, Vol. 49, No. 4, 1991/1992). In fact, the intensification of this conservative discourse can be seen as a reaction to the perceived and real changes that many educators are attempting to make to a formerly monocultural curriculum. As I argue below, the linkage between general approaches to literacy instruction and monocultural versus multicultural literacy is that transmission models of pedagogy are essential to the inculcation of monocultural literacy whereas approaches that encourage expression of student voice are essential to multicultural education.

5. There is some evidence that the constant articulation of this message by bilingual education advocates is finally being heard if one can judge by the following statement in the interim report of the National Education Goals Panel (1991) on student achievement and citizenship:

At the same time, the native language skills of immigrant children constitute a potential resource to the nation; such children will more easily than others be able to meet the objective of showing competence in two languages. There is evidence that unless schools show overt evidence of valuing native languages, many children will refuse to continue using them. We therefore recommend that children's communication competencies be assessed in two languages, beginning in elementary school. We expect that this practice will result in earlier and more intensive foreign language instruction for native English speakers and will preserve native language capacity among immigrant children (1991:48).

It is noteworthy that this statement avoids all mention of bilingual education, although this type of program is clearly implied in what is said.

6.   This has happened at Garfield School in the Milwaukee Public Schools, where the contradictions between test content and classroom objectives prompted the school to develop alternative portfolio-based assessment systems. In the words of the principal (Kery Kafka):

We stressed having the children work in cooperative groups, but we were rated on how well students did independently on standardized tests. . . . We replaced basal readers and workbooks with quality literature and children's writing, but we were rated on how well the children filled in circles on tests. We were becoming schizophrenic. (Miner, 1992:8)

REFERENCES

Ada, A.F. (1988a). Creative reading: A relevant methodology for language minority children. In L.M. Malave (Ed.), *NABE '87. Theory, research and application: Selected papers* (pp. 97–111). Buffalo: State University of New York.

———. (1988b). The Pajaro Valley experience: Working with Spanish-speaking parents to develop children's reading and writing skills in the home through the use of children's literature. In T. Skutnabb-Kangas & J. Cummins (Eds.), *Minority education: From shame to struggle* (pp. 223–238). Clevedon, England: Multilingual Matters.

Baril, A. & Mori, G.A. (1991, Spring). Educational attainment of linguistic groups in Canada. *Canadian Social Trends*, 17–18.

Barlett, D.L. & Steele, J.B. (1992). *America: What went wrong?* Kansas: Andrews & McMeel.

Bhola, H.S. (1989). International literacy year: A summons to action for universal literacy by the year 2000. *Education Horizons*, 67, 62–67.

Canadian Commission for UNESCO (1991). *Canadian Commission for UNESCO's report on the future contributions to literacy in Canada. Draft.* Ottawa: Canadian Commission for UNESCO.

Chomsky, N. (1987). The manufacture of consent. In J. Peck (Ed.), *The Chomsky reader* (pp. 121–136). New York: Pantheon Books.

Cumming, A. (1990). The thinking, interactions, and participation to foster in adult ESL literacy instruction. In J. Bell (Ed.), *ESL Literacy.* Special issue of *TESL Talk, 20*(1), 34–51.

Cummins, J. (1989). *Empowering minority students.* Sacramento: California Association for Bilingual Education.

Darder, A. (1991). *Culture and power in the classroom: A critical foundation for bicultural education.* South Hadley, MA: Bergin & Garvey.

Durkin, D. (1987). Influences on basal reader programs. *Elementary School Journal, 87,* 331–341.

Ferdman, B. (1990). Literacy and cultural identity. *Harvard Educational Review, 60,* 181–204.

Fine, M. (1987). Silence and nurturing voice in an improbable context: Urban adolescents in public school. *Language Arts, 64*(2), 157–174.

Fordham, S. (1990). Racelessness as a factor in Black students' school success: Pragmatic strategy or pyrrhic victory? In N.M. Hidalgo, C.L. McDowell & E.V. Siddle (Eds.), *Facing racism in education* (pp. 232–262). Reprint series No. 21, Harvard Educational Review.

Freire, P. & Macedo, D. (1987). *Literacy: Reading the word and the world.* South Hadley, MA: Bergin & Garvey.

Giroux, H.A. (1991). Series introduction: Rethinking the pedagogy of voice, difference and cultural struggle. In C.E. Walsh, *Pedagogy and the struggle for voice: Issues of language, power, and schooling for Puerto Ricans* (pp. xv–xxvii). Toronto: OISE Press.

Goodlad, J.I. (1984). *A place called school: Prospects for the future.* New York: McGraw Hill.

Hirsch, E.D., Jr. (1987). *Cultural literacy: What every American needs to know.* Boston: Houghton Mifflin Co.

Hodgkinson, H. (1991, September). Reform versus reality. *Phi Delta Kappan,* 9–16.

Jensen, A.R. (1969). How much can we boost I.Q. and scholastic achievement? *Harvard Educational Review, 39,* 1–123.

Kirsch, I.S. & Jungeblut, A. (1986). *Literacy: Profiles of America's young adults.* Princeton, NJ: Educational Testing Service.

Kozol, J. (1991). *Savage inequalities: Children in America's schools.* New York: Crown Publishers.

Laing, R.D. (1969). *Self and others.* London: Tavistock Publications.

Langer, J. (1989). Literate thinking and schooling. *Literacy Research Newsletter, 5*(1), 1–2.

Lucas, T., Henze, R. & Donato, R. (1990). Promoting the success of Latino language-minority students: An exploratory study of six high schools. *Harvard Educational Review, 60*, 315–340.

Mikulecky, L. (1986). *The status of literacy in our society.* Paper presented at the annual meeting of the National Reading Conference, Austin, Texas (ED 281 182).

Miner, B. (1992). Experimenting with assessment: Milwaukee school says 'No' to standardized tests. *Rethinking Schools, 6*(3), pp. 8, 23.

Moll, L. (1989). Teaching second language students: A Vygotskian perspective. In D. Johnson & D. Roen (Eds.), *Richness in writing: Empowering ESL students* (pp. 55–69). New York: Longman.

National Coalition of Advocates for Students (1988). *New voices: Immigrant students in U.S. public schools.* Boston: National Coalition of Advocates for Students.

National Commission on Excellence in Education (1983). *A nation at risk: The imperative for educational reform.* Washington, DC: U.S. Government Printing Office.

National Education Goals Panel (1991). *Measuring progress toward the National Education Goals: Potential indicators and measurement strategies.* Washington, DC: U.S. Department of Education.

Newman, A.P. & Beverstock, C. (1990). *Adult literacy: Contexts and challenges.* Newark, DE: International Reading Association.

Newman, D., Griffith, P. & Cole, M. (1989). *The construction zone.* Cambridge: Cambridge University Press.

New York State Social Studies Review and Development Committee (1991). *One nation, many peoples: A declaration of cultural independence.* Report to the Commissioner of Education, New York State.

Ogbu, J.U. (1978). *Minority education and caste.* New York: Academic Press.

Ravitch, D. & Finn, C.E. (1987). *What do our 17-year olds know? A report on the first national assessment of history and literature.* New York: Harper & Row.

Regnier, R. (1988). Indians 'R' Us: The experience of a survival school pedagogy. *Our Schools, Our Selves, 1*, 22–44.

Rickover, H.G. (1959). *Education and freedom.* New York: E.P. Dutton & Co., Inc.

Rosenshine, B. & Stevens, R. (1984). Classroom instruction in reading. In P.D. Pearson, R. Barr, M.L. Kamil, & P. Mosenthal (Eds.), *Handbook of reading research* (pp. 745–798). New York: Longman.

Rubenson, K. (1989). The economics of adult basic education. In M.C. Taylor & J.A. Draper (Eds.), *Adult literacy perspectives* (pp. 387–398). Toronto: Culture Concepts Inc.

Sayers, D. (1991). Cross-cultural exchanges between students from the same culture: A portrait of an emerging relationship mediated by technology. *Canadian Modern Language Review, 47,* 678–696.

Schweinhart, L.J., Weikart, D.P. & Larney, M.B. (1986). Consequences of three preschool curriculum models through age 15. *Early Childhood Research Quarterly, 1,* 15–45.

Shannon, P. (1989). *Broken promises: Reading instruction in twentieth-century America.* South Hadley, MA: Bergin & Garvey.

Simon, R. (1987). Empowerment as a pedagogy of possibility. *Language Arts, 64,* 370–380.

Sirotnik, K.A. (1983). What you see is what you get—consistency, persistency, and mediocrity in classrooms. *Harvard Educational Review, 53,* 16–31.

Sizer, T.R. (1984). *Horace's compromise: The dilemma of the American high school.* Boston: Houghton Mifflin.

Skutnabb-Kangas, T. (1988). Resource power and autonomy through discourse in conflict—a Finnish migrant school strike in Sweden. In T. Skutnabb-Kangas & J. Cummins (Eds.), *Minority education: From shame to struggle* (pp. 251–277). Clevedon, England: Multilingual Matters.

Statistics Canada (1990). *Survey of literacy skills used in daily activities.* Ottawa: Statistics Canada.

Stedman, L.C. (1987). It's time we changed the effective schools formula. *Phi Delta Kappan, 69,* 215–224.

Stedman, L.C. & Kaestle, C.F. (1985). The test score decline is over: Now what? *Phi Delta Kappan, 67,* 204–210.

———. (1987). Literacy and reading performance in the United States from 1800 to the present. *Reading Research Quarterly, 22,* 8–46.

Vygotsky, L.S. (1978). *Mind in society: The development of higher psychological processes.* (Eds. M. Cole, V. John-Steiner, S. Scribner & E. Souberman). Cambridge: Harvard University Press.

Wagner, S. & Grenier, P. (1991). *Analphabétisme de minorité et alpha-étisation d'affirmation nationale à propos de l'Ontario français. Volume I: Synthèse théorique et historique.* Toronto: Ministère de l'Éducation.

Waldman, M. (1990). *Who robbed America? A citizen's guide to the Savings & Loan scandal.* New York: Random House.

Walsh, C.E. (1991). *Pedagogy and the struggle for voice: Issues of language, power, and schooling for Puerto Ricans.* Toronto: OISE Press.

Weinstein-Shr, G. (1990, August). Family and intergenerational literacy in multilingual families. *National Clearinghouse on Literacy Education, Q & A Series.*

Wiggington, E. (1989). Foxfire grows up. *Harvard Educational Review, 59,* 24–49.

Williams, J.D. & Snipper, G.C. (1990). *Literacy and bilingualism.* White Plains, NY: Longman.

Willis, P. (1977). *Learning to labor: How working class kids get working class jobs.* Lexington, MA: D.C. Heath.

NOTES ON CONTRIBUTORS

Alison d'Anglejan is professor in the Département de didactique of the University of Montreal and currently associate dean of graduate studies and research in the Faculté des sciences de l'éducation. She holds a Ph.D. in experimental psychology from McGill University. Her research and publications focus on psychological and social aspects of language learning, the education of immigrant children, and language planning.

Jim Cummins is currently a professor in the Modern Language Centre of the Ontario Institute for Studies in Education. He has published several books related to bilingual education and minority student achievement including *Bilingualism and Special Education: Issues in Assessment and Pedagogy, Bilingualism in Education: Aspects of Theory, Research and Policy* (with Merrill Swain), *Minority Education: From Shame to Struggle* (with Tove Skutnabb-Kangas) and *Empowering Minority Students*.

Concha Delgado-Gaitan is professor of educational anthropology in the Division of Education at the University of California, Davis. Her research has focused on issues of literacy and the relationship between family and schools, specifically in immigrant communities. Among her numerous publications are two books, *Literacy for Empowerment: The Role of Parents in Children's Education*, and *Crossing Cultural Borders: Education for Immigrant Families in America* with Henry Trueba.

Joanne Devine teaches courses in applied linguistics at Skidmore College where she is associate professor of English. She has published numerous articles and co-edited two volumes of essays on reading in a second language, *Research in Reading a Second Language* and *Interactive Approaches to Second Language Reading*. Currently she is conducting research on the role of metacognition in second language reading and writing.

Bernardo M. Ferdman is associate professor at the California School of Professional Psychology in San Diego where he specializes in diversity and multiculturalism in organizations, ethnic identity, and organizational development. He received his Ph.D. from Yale University and previously taught at the University at Albany, State University of New York. He is a winner of the 1991 Gordon Allport Intergroup Relations Prize for his work on the dynamics of ethnic diversity in organizations.

333

Nancy Hornberger is associate professor of education at the University of Pennsylvania, where she specializes in sociolinguistics, language planning, and bilingual education, with special attention to language minority populations in Peru and in the United States. She has published widely on these topics, most recently in *Education and Urban Society, Teachers College Record, Annals of the American Academy of Political and Social Science,* and the *Annual Review of Applied Linguistics.*

Barbara McCaskill is assistant professor in the department of English at the University of Georgia. She teaches courses in African American, Caribbean, and multicultural literature and literary theories; and she specializes in the research of nineteenth-century and *fin-de-siècle* black women writers. She has co-edited *Multicultural Literature and Literacies: Making Space for Differences* with Suzanne Miller.

Arnulfo G. Ramírez is currently chair of the department of foreign languages and literatures and professor of Spanish and linguistics at Louisiana State University. He has taught at the University of California at Los Angeles, Stanford University, the State University of New York at Albany, and the University of Madrid. Major publications include *Bilingualism Through Schooling, El español de los Estados Unidos: El lenguaje de los hispanos,* and *The English of Spanish-speaking Pupils in Bilingual and Monolingual School Settings.*

Stephen Reder is director of the Literacy, Language, and Communication program at Northwest Regional Educational Laboratory in Portland, Oregon. He has conducted research on literacy and language development in a range of settings and with diverse populations, ranging from native villages in West Africa and Alaska to schools, workplaces, and communities in urban locations in the United States. He is particularly interested in understanding literacy development within broader frameworks of language and communicative choice.

Rose-Marie Weber is associate professor of reading with joint appointment in linguistics and cognitive science at the University at Albany, State University of New York. She has published on linguistic aspects of literacy and literacy instruction, including reading across languages, word recognition strategies, classroom interaction, and adult literacy, most recently in *Reading Research Quarterly* and *Annual Review of Applied Linguistics.*

Virginia Vogel Zanger's research interest is the sociocultural context of schooling for language minority students. She works as a teacher trainer, video producer, textbook author, and bilingual education activist in Boston and she is president of the Massachusetts Association for Bilingual Education.

Mark Zuss is instructor in the graduate department of specialized services in education at Lehman College, City University of New York. He is currently completing a dissertation in developmental psychology concerned with college and adult basic education students' writing strategies involving the social construction of gender and race.

INDEX

Abi-Nader, J., 173
Acculturation, 203, 260; effects of racism on, 178–79; in bicultural context, 181–82. *See also* Assimilation; Enculturation; Socialization
Acquisition: vs. learning, 90
Ada, A. F., 146–47, 148, 151, 300, 322
Adult Basic Education, 240
African Americans, 59; attitudes toward literacy among, 306; and slavery, 201–3, 206, 208, 209, 216; numbers of, in U.S., 5; literacy levels among, 303; resistance to dominant culture among, 183–84; storytelling styles of, 257–58; writers, 199–217
Age, 243
Alderson, J. C., 105, 123, 124
Allen, V., 123
American Council on the Teaching of Foreign Languages (ACTFL), 79, 82, 84–86
American Indians. *See* Native Americans
Anglo-conformity, 7, 126
Anti-Slavery Advocate, The, 212
Ardener, E., 230
Asian and Pacific Islanders: Balinese, 248; Cantonese, 249; Hawaiians, 43, 65, 189; Hmong, 43, 63, 64; Laotian, 249; literacy values of, 42; numbers of, in U.S., 5; Vietnamese, effects of racism on, 178–79
Assimilation, 7, 183, 254, 317, 320; in Quebec, 273; in schools, 182.

See also Acculturation; Enculturation; Socialization
Au, K., 65
Auerbach, E., 145
Autobiography: as literature, 213–16

Ballenger, C., 189
Baril, A., 301
Barnett, M. A., 89
Bell, J., 80
Bennett, A., 62
Berlin, J. A., 255
Beverstock, C., 303
Bicultural, 326 n.2
Biculturalism, 181
Bilingual education, 18, 123, 126, 174, 297, 326 n.5; opposition to, 7–8, 318–19; programs, 104; 130 n.10; 319. *See also* Second language
Bilingualism, 12–13, 16, 18, 38, 63, 93–94, 104, 115, 123, 128, 130 nn.10, 12; acknowledging, 319; additive and subtractive, 130 n.11, 125, 181; among the Navajo, 39; attitudes toward, 6–7; early and late, 125; and language choice, 45; and literacy, 105; programs: 191. *See also* Second language
Biliteracy, 94, 319; among the Navajo, 39; configurations, 127; contexts of, 108; continua of, 105–128; development of, 116–24, 119, 121, 124, 126, 128; media of, 124–27; and power, 112; social contexts of, 109–110, 112–13, 114–15; understanding,